AFRICA & AFRICANS
FOURTH EDITION

AFRICA & AFRICANS
FOURTH EDITION

Paul Bohannan

Philip Curtin

WAVELAND

PRESS, INC.

Long Grove, Illinois

For information about this book, contact:
 Waveland Press, Inc.
 4180 IL Route 83, Suite 101
 Long Grove, IL 60047-9580
 (847) 634-0081
 info@waveland.com
 www.waveland.com

Figures on pages 21, 38, 160, 212, and 223 used by permission of Longman Group UK Limited. Figure on page 38 used with permission by Claudine Vansina. Additionally, various line illustrations found in this edition were originally prepared by the Graphic Arts Division of The American Museum of Natural History.

10-digit ISBN 0-88133-840-0
13-digit ISBN 978-0-88133-840-9

Printed in the United States of America

18   17   16   15

CONTENTS

I. AFRICAN BACKGROUND

1. Myths and Facts   5
2. The African Continent   17
3. Mapping Africa   33

II. AFRICAN INSTITUTIONS

4. African Arts   49
5. African Families   63
6. Land and Labor   77
7. African Politics and Courts   87
8. African Trade and Markets   101
9. African Religion   115

III. AFRICAN HISTORY

10. The Peopling of Africa   129
11. Farms and Iron   139
12. Africa in World History   151
13. The End of Isolation   165
14. The Era of the Slave Trade   179
15. Secondary Empires of the Pre-Colonial Century   191
16. Commerce and Islam:
     The Dual Revolution in West Africa   205
17. Forms and Conditions of Conquest   217
18. The Colonial Era   229
19. Toward Independence   239

IV. EPILOGUE

20. Africa Since Independence   253

     Photograph Captions and Credits   270
     Further Reading   271
     Index   279

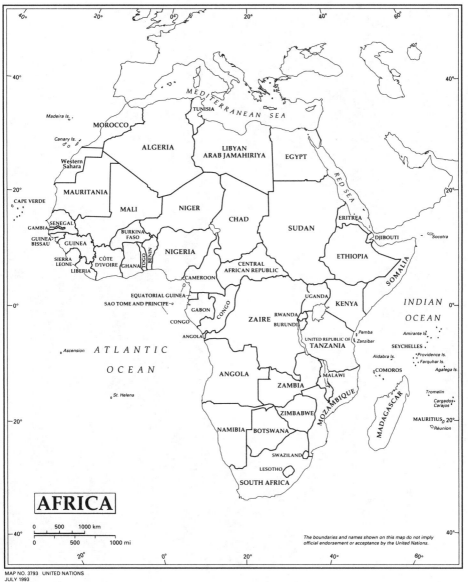

AFRICA

| 0 | 500 | 1000 km |
| 0 | 500 | 1000 mi |

The boundaries and names shown on this map do not imply
official endorsement or acceptance by the United Nations.

Part I

AFRICAN BACKGROUND

1
MYTHS AND FACTS

Africa has for centuries been seen by Europeans and North Americans through webs of myth. The myths change from time to time and place to place, depending far more on the needs and prejudices, even the ignorance, of the myth-makers than on the facts in Africa. The process of myth-making is still going full tilt, but the myths are quite different from those of only a few years ago. Understanding the reality underlying such pervasive and glib myths helps to strip them away so that we can see what is in fact there.

Africa was long known as the "Dark Continent," but the darkness was in the ignorance of the outside world, not in Africa. Europeans and Americans knew a great deal about the geography of most other parts of the world before explorers began the systematic penetration of Africa in the nineteenth century. During the colonial era—for tropical Africa, roughly 1880 to 1960—Europeans who went to govern Africa or to do business there began to learn more, and the new familiarity percolated down to the rest of the population back in Europe. British and French school children learned about great missionaries like David Livingstone or Cardinal Lavigérie, as well as military leaders like Kitchner or Archinard.

Americans were spared this familiarity with "colonial history"— the history of Europeans in Africa. Few Americans went to Africa. Until the 1950s, American diplomats went only to the few independent countries like Liberia or Ethiopia. Elsewhere the United States had only a few consulates, attached to the embassies of colonial powers in their European capitals. The State Department dealt with Africa as a minor facet of European affairs.

By the late 1950s, a change was evident. The "third world" came to include Africa as well as Asia and Latin America. African Studies programs emerged at several universities both in the United States and in Europe. The politics, economics, and history of the continent joined the study of African culture, already begun by anthropologists. In North American universities before the mid-1950s, African history was taught only as a part of "Negro history" in a few predominantly Black colleges. By the mid-1980s, it was a recognized part of historical knowledge. African art and culture are prominent in American museums, most recently the brilliant Museum of African Art associated with the Smithsonian in Washington. The continuing importance of the African heritage in shaping American popular music from jazz to rock came to be generally recognized. With the civil rights movement of the 1950s and 1960s and the independence of most of tropical Africa, Afro-Americans began to be interested in their African heritage. Hundreds of them went to Africa as tourists to see for themselves the land of their ancestors.

In spite of the more systematic search for knowledge about Africa, the old myths lived on and new myths were added. Part of the problem comes from the way the news media report African affairs. From the American perspective, the important foreign news comes from Western Europe and Japan, from China and Russia, with only an occasional crisis drawing concern to other areas. The Viet Nam War brought Southeast Asia into the news in the 1960s; both Central America and the Middle East got media coverage in the early 1980s; the festering struggle over apartheid in South Africa from the mid-1970s onward, and pictures of starvation in Somalia in the early 1990s, assailed us. The rest of Africa, however, makes the news only when some especially troublesome event draws attention—most often negative attention—to it.

Over the past thirty years, ordinary newspaper readers and TV viewers would have been conscious of the Congo crisis beginning in 1960, which led to the creation of an independent Zaire. They would have read about the military coups and the general failure of newly independent African states. In the 1970s, tyrants like Idi Amin in Uganda or "Emperor" Jean Bedel Bokassa of the Central African Empire got more space and air time than the spectacular but peaceful economic progress and comparative freedom of Ivory Coast or Cameroon.

Natural disasters like the great drought in the sahel, which stretches across Africa from Senegal to the Sudan and Ethiopia, were publicized—in 1973 alone, more than a hundred thousand people died of starvation and disease brought on by malnutrition. A decade later, drought returned—this time to Ethiopia, the Sudan, and south as far as Zimbabwe and South Africa. Worldwide television showed dramatic starvation in Ethiopia. The disaster itself attracted some press and TV coverage, but internationally-famous rock stars attracted far more attention with concerts to raise money for the victims.

Exposure to such spectacular events did nothing to erase many of the old myths. In the popular mind, Africa is still associated with lions, and lions with jungles. In fact, lions don't live in the rain forest, but in open grasslands. Only about 5 percent of the African landmass can be classified as "jungle," if jungle means rain forest—

and for centuries, Africans have been clearing undergrowth in the rain forest to cultivate crops. Destruction of the remaining rain forest is one of the most pressing threats to the environment.

Animals of the open savanna of Kenya and Tanzania, which have attracted tens of thousands of tourists, appear weekly in TV nature series and, from time to time, in spectacular films like *Out of Africa*. Neither the nature films nor Karen Blixen's picture of settler life in Kenya are inaccurate. They tell what they want to tell very well. But, because they tell next to nothing about the life of ordinary Africans, about all they achieve is reinforcing the view of Africa as the place on earth with the most wild animals. The North American public now knows a lot about those animals. Yet none of that knowledge dispels an older and more deeply ingrained myth of Africa as a savage continent. An accurate picture of animal life high on the slopes of Mount Kilimanjaro coexists easily with the cartoon image of the missionary in the cannibal stew pot.

That myth of savage Africa has been part of Western thought since the seventeenth and eighteenth centuries. Even in those days, it was created out of philosophical necessity, not out of observations. The European view was that "we," the Europeans, had the one true religion and the one true civilization in the world. If that is the case, then someone else, somewhere, must represent the other extreme—the non-civilized extreme. Such philosophically necessary "savagery" could, of course, be located anywhere Europeans knew little about. Africa was a favorite place.

The opposition of savagery and civilization got confused with other oppositions: bad and good, depravity and virtue. Europe had long had a vision not only of the "achievements" of civilization but of the accompanying idea that civilization also brought with it perils of the soul that had been unknown in earlier times and "simpler" places. The confusion is mapped in the diagram below.

A Model of Confusion

	Savagery	Civilization
Good	The Noble Savage	Achievements of Civilization
Bad	The Depraved Savage	Civilization and its Discontents

The savagery that Europeans imagined at the opposite pole from themselves could be seen as either good or evil, in large part in terms of the distinction they made between the good and evil of their own position. Just as Europeans needed a distant, bad example, however imaginary, as a measure of their own attainments, so they needed a good example to measure their own shortcomings. The image of unenlightened people who nevertheless had a natural nobility served both purposes. The noble savage myth took several different forms. As the Europeans struggled with the problems of a complex and increasingly technical society, they found it useful to imagine people who were free to practice the simple virtues born of innocence. They postulated (with little or no evidence) people closer to nature, free of the incessant struggle for power and domination that marked European class and international relations. The Christian virtues of faith, hope, and charity were said to come easily to such people.

Depending on which need was greatest, Europeans could invoke whichever part of the image best suited their purposes. They could postulate people with only the most rudimentary technical knowledge—without fire, virtually without language, practicing unspeakable cruelties on one another—although none of this picture had ever been true. European familiarity with cannibalism came from the Caribbean and the South Pacific, not from Africa. Non-agricultural hunting and gathering societies were very few in Africa, even before Columbus—they were far more common in the Americas and in Australasia.

The myth of savage Africa was further distorted when Europeans traded in African slaves. Most of the slaves shipped to European dominated plantations in the Americas were Africans. The need to justify the trade as compatible with Christian morality reinforced the savage myth. After all, the myth said, taking people out of such savagery was a step up for them, even if that step took them and their descendants into a life of slavery.

Later on, as the slave trade began to taper off and Christian missionaries appeared in Africa, the value of the myth of savagery changed its focus, but not its content. The more "savage" the place they worked, the greater the missionaries' mundane as well as supermundane rewards. Many of these missionaries were levelheaded observers who did not depict a savage Africa. Yet they cast before them the image of heroes doing battle with cannibalism, lust, and depravity—the forces of "darkness." Their undeniable fortitude, and the hardships they bore, were translated into the imagery of "savagery" by home congregations and missionary societies.

The myth of a savage Africa lives on today in the same way that racism in the United States lives on despite the civil rights revolution of the 1950s and 1960s. Like racism, the savagery myth takes subtle forms. For example, the news media report African affairs using terms like "tribe" and "tribalism"—the only other place they do that is Native American affairs. The term "tribe," in European writing about Africa, became common only in the nineteenth century. In the era of the slave trade, Europeans usually talked about different African "nations" (although that word, too, meant something different at that time than it means today).

The confusion mapped in the diagram also shows up in the opposite myth: the "noble savage" had no more empirical basis in reality than did the myth of the depraved savage. Various forms of this image turn up in Western literature about Africa and Africans. Slaves like Eliza and Uncle Tom in *Uncle Tom's Cabin* showed natural innocence and Christian virtues, as contrasted with the moral failings of the drivers and planters (who supposedly had the benefit of the full Christian message, yet failed to measure up to its demands).

A similar myth is still alive—only a few years ago, Alex Haley's *Roots* portrayed an eighteenth century African society on the banks of the Gambia River as innocent of the evils of the slave trade. The people (the myth goes) went about unarmed, while European slavers filled their ships by kidnapping. In fact, the Gambians not only bought and sold slaves, they were heavily armed. The Gambia River had been an artery of the slave trade for more than three hundred years. In the eighteenth century, the hometown of Haley's hero, Kunta Kinte (the presentday rural village of Jufure) was a thriving center of that trade. The Kinte family have been traders by tradition and were no doubt involved in the slave trade themselves. One can only guess that Haley used the innocence of the Africans as a literary device to highlight the crimes of the European slavery and planters, much as Harriet Beecher Stowe had done more than a century earlier.

Only a few years after *Roots* appeared as a television spectacular, a similar picture of innocence with more obvious political intent appeared in the South African movie, *The Gods Must be Crazy*. There, the San people of the Kalahari (whom the movie called Bushmen, though the word has fallen out of anthropological use) were shown leading an innocent and good life, in tune with nature, so far removed from any understanding of the modern world that they could not even recognize a Coca-Cola bottle. The implication was clear: such people could not face the modern world on their own, and were hence better off under the benevolent guidance of an apartheid regime.

Both versions of the myth of a savage Africa neglect one important fundamental fact. European and African culture and social organization have a great deal in common, developed over a very long run of history. They have more in common, for example, than either does with the cultures of eastern Asia or native North Americans or Australians. Agricultural techniques and traditions belong to a single cultural sphere. Market organization was similar. Religions were variations on the same basic themes. Family organization reflects pretty much the same values, even though Africans tended to be polygynous and Europeans claimed to be monogamous. The same kind of similarities are not found among the Chinese or the Aztecs. Europeans and Africans share a common set of diseases and immunities to disease that Native Americans and the peoples of the Pacific did not share. This deep similarity was to become one of the fundamental reasons the Americas today are occupied by descendants of Africans and of Europeans.

Among all the other myths, one of the most generalized and difficult to tear away hovers around the matter of race. Americans, both black and white, live in a society that is extremely conscious of race. Yet Europe too was a racist society from the nineteenth century onward. Europe is now increasingly troubled by racial conflict that grows out of the great immigration from overseas after the 1950s. There, as in North America, color and physical appearance far too often carry social implications.

The cultures and the histories of sub-Saharan African societies have much in common. Many commentators in the past have associated this common experience with common race. Yet all sub-Saharan Africans do not belong to a single race—not even if comparatively recent arrivals like the European-derived minorities of Zimbabwe and South Africa are left out.

The problem of race and Africa is not an African problem. Africans note racial differences, but Europeans and Americans are hung up on what they call "race." No scientifically viable measures exist for defining a similar group of people as a "race." For geneticists, the word "race" means an interbreeding population with distinct and heritable characteristics. In ordinary usage, the characteristics are not genetic but are a cultural classification of visible, physical appearance. There is no scientific reason for "counting" the shape of a person's nose and not his or her haemoglobin characteristics or proclivity for heart disease as "racial" characteristics. As an everyday badge of racial identification, North Americans recognize as "Black," "Negro," or "African-American" anyone with any degree of African descent, measured by skin color, facial configuration, hair texture, and so on. In Liberia, "white" is measured in exactly opposite terms. A person can be "Black" in the United States and "White" in Liberia. Obviously, definitions of race can only be cultural. Geneticists estimate that about 25 percent of the gene pool circulating within the African-American community is European, predominantly from the British Isles. This means that more of the ancestors of the "typical" African-American come from Britain and Ireland than come from any one particular region of Africa.

African assessment of race is as socially conditioned as is American assessment. In the past, before anthropology was able to separate race, language, and culture and to demonstrate that the three may be connected by history, but never by genes, Westerners postulated that cultural characteristics like language were heritable. When Africans think about race, they too tend to include a lot of learned characteristics. Even the most stereotypically African-appearing of African-Americans cannot easily "pass" for African in West Africa. Africans will almost universally classify them as "European," from the way they walk, talk, and carry themselves.

Africans tend to see quite a different set of physical traits from Americans and Europeans when they examine "racial" differences. There are, within Africa, physical differences that Europeans and Americans are not conscious of. Sometimes this recognition is no more significant than the ability to guess a stranger's nationality—whether Swede or Italian, Pole or Spaniard. In other instances, recognizable physical appearance marks ancient social divisions between superiors and inferiors. Rwanda and Burundi in central Africa have a common, Bantu language and a common culture, but the physical difference between the Tutsi, the former masters, and the Hutu, the former subordinates, is usually clear even to outsiders. On the Kenya coast, nearly everyone is conscious of the physical differences among the socially dominant Afro-Arabs, the descendants of former slaves from the region of Malawi, and the up-country Kikuyu and Luo who now hold many government posts—to say nothing of the Wazungu, or European tourists, whose spending helps to support the economy. Differences in physical type also go along with important social distinctions in Ethiopia.

The point is that the racial myth—the belief that physical type is a guide to inherent ability or cultural characteristics—is completely exploded. What remains is the fact that physical appearance serves to demarcate certain social groupings. It is something like the various accents in Great Britain: English people use accent to rank others—distinctions that are totally lost on most Americans.

In North America, the African cultural heritage and African racial heritage have mixed in a very complex way. We tend to think of the United States as settled mainly by Europeans, which is true; however, our common myth fails to distinguish the timing of the European arrival. The median date for the arrival of America's African ancestors—the date by which half had arrived and half were still to come—is remarkably early, about 1780. The similar median date for the arrival of our European ancestors was remarkably late—about the 1890s. It was not until the 1840s that more Europeans than Africans crossed the Atlantic each year.

This early arrival of our African ancestors had important cultural consequences. Anthropologists used to write about the survival of "Africanisms" in African-American culture. They sometimes failed to point out that cultural Africanisms were not a part of physical inheritance. They were brought by the African immigrants through the slave trade and remained strongest within the African-American community, although many became part of American culture at large, first in the South and then in the rest of the country. African-American cooking, for example, has many traits from Africa; but gumbos with their African-derived okra are now part of a much broader tradition of "Southern" cooking, partly traceable to Africa, partly not. African music made an enormous formative contribution to jazz and its successors in American popular music, which has done much to set the tone of popular music throughout the world. Just as African-Americans share a racial inheritance from the British Isles with Euro-Americans, all Americans share a cultural inheritance from Africa.

One of the most difficult and persistent sources of myth about Africa comes from a blind spot in American thinking about the rest of the world, caused in part by the long-term rivalry between the United States and the Soviet Union that dominated world international relations for forty-five years after World War II. American political leaders tended to see Africa as a group of small countries that could help or hinder the rivalry with the Soviets. The polarization made both the Americans and the Soviets see African nations either "with us" or "against us." Africans never did see the world that way—they were never much concerned with big-power rivalries. Rather, they have been and are *for* Africa, sometimes defined as their own country, or even for some smaller group within it. They were thus "for" anybody who was "for Africa" defined that way. They were against anybody who was "against Africa."

Western courting of African countries to keep them out of the clutches of "the Communists" rose and fell with changing administrations in Washington. The Reagan years were peculiarly blind to the fact that regimes labelled "Marxist" were not automatically captives of the Soviet Union. Nor were regimes that found it to their interest to support the United States, like Mobutu's Zaire, genuine friends of democracy as we understand it. Many African governments "changed sides." Egypt switched from Russia to American support in 1972, Ethiopia changed from American to Soviet support in 1974, and Somalia changed from Soviet to American support in 1975.

Several African governments have adopted names like the People's Republic of Benin or the People's Republic of the Congo, but that never did mean that they had "gone Communist" in the sense of modelling their institutions on those of the Soviet Union or joining the Warsaw Pact. Neither had those who claimed to be friends of the United States "gone Western" in the sense of instituting Western-style democracy.

In the years since the demise of the Soviet Union, the images of Africa that have appeared on our television screens have been of starving Ethiopian, Sudanese, and Somali children, and of "warlords" and "clan fighting." We have seen crowds of demonstrating South Africans mowed down by gunfire. Yet, during the same period, forward-looking African business people have been profiled in *Forbes* magazine. The task still remains: to look at Africa whole, without the myths and without the images built on our own ethnocentrism.

One last point must be made clearly, although it is easier to do today than it was a few years ago. The West does not so much have an African problem as Africa has a European problem. The white South Africans talk about a "native problem," but it is they who are the troublesome minority in that African country. Elsewhere European settlers have tended to make the best of African rule, and few African governments have been more than temporarily anti-European.

Well before the period of colonial conquests, the West began extending its cultural influence into the rest of the world. Christianity was and is an expanding, proselytizing religion. Perhaps more important, nearly simultaneously with its overseas conquests, the West discovered the power of industrial technology, which made it possible for people to produce and consume material goods on a scale completely unprecedented in the world's earlier history. The rest of the world, including Africa, wants to have control of this technology for its own purposes. Once they see how rich others have become, they are no longer content to be poor. Even if they are better off than they were before the colonial era, the contrast between their relative poverty and the wealth elsewhere makes them deprived.

Lives of tremendous dignity and valued rewards can be lived without the trappings of Western civilization. However, once the technological possibilities are known, a new day has arrived. The relative deprivation in Africa is not simply in contrast to Europe, North America, and Japan; Africans are also conscious of what has happened in recently industrializing countries like Korea, Taiwan, and Singapore. They see other peoples becoming comparatively rich without becoming completely Westernized. Africans do not want to become European or American in their culture; they want to keep what they value in their old way of life.

Our task in this book is to present briefly and as accurately as we can the facts about African society past and present. We know that we must, necessarily, be affected by the needs and myths of our own times—but we also hope to be among the first to correct whatever distortions appear as time passes, as more research is done, and as we all live longer and learn more.

2

THE AFRICAN CONTINENT

To understand Africa, you have to understand its ecological environment, its history, something of African achievements and aspirations, and the cultural values and outlook with which Africans view the world.

Africa is immense. It is fifty-two hundred miles from Tangiers in North Africa to Capetown in the far south—approximately the same distance as from Panama City to Anchorage, Alaska. It is forty-six hundred miles from Dakar in the far west of Africa to Cape Guardafui, the easternmost point of the African horn—only sixty-five miles less than the airline distance from New York to Moscow. Africa is a big place—three times the size of the contiguous forty-eight states of the United States.

The African continent is a vast plateau of ancient hard rock. Only 10 percent of its land area lies at less than five hundred feet above sea level, compared to 54 percent for Europe and 25 percent for North America. It has been a land area since Pre-Cambrian times—more than five hundred million years. The entire continent has been raised and lowered at various times in geological history, but only in the extreme north and south has there been any building up of great folded mountains like the Rockies or the Caucasus. The main form of land movement has been the faulting that produced the Red Sea and the Great Rift Valley that is now filled by Africa's Great Lakes.

The Arabian peninsula can be seen as a part of the African continent—the Rift Valley that cuts through it beginning in northern Turkey stretches through the Jordan Valley and the Dead Sea. It then follows down the length of the Red Sea (which can be thought of as an inland lake with a small opening into the Indian Ocean) and down through Lake Rudolf. Then, at the south of Lake Rudolf, the rift divides and spreads out around Lake Victoria. However, it joins again at the head of Lake Nyasa, runs down the Shire and Zambezi rivers, and finally out to sea, where it continues as a valley in the ocean floor. It extends through more than seventy degrees of latitude—almost one-fifth of the way around the world—and contains some of the deepest lakes on earth.

The rivers and the basins of Africa are prominent. The vast basins of the Niger, the Nile, the Volta, the Zambezi, and the Congo empty into the sea, but those surrounding Lake Chad and the wastes of

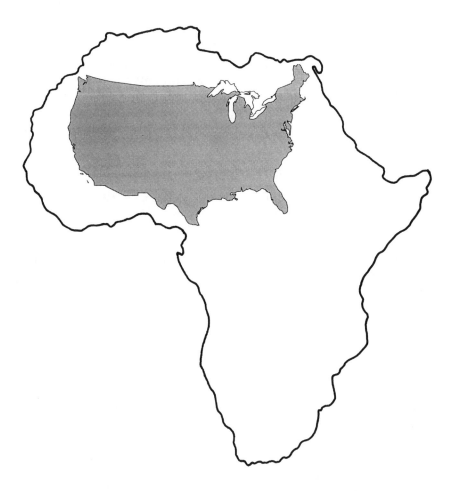

Figure 2. Africa, with the United States superimposed.

the Kalahari have no such outlets. Most African rivers fall off, in steep escarpments, to the narrow coastal plain that surrounds the entire continent. Only the Niger-Benue and Zambezi-Shire do not plunge in falls and rapids over the scarps, making effective navigation from the sea impossible.

Climates and Vegetation

If we oversimplify, Africa can be divided into five major physical and vegetational zones. The north and south ends of the continent, occupying only a small portion of its surface, enjoy Mediterranean-type climates and vegetations, much like central California. Coming inland, vast desiccated deserts and arid plains appear. Still closer to the equator are wide savanna regions, covered with tall grass and widely spaced trees. Along the equator lie humid and forested lands. Finally, highland areas throughout the continent respond to natural forces that override the climatic effects of latitude and of rainfall.

The humid forested lands straddle the equator in the Congo Basin and appear again in the coastal areas of western Africa that have the highest rainfall. Many of the most densely wooded areas take the form of gallery forests along streams and, at certain altitudes, surrounding the high hills. The forests vary from dark tropical rain forest to wooded areas so open that they can be distinguished from savanna only by scientific criteria.

North and south of the humid zone lies the savanna, which occupies by far the greatest number of square miles of Africa's surface. Savanna landscape is typically made up of rolling stretches of tall grasses, with intermittent bush and scattered trees. The inland valleys are broad, with gently sloping sides. Only where the streams rush over the scarps from the highland areas is that pattern broken.

Going still farther from the equator in both directions, the dry lands of Africa are encountered. In the south is the Kalahari Desert, and in the north, the Sahara. Some of the semi-arid African regions, where the desert and the savanna blend into one another, are reminiscent of the American Southwest. The deserts themselves—the center of the Kalahari and the several vast dry centers of the Sahara—are comparable to conditions found in Death Valley of North America.

Cities such as Algiers and Cape Town enjoy a climate much like that of southern France. The crops and cultures, where they have been subjected to European influence in these areas, are much the same: livestock, grain, and grapes.

The climatic areas of Africa might be seen as parallel belts stretching from east to west, a mirror image on either side of the equator, were it not for the fact that the pattern is seriously upset in the eastern part of the continent (and a few other parts) by highland areas in which altitude overrides latitude. The highland areas of Africa are divided between steeply mountainous terrain like that found in Cameroon and the Ruwenzori and the high, rolling plateaus such as are found in Ethiopia and Kenya. Here the climate may be cool and temperate; Mt. Kilimanjaro and Mt. Ruwenzori bear permanent ice fields on their caps. Vegetation varies from humid

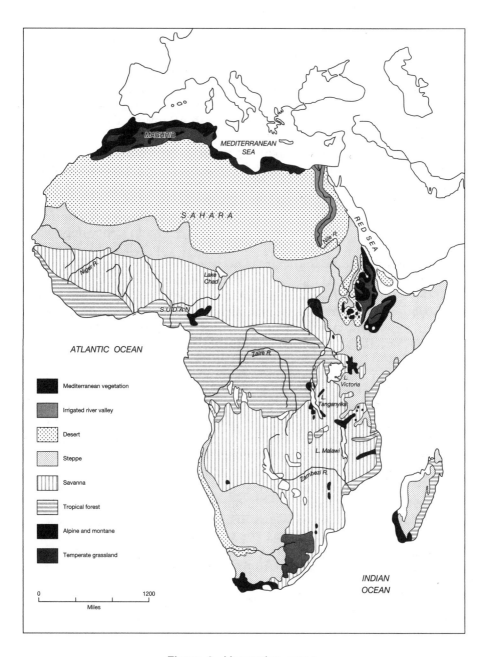

Figure 3. Vegetation zones.

forest or savanna at the foothills to Alpine mountains and tundra adjoining barren glaciers.

One of the most distinctive aspects of the African landscape is that, once the scarp is climbed, few impassable barriers are present. The climates of eastern Africa are complicated by the monsoon winds coming in from the Indian Ocean, as well as by the high altitude. Along parts of the west coast, the pattern is disturbed by winds created by the currents of the South Atlantic and the drought of the Sahara.

The climate therefore depends primarily on winds, the position of the sun, and altitude, more or less modified by the changes wrought by human beings. Because the barriers of terrain are neither sudden nor insurmountable, the weather can ''follow the sun.'' When the sun is far north in June, July, and August, it brings rain to the lands that lie between ten degrees and twenty degrees north of the equator. Similarly, during November, December, and January, rains come to the areas between ten degrees and twenty degrees south. Each enjoys a long dry season during the wet season of the other. In the humid forested lands, rain is often well distributed throughout the year, although short dry seasons may occur, depending primarily on the winds. As a general rule, rainfall throughout the continent tends to be heaviest when the sun is overhead.

The actual amount of rain is less important than its distribution through the year. Agriculture is possible only during the rainy months. The savanna zones get from five to twenty-five inches per year, but high temperatures and pronounced dry seasons lead to rapid evaporation and hence limit the types of agricultural activity that can be pursued. The most typical savanna trees are those that are drought-resistant, such as the acacia or the locust bean. On the other hand, the areas of heaviest rainfall along the equator have broad-leafed evergreen trees. As one goes away from the equator in either direction, or as one gains altitude, evergreens give way to deciduous varieties. Along the equator, there is little range of variation in temperature from one season to the next; temperatures drop only a few degrees at night. Rainfall may go to over one hundred inches.

The dry lands may receive less than five inches of rain a year, and sometimes the heart of the desert areas may go for years with no rainfall at all. When rain does fall, it may come in torrents that dump several inches within a few hours, creating floods and erosion that give way again almost immediately to desiccation. This high variability in annual rainfall causes Africa's periodic droughts. In some regions, rainfall will vary 20–40 percent from the mean in any year. A belt of highly variable rainfall covers the Sahara; south of the Sahara, a similar region of variable rainfall runs along the west coast from the Congo mouth southward, and inland far enough to include most of Angola and Namibia. The belt of savanna country reaches from Senegal on the west through to southern Somalia on the east, including all of Ethiopia.

Soils and Agriculture

Most African soils are typical tropical soils with little humus. Humus is the vegetable mold in the soil that results from slow decomposition of organic matter. In the so-called temperate zone there are at least some months during the year in which the oxidization of vegetable matter is slowed to a near standstill—winters enrich the soil not merely by the aeration that results from alternate freezing and thawing, but also from the fact that humus can decompose at a rapid rate only for half the year. The soil thus remains enriched. In tropical climates, humus oxidization goes on the year round, which means that much of the fertility that might be used by plants is wasted. Tropical soils have a humus content of 1.8 percent of total volume, or less. The humus content of soils in upper New York State or in Ohio runs from 10–12 percent, and in the richest Iowa farmland, as high as 16 percent. African soils are indeed poor.

Tropical soils are also easily leached. That is, the nutrients and minerals are washed out of them and flow away, either into the subsoil or into the sea. The lack of humus content and the ease of leaching interact with one another to ensure that thin tropical soils never achieve the richness of the soils of the temperate zones. The only exceptions in Africa are to be found in the Nile and Zambezi valleys and a few other areas in which there is a permanent, rich, alluvially deposited soil, maintained by seasonal flooding.

Since poor soils are easily exhausted, they can be worked only for short periods unless expensive and tedious steps are taken to maintain them. Few tropical peoples have ever had the technology or the knowledge to take the required steps. Rather, they have mined the soil of its nutrients by a method of farming known as "shifting cultivation."

Shifting cultivation is a method of farming in which land is cleared, either of the forest or of the grass that grows on it, and farmed without artificial fertilization. When the natural fertility of the plot has been exhausted, the farmer clears another patch and repeats the process, while the first patch is allowed to revert to fallow, and ultimately to regain fertility by natural means. The entire process may take as few as five or as many as thirty years. Some authorities (and some African farmers) claim that never again is the land as good as the first time it is cleared. This method of dry farming is widespread in the tropical world: in the Philippines and Southeast Asia, in much of India, and in tropical America. In Africa, farmers in some areas remove grass or tree limbs, burn them, and use the ash as fertilizer. In parts of central Africa, notably in Zambia and the surrounding areas, branches are cut off the large trees, burned, and corn planted directly in the ash beds.

Seen from the standpoint of modern technology and the needs of the modern world, shifting cultivation is a wasteful method of farming. Agricultural experts of the world, including tropical Africa, are working to improve the system. However, the method does provide short-term security. Africans are willing to make changes, but they must first be convinced that the changes are actually for the better—that greater plenty and fuller security will result. Mere introduction of the plow, for example, is not sufficient: deeply plowed land leaches faster than land which is merely scratched on the surface, and the oxidization of humus is speeded up by aeration. Fertilizer is expensive; green manure crops require as much labor as do crops from which a more immediately apparent return is reaped. Compost requires new and improved means of cartage in a continent still accustomed to head-loading. Moreover, the new cartage would require more, and different, animals, differently used, which in turn would require new types of roads and paths, not to mention control of animal diseases. Changing the pattern of African agriculture is a monumental task.

Some peoples in the African savannas—most of them are nomadic or transhumant—are primarily dependent on their herds. Nomads do not merely wander, but rather proceed in more or less fixed patterns of routes that may take several years to complete. If the cycle of movement is one required by the seasons and is repeated in an annual cycle, it is called transhumance. Mixed farming and herding is found; in other places herders and farmers cooperate to the point of mutual dependence. Herding is restricted to the savannas and some of the highlands. Only goats can be kept in the humid forests, where in a few places even goats cannot thrive. Goats and donkeys can live in any parts of the desert that will support human populations, although a few of the human populations do not keep them. Chickens are ubiquitous among the settled peoples, many of whom also keep ducks and pigeons.

In the past the major hazard for livestock has been endemic sleeping sickness. The problem has not been fully solved, although more research and effort have been expended on controlling sleeping sickness than on any other single health factor.

In Africa, as everywhere else, resources must be available in two senses: they must be physically present, and they must be culturally valued and used. This cultural availability may change rapidly.

In the decades just after World War II, much of the tropical world passed through what was called a "green revolution"—agricultural production rose rapidly even in the face of rapidly rising populations. In India and Latin America, such gains were made possible by new fertilizers, new varieties of seed, and new knowledge of tropical agricultural techniques. However, the green revolution by-passed Africa. The African environment is not well suited to the technology that created the green revolution. New seed varieties were tried, but it often turned out that the African seeds and techniques were already the best available for their peculiarly bad conditions.

In all the so-called "developing world," sub-Saharan Africa is the only major region where per-capita income and per-capita food production declined after about 1960. One important factor is the rapidly rising African population. When one of us studied the Tiv of central Nigeria in 1949–53, they numbered about 800,000. Today there are three and a half million of them. The current growth rate is estimated at about 3.2 percent per year for sub-Saharan Africa as a whole, and as high as 4 percent in countries like Kenya. Though total agricultural production has increased, it has not increased as fast as the population. Because many countries rely on agricultural exports like coffee and cocoa as a source of revenue, less food for local use can be grown. It has been estimated that per-capita food production in 1982 was 11 percent less than it had been in 1969. After the serious drought of 1983–84, it was down 16 percent.

Another factor is that many people who had worked the land moved into the cities where they were often unemployed or under-employed. At independence, around 90 percent of the population was rural; by the mid-1980s, only an estimated 77 percent still lived in rural areas, and only 71 percent was involved in agriculture.

In spite of the sad record before and into the early 1980s, some improvements began to show a more hopeful future after the drought years. When African countries became alarmed about declining food production, they took steps to make sure that the price structure was not rigged against the farmer. The government of Rhodesia under white rule had given favorable treatment to white farmers. After Rhodesia became the independent Zimbabwe under African control in 1980, the government set out to help the black farmers as well. By 1985 they had more than doubled their yield per acre in maize, and produced three times as much maize as they had done in 1978.

Minerals

Mineral resources other than gold were not much used by African societies before the beginning of the Christian era. Beginning about the twelfth century, perhaps even earlier, gold from sub-Saharan Africa began to reach the outer world in three separate streams. Gold from West Africa was carried across the Sahara by camel caravan to be minted in Morocco into coins that circulated throughout the Muslim world and even in Europe. A second stream moved overland from Ethiopian highlands to Egypt. The third, from placer gold diggings in Zimbabwe, was exported overland to the east coast and then north by sea in the hands of Muslim shippers mainly from Arabia, who sold most of it to India, though some reached the Muslim world as well. We cannot be precise about the size of these streams. However, the Zimbabwe and Ethiopian sources each exported on the order of five hundred kilograms in a good year. The West African supply was somewhat larger, perhaps fifteen hundred kilograms a year. The total may have been as high as 2.5 metric tons in a good year, though probably closer to 1 to 1.5 metric tons as an annual average. For the time, that was an enormous quantity of gold. It had a significant influence on monetary systems from India to Gibraltar.

Then in the 1880s, Europeans discovered gold on the Witwatersrand in South Africa. It lay in comparatively small, vertical deposits of low-quality ore, but in enormous quantities. If it had been discovered earlier, neither Africans nor Europeans would have had the technology to work it, but in the 1890s the machinery was available. South Africa rapidly became the most important source of gold anywhere. In the mid-1980s, South Africa alone produced more than 70 percent of the world's gold; additional supplies came from Zimbabwe, Zaire, and Ghana, among others.

Other metals had an early importance in long-distance trade. Copper mining began in central Africa in the second or third century of our era. By the time Vasco da Gama visited the East African coast in 1498, copper objects from either Zaire or Zambia were available for sale there. In West Africa, the copper trade was even more important, since West Africa lacked its own supplies. The trans-Saharan trade before A.D. 1500 included large copper shipments, mostly from North African or Saharan mines, but some from as far away as central Europe. The famous bronze statues of Ife in Nigeria were produced at this time out of copper from the Sahara or from Europe combined with tin from northern Nigeria.

As with gold, the quantities of copper mined increased enormously with the coming of the Europeans and their machines for digging deep mines and working the ore. By the mid-1980s, Zambia, Zaire, and South Africa together supplied about 17 percent of the world's copper.

Africa is almost a solid chunk of iron ore—most of it low-grade, though in some areas of Liberia and Guinea-Conakry, the content runs as high as 84 percent. The early mining technique in the Nimba Mountains on the Guinea-Liberian border was merely to cut down the trees, let the thin topsoil wash away, and use surface mining methods on the naked, rusting hills. In the mid-1980s, however, Africa accounted for only about 9 percent of world iron-ore production, mostly from South Africa, followed by Liberia and Mauritania.

Iron was forged in many parts of pre-colonial Africa. The southern fringes of the Sahara are littered with the remains of earthen furnaces which could turn out either wrought-iron or steel. In a few places in West Africa, smiths still make their own iron using the old methods, though today they are likely to recycle truck springs to make tools in the traditional shapes. Most iron used today is a product either of Africa's new iron industry or is imported from Korea or Japan.

Diamonds are one of the continent's most important assets. In the mid-1980s, Africa accounted for more than 80 percent of world diamond production, both industrial and gem stones.

All of these minerals—the gold, diamonds, iron, and copper—were explored and set into production before the colonial period ended. Oil, however, was new in the post-colonial era. Especially during the period of very high oil prices, from 1974 to the early 1980s, oil had an enormous influence on African development. Those countries that had large supplies readily available, like Nigeria, passed through an economic boom followed by a bust. Countries that had no oil found their economic development sharply curtailed by the rising cost of energy that was essential for transportation, industry, and modern agriculture. The extent of Africa's potential wealth in oil is still uncertain. By the mid-1980s, Africa produced about 4 percent of world crude oil, much of it from the off-shore continental shelf of the Gulf of Guinea in southern Nigeria, Gabon, and Angola.

Since the Second World War, many minor minerals from Africa have also increased in importance. These include mica, quartz, tungsten, bauxite, uranium, chrome, tantalite, columbite, cobalt, zinc, and manganese.

Africa's main economic claim to world attention has been minerals. That situation will probably continue for some time to come.

Diseases

Africa was long called "the white man's grave," and with reason. Strangers arriving on the tropical coasts once died at rates as high as 50 percent in the first year of residence because they lacked immunities to tropical diseases. People of African ancestry born in and raised in North America or the West Indies died at the same high rates if they came to Africa as adults.

Lowland, tropical Africa may well have the most intractable disease environment in the world. Over the past century or so, the struggle of modern medicine to deal with that environment shows some victories and some defeats. One victory during the early decades after the Second World War was won over yaws, which is, in its primary phase, a skin disease of the wet tropics (tertiary yaws affects the bone). It is a close relative of syphilis, but it is spread by skin contact rather than sexual transmission, and it was one of the world's most prevalent diseases before 1949, when the World Health Organization began a campaign of mass treatment with penicillin. The anti-yaws campaign was dramatically effective in the 1950s, and the disease nearly disappeared in some places. Continued surveillance was necessary to sustain the victory, however, and yaws began a revival in some parts of West Africa in the 1970s, in much the same way tuberculosis revived in the United States in the 1990s. The most notable victory, however, was the eradication of smallpox. In 1980, the World Health Organization announced that smallpox had disappeared worldwide, the last cases being in eastern Africa.

Another notable victory came in the early 1980s, when teams from the World Health Organization and cooperating African governments managed an immense reduction in the incidence of onchocerciasis or "river blindness." This disease exists in many parts of the tropical world, where it is carried by a fly with the descriptive name of *simulium damnosum*. In Burkina Faso and parts of northern Ghana, it used to be so serious along certain rivers that as many as 50 percent of middle-aged people had been blinded for life. Many other fertile valleys were left unoccupied because of the disease. The international campaign against its carriers and intermediate hosts, however, seems to have reduced it to minor proportions in West Africa.

Some diseases are easier to control than others. Yaws has been stamped out in wide regions of the continent. The curative drugs are cheap and can be distributed on a mass basis wherever health services reach all those who are infected.

Schistosomiasis is quite different. It is said to be the most widespread of all human diseases; 150 million people suffer from it chronically. It is caused by parasites of the genus *Schistosoma* that live in fresh water. They enter the human body through the skin and lay eggs which pass back into the water through human waste. After a complex cycle in the water, with snails as an intermediate host, the parasites are again ready to infect anyone who goes wading to fetch water, to wash clothes, or merely to cross a stream. Clean, piped water and efficient sanitation could end the disease, but these simple controls are far too expensive for most African countries. In the past, most of the drugs available against schistosomiasis had serious side effects or were very expensive. In the late 1970s, however, a number of new drugs appeared, which were both cheap and harmless to most patients.

For Africa as a whole, about half the population suffer from schistosomiasis; in some rural areas everyone over the age of two is infected. The disease is rarely fatal and may not be incapacitating for many years. Thus, it escaped notice until recent decades. Doctors now realize that progressive damage to the intestinal tract, lungs, and liver seriously affect the victim's vitality and contribute to early death. The new drugs show some possibilities of control, but general eradication is still years away.

Tropical Africa's bad reputation for health comes mainly from such insect-borne diseases as malaria and yellow fever. Yellow fever (which probably originated in Africa) is carried by *Aedes aegypti*, a mosquito that is fairly easy to control. A simple inoculation can protect the individual. Yellow fever is not likely to be a serious threat in the future, but it played an important role in African history. Infection in childhood is seldom fatal and produces a lifelong immunity. Only strangers who came to Africa as adults died at the first infection.

Malaria was equally dangerous in the past and continues to be a serious problem, harder to control than yellow fever, yaws, or schistosomiasis. It has been wiped out by effective mosquito control on some of the African islands like Mauritius and in North Africa. In tropical Africa, however, intensive mosquito control was tried for fifty years and failed. For a time people hoped for success with DDT, but resistant strains of mosquitos appeared. After World War

II, treatment of malaria with chloroquine looked promising, but the parasite evolved new resistant strains. By the early 1980s, an anti-malarial vaccine appeared to be theoretically possible, but it is not yet tried in practice.

The principal carriers of malaria in tropical Africa are the mosquitoes *Anopheles funestus* and *A. gambiae.* Together they guarantee that most of tropical Africa is a hyperendemic area, where virtually everyone suffers an infective bite. In addition, Africa is one home of falciparum malaria, the type that is most often fatal. Every African child therefore fights a life-and-death struggle with the malarial parasite during the first years of life. As many as half may die before reaching the age of five. The survivors are infected during the remainder of their lives, but rarely suffer from clinical symptoms. They acquire an apparent immunity that hides the progressive damage to the liver and other organs. Before the development of tropical medicine, strangers paid a price in adult mortality similar to that paid by Africans in infancy. With modern drugs, Africa may no longer be the "white man's grave," but it continues to be the "black child's grave" to a degree far beyond the range of recent Western experience.

Sleeping sickness, or trypanosomiasis, is also an insect-borne disease. The vector is the tsetse fly—actually several different flies of the genus *Glossina* carry several different parasites of the genus *Trypanosoma.* Both the disease and the flies are peculiar to Africa; even there they are confined to restricted regions in the humid tropics. Some are found in the forest, while others thrive in wooded or brush-covered savanna. Because these flies cannot survive in open grassland, clearing the brush is one means of control. Like other forms of disease control, this one requires expensive and continuous effort.

Unlike malaria or schistosomiasis, trypanosomiasis is not, in most areas, a direct problem for the human population. Although most types are fatal to people, people are not infected as often as domestic animals or wild game. In the past, epidemics have killed as much as two-thirds of the human population of some small regions, but such occurrences are rare. The continuing and serious problem is with animals. Without cattle, a diet containing enough protein is difficult to acquire. One result of insufficient protein is the prevalence of kwashiorkor, a form of malnutrition caused by the lack of milk and meat that domestic animals could provide. Kwashiorkor in infancy can be permanently damaging.

These diseases are an obvious hindrance to African development today, and they have played an incalculable role in the African past. Three quarters of all the world's cases of schistosomiasis are in

Africa; Africa appears to have far more than its share of hyperendemic falciparum malaria; yellow fever originated in Africa; and trypanosomiasis is still confined to that continent.

Tropical Africa has also had—and still has—the full range of diseases common to Europe and North America. This kept Africa from suffering as South America did on its first contact with European diseases, but one of Africa's most serious disease problems is one it shares with other continents. This is the world-wide emergence of AIDS, the acquired immune deficiency syndrome. Some authorities believe that AIDS originated in Africa, but that theory of origins is only one of several. AIDS did, however, spread at first most rapidly in Africa and North America—among homosexuals in America and through heterosexual contact in Africa.

The first appearance of the new disease was deceptive because it led to its public characterization as peculiar to homosexuals and Africans. Ten years or more can pass between the first infection with the human immunodeficiency virus (HIV), which causes AIDS and the appearance of the disease itself. Another delay of several years can take place before the victims die, which all of them do. This means that the present number of recorded AIDS cases is only a small indicator of a much larger number of people already infected. The incidence of HIV infection in the mid-1990s showed that it was spreading heterosexually in Europe and North America and that it was spreading rapidly in southern and Southeast Asia, which could soon replace Africa and North America as the principal focus of the disease.

The spread elsewhere does not alter its seriousness for Africa. For 1990, the World Health Organization has recorded 283,000 actual cases of AIDS in Africa, but it estimated that the number actually infected was more likely over five million. The special African problems with HIV infection are poverty and education. It has long been known that the use of condoms can slow the spread of AIDS, but it is hard to convince people of that fact. Even if they were convinced, condoms are very expensive for people with the income levels common in tropical Africa. Poverty also stands in the way of using what treatments are known. The drug AZT can slow down the consequences of the disease, but AZT is expensive and only a tiny minority of Africans with HIV infection have been able to use it. To keep the AIDS epidemic in perspective, it is important to remember that as of 1985, more people died of malaria than died of AIDS. But the long-run picture is more serious, though it is hard to predict from the evidence available. A significant population downturn is possible in the areas that are most severely afflicted.

In addition to the impact of disease on Africans themselves, disease contributed to Africa's isolation by keeping visitors away. Traders who crossed the Sahara from North Africa found that residence in the sudan areas brought disease and death. When they therefore stopped at the desert's edge, tropical Africa lost an opportunity to keep in close contact with the world north of the Sahara. After the fifteenth century, when European traders began to arrive by sea along the African coast, they made the same discovery—that their death rates were astronomical. A few—but only a few—found it worthwhile to take the risk in order to buy gold and slaves. Africa thus remained largely isolated from the inter-communicating zone that stretched from Spain and Morocco to China.

MAPPING AFRICA

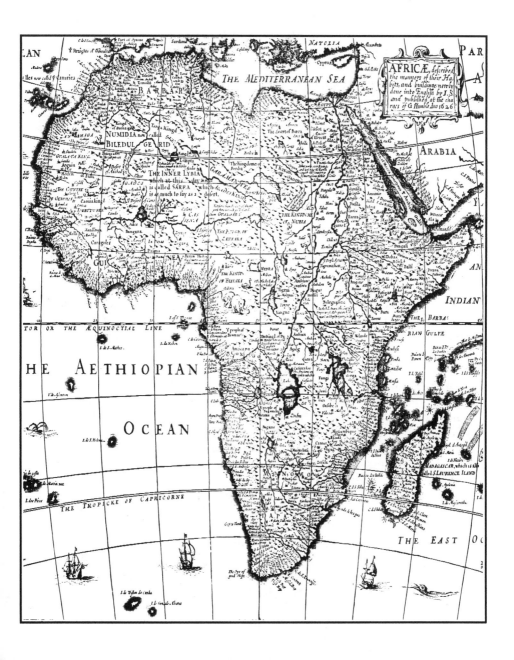

Early scholars of and travellers in Africa made several assumptions that remained fixed until fairly recent times. The most telling of those assumptions was that everyone in Africa belonged to some "tribe" or other, and that each of those tribes was territorially delimited. Colonial administrators, when they got to Africa in the late 1800s and early 1900s, found such assumptions congenial because administration was easier if each group could be "put into its place." Museums could arrange their displays better if they knew the juxtaposition and historical relationships of the people whose artifacts they displayed.

Such a concern with territorial areas also worked for anthropologists of the early era, who were concerned with what they called "culture areas." The idea of culture areas began in an effort to straighten out the cultures of Native Americans whose cultural traditions had been badly beaten or destroyed. Early anthropologists were in the business of reconstructing them before the memories of older people were completely gone. Mapping culture areas was in the air.

However, maps cast a long shadow: anthropologists, without serious consideration of the results of what they were doing, tried to get a picture of Africa "as it must have been" in what they conceived, erroneously, as a long period of stability before contact with the outside world.

The trouble with mapping is that somebody has to draw a line some place. Those lines—like the international boundaries that were drawn in the early days of colonialism—had an immense effect on our understanding of the situation in the years following. Nobody questions that there are significant differences between the cultures found in coastal West Africa and those found in the sahel, or between the cultural traditions of the Congo Basin and those of the East African Highlands. The trick is in deciding just what criteria you use to draw a line on a map. Those lines are the equivalent of boundaries. Thus maps separating one people from another, no matter how carefully they are made, give a false idea about the relationship of peoples who were separated by those phony lines. Cultural reality is too complex for a simple map—distribution of house types, myths, language, art styles, crops, and market places do not necessarily coincide. Lines on a map, if we read them too

34

literally, dull our realization of relationships among peoples.

There were time boundaries as well as space boundaries—and they were just as misleading. Too many early anthropologists, under the influence of the reconstructors of Native American cultures, failed to note anything about the colonial administrators, missionaries, traders, and the African men who, in the new situation, had to migrate to the mines or to European farms to earn money to support their families. They also left out "minorities," many of whom had been there for centuries—foreign fishing villages in the midst of farming communities, nomads who crossed and recrossed the territory of settled people, traders belonging to trade diasporas that could stretch for hundreds of miles. Only when these others had been excluded could any subject group be placed within boundaries on a map. The mapmaker's problem was to get all people located in the right place, either to govern or to study them. They left out many minorities; even more important, they left out the relations among the various peoples they divided.

Maps are, however, convenient for providing generalizations—if you do not misuse them. Here we present only two maps, one for the languages of Africa and the second for ecological adaptation. Both represent snap-shots taken at the time of colonial conquest in the late nineteenth century. We also discuss the peoples of Africa briefly, but specifically omit maps of "the races of Africa" of the sort common around the 1930s because the fuzzy idea of race and the precision of lines on a map are simply incompatible. Maps of "the culture areas of Africa" are also omitted; they were important for a few years after the middle 1930s, but they too impart as many falsehoods as they do truths.

The Peoples of Africa

It is always wise to be suspicious of any list of "races," but it is convenient—no matter how unscientific—to mention seven principal physical types in present-day sub-Saharan Africa. In approximate order of their numerical importance they are: 1) Negro, 2) Ethiopian/Somali (formerly called "Hamite," sometimes Erythriote), 3) Caucasian, 4) Indian, 5) Khoisan, 6) Oriental, and 7) Pygmy.

The physical types on our list are those visible to any superficial observer. Negro and Caucasian types are familiar throughout the world. Negro-appearing people are the dominant population in sub-Saharan Africa. People of the other types are either scattered or dominant in a small region.

The Ethiopian/Somali type is dominant in those two countries and in Djibuti—broadly the eastern peninsula called "the Horn of Africa." They are probably a stabilized mixture between people from Arabia and from Africa, but they are a different physical type from either. Past authorities had them classified as a separate "Hamitic" race, sometimes called a sub-class of Caucasian because Amharic, one of their main languages is similar to Arabic and Hebrew. That myth had to be abandoned after the fact sank in that languages are learned, not inherited.

The Khoisan people are another distinct physical type of purely African origin, fairly short, with kinky hair and a yellowish skin. They are found mainly in the southwest—in parts of Botswana, Namibia, and the Republic of South Africa. The name "Khoisan" is a made-up word derived from San (the hunting and gathering peoples formerly called Bushmen) and the Khoikhoi (the cattle-keeping people who once occupied the hinterland of the Cape of Good Hope and were once called by the now-insulting term "Hottentot"). Most authorities think that they and the Pygmies of the forest belt farther north may well represent the remains of a broadly scattered but sparse population that occupied the whole of central and southern Africa before the Negroes moved in from the north during the past three thousand years or so. Pygmies live mainly in the tropical forest, where they continue to specialize in hunting. They are today mixed physically and culturally with their Negro neighbors. Pygmies and Khoisan may have descended from common ancestors, but they look different today.

The groups we have called Caucasian, Oriental, and Indian are all recent immigrants from elsewhere. The main Caucasian group is the settler minority in South Africa and Zimbabwe, descended largely from Dutch and British settlers. Other Caucasian immigrants, largely of French ancestry, are found in North Africa. In the Nilotic Sudan and scattered down the East African coast, the immigrants came from Arabia. They have intermarried with their Negro neighbors for several centuries. In cities everywhere, scattered Caucasian communities from Europe and North America are more numerous than they were during the colonial periods. They tend to live concentrated near buildings labelled "Hilton" or "Novotel."

The largest and oldest settlement of Orientals came earlier to the large island that is now the Malagasy Republic. They came by canoe from Indonesia and settled on the then-uninhabited island. Negroid peoples from the African mainland came later, so that most Malagasy today are mixed, though their Southeast Asian origins are visible. Other Orientals are the Chinese communities of South

Africa and the Mascarene Islands—Reunion and Mauritius —and, in smaller numbers, in most African cities.

People of Indian descent are mostly urban people, except in South Africa, Reunion, and Mauritius, where they represent the descendants of migrant sugar workers. Substantial Indian communities, mostly engaged in commerce, are found up and down the East Africa coast and its hinterland. Kenyans of Indian descent are about 3 percent of the population and are important economically. Other, smaller and more scattered Indian communities are found in West Africa as well.

Some authorities would like to sub-divide the Indians into several different physical types, just as others in the past have tried to distinguish "true Negroes," "Bantu," or "Nilotes" among the Negroid-looking Africans. The effort has some merit for trying to trace prehistoric migrations across Africa or India, but such distinctions have little value for understanding recent African history. Race is, after all, in the eye of the beholder.

The Languages of Africa

African languages have sometimes, in the past, been said to be so simple that they contain vocabularies of only a few hundred words or so difficult as to be unlearnable by ordinary Europeans or Americans. Both statements are absurd. African languages are fine instruments that can be as expressive and as expandable as their speakers care to make them.

Some African languages contain consonantal sounds not found elsewhere: the four clicks of the San languages (which have been taken over by some of the surrounding Bantu-speakers) are probably the most famous. The double consonants of some west coast languages occur only there—for example, gb, pronounced by releasing g (with the tongue and roof of the mouth) and b (with the lips) at the same time. African vowel systems tend to be simple like Spanish or Japanese rather than complex as in such languages as French and English.

Many African languages are tonal—a fact that scares off anyone who is preconvinced that tone is difficult and who hence refuses to relax and sing. But anyone can, if they lose their self-consciousness and try, learn to speak African languages. Speakers of Indo-European languages can learn most African languages with somewhat greater ease than they can learn Arabic or Chinese or Hungarian. On the other hand, they should not confuse a smattering of what is called "kitchen Swahili" or "trader Hausa" with knowing an African language.

There are many languages in Africa: over 1,400 even if one allows for possible misclassification when several dialects of a language are counted as separate distinct languages. Joseph Greenberg made the current classification in the 1960s. His classification recognizes five major language groups, shown on figure 4. Far and away the

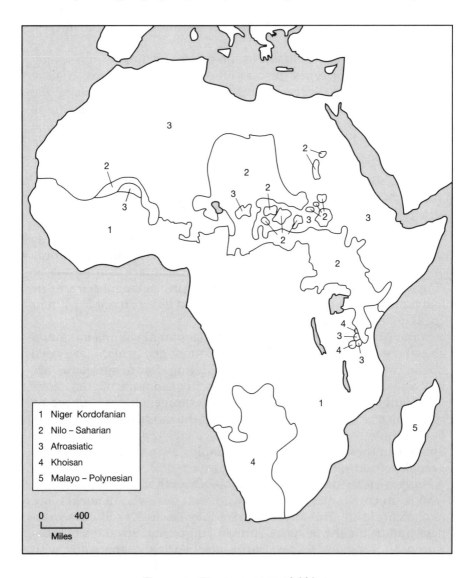

1 Niger Kordofanian
2 Nilo – Saharian
3 Afroasiatic
4 Khoisan
5 Malayo – Polynesian

0   400
Miles

Figure 4. The languages of Africa.

largest of the language groups is the group that Greenberg calls the Niger-Kordofanian group of families. Its most important member is the Benue-Congo family of languages, which subdivides into six subfamilies. One of these subfamilies contains the well-known "Bantu languages" which cover most of central and southern Africa—but all are closely related to one another, reflecting the fact that it has been only in recent centuries that the Bantu peoples have spread into the forest regions and down the eastern and southern highlands.

The second large group, called the Nilo-Saharan, includes the languages spoken by the Nilotes as well as many spoken in the western sudan and the area of the middle Niger River.

The Afro-Asiatic group of languages contains Semitic languages that are spoken in Southwest Asia as well as in North Africa; it also contains Arabic, Hebrew, Berber, and Cushitic languages, as well as various languages spoken today around Lake Chad, of which the most significant is Hausa. Of the four major branches of this group, only the Semitic languages extend into Asia. The others, with their many individual languages, are spoken in Africa. This does not mean, of course, that the ancestors of the people who speak Hebrew or Arabic ever came from Africa. Languages can be learned. The only language group that even vaguely corresponds to physical appearance is the Khoisan—and even here the distinctive clicks have worked their way into the languages of their neighbors like the Zulu.

The final African language group is Malagasy, spoken all over the island of Madagascar. Malagasy is the first African language to be written in Roman script (several before it had been written in Arabic script)—missionaries reduced it to writing in the 1820s. As a result the Malagasy national archives today contain government documents in that language going back a full sixty years before the French conquest of 1895.

In most of Africa, colonial languages became the official languages of law, politics, journalism, and education. Africans educated in Europe began using them well before the colonial period had even begun. Africans have published books in European languages since the eighteenth century, several dozen of them before the colonial period. They still do. English and French have become the ordinary vehicle for African authors who want to reach a wide audience, and the names of Chinua Achebe, Amos Tutuola, Wole Soyinka, and Ousemane Sembene have become internationally known. Only recently, the first Nobel Prize in literature to be awarded to an African went to Wole Soyinka—for works written in English.

The presence of foreign traders—in some numbers since the

seventeenth century—led to new, mixed languages called "pidgins" (from the pidgin-Chinese word for business). In time they came to be established as the first language for some speakers. When that happens, the languages are called "creoles," after the similarly mixed Afro-European languages of the Americas.

In the Cape Verde islands and in Guinea-Bissau, Portuguese-African creoles have existed for centuries—formal languages with their own grammars and dictionaries. In the Indian Ocean islands of Reunion and Mauritius, the normal language is an Afro-French creole, though the official languages are French and English respectively, despite the majority of the population being descended from immigrants from India. In Sierra Leone, a similar creole, called Krio, is the language of discourse in the Freetown area; it serves as the language of trade in the interior markets.

Krio is not only a creole, but a *lingua franca*. Although the original lingua franca was that variant of Italian which served as the language of commerce in the Medieval Mediterranean, today the term means a language used for communication by people for whom it is not the home language. In East Africa, Swahili (a Bantu language with many Arabic and English loan-words) is the language of the coast of East Africa. It is the home language of comparatively few people, but serves as the second language for many millions. It is the official language of Kenya and Tanzania. In Tanzania all children must be educated in Swahili through primary school.

Language is an important policy issue all over Africa. African governments and intellectuals know that they need access to one of the world languages, preferably English. At the same time, they want to preserve their African heritage. Thus all Tanzanians learn two languages in school: Swahili and English—and that may be in addition to whatever language they speak at home (although the home language of urban children is likely to be Swahili).

Other countries began with English, or even switched to English. Ethiopia has Amharic as an ancient written language, but it adopted English-language education after the Second World War because Amharic was not popular with the non-Amharic-speaking majority, and because English provided an easier and quicker access to the broader world.

In mapping African languages, we placed them where they were about the beginning of the colonial period. But languages move when people move, and sometimes they spread without any migration. The actual languages spoken in Africa have shifted a little with the massive movements of people in the twentieth century. Most Africans already spoke two or more languages with varying degrees of competence. As they move, they learn to speak more languages, and with years of residence in a foreign place to speak them better. This is one reason why the use of European languages and other linguae francae has become so important in this century.

Subsistence Areas of Africa

The next area of mappable culture in Africa is the overlapping zones or belts of traditional subsistence crops, determined in part by the patterns of weather and climate shown in figure 5. However, no map can give a clear account of a country like Nigeria, which exports oil and imports much of its food. We can, however, show areas of African subsistence before extensive trade and importation began.

The subsistence areas are important for some other aspects of culture. Subsistence activity shows a close correspondence with the working habits of both sexes; with the size and composition of work groups; with trade; with diet patterns; indeed, even with musculature of the body. It is also true that subsistence patterns were relatively little changed by the colonial experience.

Foraging

There are—or were until very recently—a few remnant groups who subsist on a foraging economy. The Pygmies of the forests of Zaire are primarily hunters and gatherers (although trade with neighboring farmers brings them part of their vegetable food); so are the San of southern Africa. The most important group of foragers are the fishermen on the coasts and rivers. Fishermen are among the few Africans who do not show dietary deficiencies. They usually trade a part of their catch for vegetables and one or more of the starchy staples. Women of the group grow some grain or tubers.

Herding

African herders are primarily cattle herders, although the Sahara shelters a few peoples who keep camels, and the Serengeti plain and other areas in East Africa are the home of peoples who keep large flocks of goats (that animal being all but ubiquitous on the continent, in any event). Herdsmen's diets may center on milk as a staple, but almost all herding peoples add starchy staples, either by harvesting their own crops or, more commonly, through well-integrated systems of trade with settled agricultural peoples.

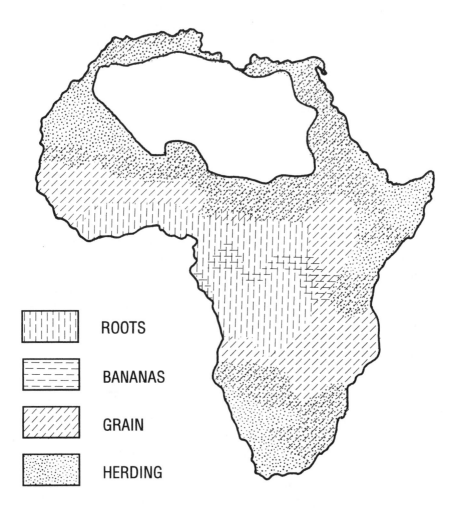

Figure 5. Subsistence areas of Africa.

Camel herders are found throughout the inhabited Sahara and on both its northern and southern fringe, as well as in the eastern Horn. The "cattle belt" of Africa runs from the Atlantic in Senegal, along the corridor between the forests and the desert with only a few breaks, then turns south along the Nile. From Lake Victoria it proceeds southward, eventually swinging back to the Atlantic in Angola, south of the forests of the Congo but north of the Kalahari Desert. Much of the area of East and South Africa, where cattle are the greatest concern but do not actually form the subsistence base or provide the staple part of the diet, must be included in the "grain belt,'' the staple being maize or sorghum. Cattle do, however, form the basis of the morality and prestige activities of the men of that area, and many pastoralists exchange dairy products for grain.

A great deal has been written about the East African herding peoples who tap blood from the neck veins of their cattle, mix it with sour milk, and eat the mixture. Actual studies by food economists, dieticians, and geographers, however, have recently indicated that blood accounts for at most a few hundreds of calories a week. Milk and butter are much more important. People seldom kill animals for meat, but do of course eat those they sacrifice.

Agriculture

By far the greatest number of Africans are farmers. They can be sensibly divided into three groups: those among whom grain crops are the major staple, those who grow root crops, and those who grow tree crops. Bananas, a tree crop, are the basis of the diet in a belt stretching westward from the vicinity of Lake Victoria to the Atlantic. These bananas are not the sweet bananas that Americans and Europeans eat for breakfast or dessert, but are plantains— scarcely sweet, much starchier, and of a less oily consistency. Plantains are cooked and, like the grain and the roots, made into porridge. Dates form a staple in a relatively large area of the Sahara.

The grain belt forms a crescent, inside of and overlapping with the herding crescent. There is another, smaller grain belt along the Mediterranean coast, where the staple grains are barley and wheat. South of the Sahara, however, the grains are of a different sort. Farmers from Senegal south through Liberia and into the Ivory Coast grow an indigenous African variety of rice as their staple food. They grow it either as upland rice or sow it into patches which they have cleared out of the forest. Although African rice has remained a staple in this area, much of the acreage has been put into Asian rice, which Africans consider superior.

As one proceeds eastward from Senegal, the grain changes to sorghum and millet. Still farther east, in the southern sudan and Ethiopia, the primary grains are eleusine, teff, and fonio. As one turns south, east of Lake Victoria, maize and sorghum are the staples; there is some pearl millet in the southern Congo area and in a few others, but aside from that, maize and sorghum form the staples all the way to the southern end of the continent.

Throughout the grain-producing areas of Africa, the mode of agriculture and the nature of the diet are similar. The chief agricultural implements are the hoe—short-handled in most places but long-handled in parts of Zimbabwe, Zambia, and Zaire—and the long knife called a *matchet* in western Africa and a *panga* in Swahili-speaking areas. In some places the digging stick, with or without a metal tip, is still to be found. The plow, pulled by oxen, is found today in parts of eastern and southern Africa. In most places—but there are, as usual, exceptions—the heavy work of clearing the land is done by men, who also prepare the fields for planting and may do the planting. The women then take over—if they have not indeed been doing the work already—and take care of weeding and harvesting. It is also the women who carry the grain back to the homestead or to the drying platforms. It is stored in granaries which are made, in most areas, something like the houses but smaller and usually set up off the ground to give some protection from termites, rats, and other pests. These granaries— and the food in them—are often the property of the household head, but the food is just as often considered the property of the woman who is obliged to feed her children from it as well as her husband, who provided her with land and cleared it for her.

Except for rice, which is cooked whole, grain in Africa is ground— traditionally by hand on stone, today often by hand-operated mills or power mills at the village or town center—and cooked into porridge. A thick, malleable porridge is Africa's bread, providing most of the calories of most African diets. It is eaten dipped into a sauce of meat or vegetables or both. Oils and fats are plentiful— the particular one varies with the part of the country—from shea butter to palm oil to peanut oil to sesame oil and many others. Oils are part of the sauce, not of the porridge.

The subsistence area based on root crops forms a core in the Congo basin, with a long strip along the Guinea coast. Crops are yams, manioc, taro, sweet potatoes, and a few other minor root crops. None of these roots, it would appear, is indigenous to Africa. The yam is Malaysian (not the sweet potatoes that Americans call yams, which are also present); manioc is South American.

Root crops, as food, are generally considered by Western dieticians to be inferior to grains, because they lack some of the essential vitamins and minerals. Growing root crops puts a little more work on the men, who must, in the shallow soil, make two-foot mounds in which to grow yams, or smaller ones in which to grow manioc or sweet potatoes. Roots are either cooked green or else dried and made into a flour, then mashed or stewed into porridge and eaten with sauces.

Drink as well as food follows the same mapped areas. Again to oversimplify, herders drink honey beer, although some of them make beer from traded grain. In the grain belt, arguments rage about the virtues and faults of beer made with maize, sorghum, and millet. In the banana country, bananas are mashed and made into beer. Root crop country is approximately the same as oil palm country; there the staple beverage is palm wine.

Westerners who are thoroughly familiar with market economy and with the particular tensions and insecurities it brings would do well to remember that subsistence economy also brings its own tensions: food during the next year is totally dependent on one's own labors and on the fruits of one's fields, more or less ameliorated by dependence on kinsmen. Droughts and floods, locusts and birds are personal enemies. Religious myth and ritual, like insecurity, center around food production. Africans who have entered a market economy are adjusting to new types of insecurities: unemployment, boring jobs, loss of self-determination. Yet with most Africans, even now, subsistence is a major psychic as well as practical pursuit. In creating subsistence, one must work with and cooperate with kinsmen, neighbors, and the forces of the gods.

Part II

AFRICAN INSTITUTIONS

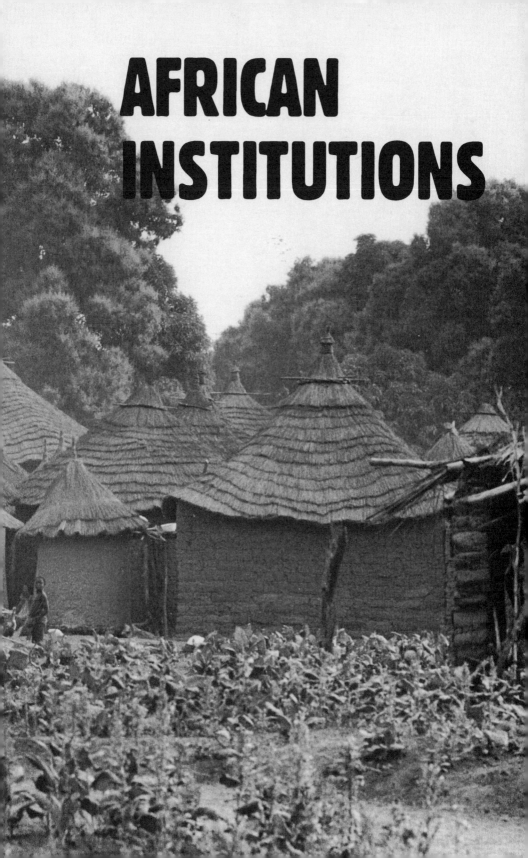

4

AFRICAN ARTS

All people grow up with cultural institutions that provide them with models they use when looking at the world around them. In order to understand the institutions of a foreign culture you must be sure that the institutions you already know do not hide the alien ideas. If you look through the lenses of your own culture without being aware of those lenses, you are likely to see nothing but inadequate reflections of what you already know. Certainly you cannot see any other culture as do those who use it. Looking at unfamiliar cultures, thus, is an exercise in stereoscopic vision. You achieve that stereoscopic vision by learning more and more about the lens through which you were taught, as a child, to look at the world. The more complex the world becomes, the more you must learn about living with other people and their very different cultures—and hence the more you must learn about your lenses.

Each of the chapters in this section makes almost as many observations about American and European cultures as about African cultures. The point is to help you get your own convictions and opinions out of the murk of unexamined assumptions. When they are made overt, they will no longer hinder your understanding of African institutions. Learning about African institutions also clarifies and explains a lot about Western institutions.

Grammatical tense is a problem in talking about African institutions. To put everything in the present tense falsifies statements for two reasons: it makes it seem as if all Africa and Africans are more alike than they actually are and also obscures the processes of change and development that constantly occur in African society, as in any other. Yet, to put one's description into in the past tense is even more falsifying. The African past continues to inform the present. It presents a set of premises Africans use to understand their own changing and developing.

The compromise we have reached is to write about cultural institutions in the present tense, asking readers to understand that what is described here is a summary of some of the ideas out of which today's African institutions have grown, and which to a degree persist. As Africans participate in global society, these ideas get altered. They nevertheless form the basic values—the lenses— through which Africans look at what goes on in that global society.

Today, of course, all educated Africans have good English or French or both, often as mother tongues. However, most European and American students do not yet have the advantage of the bicultural style that is second nature to these educated Africans. We have tried to tackle this problem head-on, pointing out ideas in our own culture that are comparable to African ideas—ideas that must, however, be fully examined if we are to translate African ideas into English successfully.

All art can be said to have two sweeping characteristics: it embodies a message within an idiom of communication, and it arouses a sense of mystery—a feeling that it is more than it appears to be. "Good" art, no matter what its cultural origins or uses, can arouse this sense of mystery in many persons, from many cultures. In that sense, Africa has an extensive "good" art. It has taken its place in museums and in the collections of many art lovers throughout the world.

Yet art also bears a "message" from artist to viewer. It is impossible for an artist *not* to convey a message. For some the métier may be the kind of measured realism that can call up the calm of a forest twilight; for others, it may be an abstract about art itself.

Art may be valued either as a message-bearing comment or as mystery. It may in fact be valued for both of these things at once. Yet, too often art appreciators—those who prize the mystery for itself—object to the people who intellectualize and put the messages into words. Anthropologists and others who use art to get at the temper of a culture (much as critics use it to get at the temper of an age or of a creative mind) usually denigrate the mere appreciator. Fullest comprehension implies both.

The mystery of good art crosses cultural barriers. The message may not. Therefore, in order to appreciate the art fully, something of the cultural background must be known to make the message clear.

African art is to be understood on at least three levels. It can be studied as form and technique. Second, the purpose and the meaning—the aesthetics, indeed—must be garnered not only from the artists but from the critics. Finally, the impact of African art on Western (or some other) art can be examined.

The Forms and Techniques of African Art

African arts are known and appreciated far beyond Africa. African music is one of the world's great musics. The most dramatic of its contributions lies in its polyrhythmic structure. European music specialized in polytonality, using several tones at once, while African polyrhythms are complex combinations of fairly simple but different rhythms, all played at once. Western music may use "two against three"—the triplet played against two "full-value" notes during the same time span. Rarely, in Western music, a third rhythm may be added. In African music, on the other hand, five such rhythms are common, and as many as a dozen at a time have been used.

African dancing follows those polyrhythms. Different parts of the body take up one of the different rhythms in the orchestra. The polyrhythms in the orchestra are thus duplicated by the dancer's body. The head moves in one rhythm, the shoulders in another; the arms in still a third, the trunk in another, and the feet in still another. A viewer who has learned to see and feel the polyrhythms in the dance as it reflects the music can appreciate that African dancing both demands great precision and allows great freedom of expression to the dancers. African dancing is still a folk art; there have been a few attempts to produce it for the stage, notably the ballet companies sponsored by several African countries. Too often, however, the individual dances have been cut short so as not to bore European and American audiences—and in the process deprived the dancers of extended play for their imagination and the variations that each dance requires if the rhythms are to be fully explored.

The central form of African literature is the dramatic tale. African tales have affected the literatures of many lands, particularly the southern United States and the Caribbean area, where the so-called Brer Rabbit stories have caught on. Collections of African folk tales are also plentiful, but in all of these versions the true quality of the original has been left behind in Africa. A mere tale on a printed page produces little more than would retelling the plot of *As You Like It* in two paragraphs, with a moral tacked on at the end, fable-fashion. African dramatic tales, in Africa, have a theatrical quality. They are told and acted out before audiences who participate in musical choruses and spoken responses. Individual taletellers may be assisted by a dozen or more people who are costumed and "cast," as in any other theater art. The taleteller makes up songs, centering around the situation of the tale, and teaches the choruses of the songs to the audience, thus assuring audience response. The stories of the tales are well known. The achievement of the individual artist is to be found in the music, in the particular version of the tale, and in the way the teller manipulates the dramatic elements to enlarge or highlight the moral. The result is living theater. It cannot be overemphasized that African folk tales, written on half a sheet of paper in a Western language, lose all but the stalled "plot" of the original. The art is gone.

Africa has produced world-renowned novelists like Chinua Achebe. Playwright and poet Wole Soyinka, whose plays have been produced in Africa, Europe and North America, won the Nobel Prize for Literature. A host of young writers in English and French—and a few in African languages—are garnering fine reputations today. Several American and European universities have added courses in African literature, and in the last twenty years African universities have also added them.

African painting has a long history, but is comparatively unknown in the West. The earliest cave paintings go back several thousand years, but as yet have not been dated with any great precision. Experts do, however, know the marks of various periods of such paintings—some of the earliest are huge representations of human beings eleven feet high and animals as much as twenty-six feet long. Rock painting in the Sahara is still being done today, but the figures are miniatures rather than gigantic murals. Rock paintings have been found and studied in most parts of the continent. Expert opinion says that it will be some decades before a real "history" of African painting can be written. Since the middle of the twentieth century, African painters have appeared in great number, and some have acquired international reputations.

The best known of African arts, outside of Africa at least, is sculpture. Most African sculpture, except that done in terra cotta, is produced by a subtractive process—material taken away from a core instead of added to a core. Soapstone carvings are to be found in areas of Sierra Leone, and iron sculpture in several isolated places in Africa. Ivory was a favorite medium in the Kingdom of Benin and in Zaire, and ivory sculpture is carried on in some areas today. However, the major media for African sculpture are wood and various alloys of copper, tin, and zinc that hover around bronze and brass.

African carvers work almost exclusively in green wood. The carver must know a great deal about the qualities of different woods, so that they will not crack too much when dry, although cracks appear in most pieces of African art even in Africa. Cracking is a common problem when the pieces are subjected to the high and dry temperatures of American and European homes and museums.

Woodworking is done with an adze and finished with a knife. In some parts of the continent, some sculptors traditionally use rough leaves as sandpaper. Today many use sandpaper. The carvings may be painted with mineral and vegetable colors (and today with imported paints), the most common being lampblack set by the sap of any of several trees.

Indigenous African sculpture falls into three main sorts: one is the figurine, which may vary from small and simple figures only a few inches high to elaborate carved house posts, stools, or other functional forms. The figurines are fundamentally adaptations from the tree trunk, with the heaviest weight at the bottom. The next form is the mask. African masks are among the best known in the world and artistically are among the most satisfying. They come in three main shapes: those that are worn over the face, those worn on top of the head, and the helmet-type masks which fit down over the head. The third form is decoration of various useful objects, ranging from doors to spoons to bobbins.

African bronzes are all cast by the lost-wax method. Each piece is therefore unique. In this method, the technique is fundamentally additive, rather than subtractive. Over a core of some sort—usually dried mud in the traditional forms—the sculptor models in wax whatever he wants to reproduce in metal. To this he adds, also in wax, several long, tentacle-like appendages. When the core is thoroughly dry and the waxen model completely set, it is covered by several coats of the finest pottery slip clay available. The whole is then covered with coarser pottery clay. When the mold is heated, the melted wax runs out through the tentacle passageways. Then molten metal is poured into the hot clay mold—a skilled task if one is to avoid air bubbles—and exactly fills the space left by the melted wax, thus reproducing the original image.

The History of African Art

In a fairly narrow area between Katsina and Katsina Ala in northern Nigeria from about 600 B.C. to A.D. 200, the Nok culture was the home of the earliest sculpture (except for Egypt) that we know to be unequivocally African. It was discovered in the course of tin-mining excavations. Nok art, as we know it, is almost entirely a pottery or terra cotta art. Most terra cotta, even in Africa, is done by an additive technique in which the sculptor starts with a core and adds more clay as the sculpture progresses. However, some examples of Nok terra cotta showed forms more suitable to a subtractive technique, like carving. It was hence inferred that carving in wood (necessarily lost to time and the elements) was also present. Nok art which has been preserved is done in fine pottery, excellently fired: hollow figures, three-quarter life size, in some cases. Such an art is technically very demanding. Nok culture is now represented by several score of examples—heads, limbs, and some furniture.

The earliest bronze sculpture so far found in Africa is from eastern Nigeria, and is known as the Igbo Ukwu style. It has been dated to the tenth century A.D. Among the finest pieces of measuredly naturalistic sculpture ever produced anywhere are the bronze heads of Ife in Nigeria, which date from about the twelfth century A.D. Because they are in a classical naturalistic style, it was assumed when they were found (in the early twentieth century by Frobenius, the German ethnologist, folklorist and adventurer) that Africans could not have made them. Therefore, "obviously" it was the Portuguese who did them. The fact that there was no technique of this sort known to the Portuguese at this time was not allowed to belie the stereotypes. Once carbon-14 dates made the age fairly precise, it was necessary to admit that they could only have been done by Africans.

Frobenius turned up a good many of these Ife heads in terra cotta and one in brass. The brass piece that he discovered he "bought" (in a manner of speaking) from the family in charge of the Olokun Grove. The British administrative officers on the spot refused him permission to export it. After considerable contretemps, Frobenius returned the bronze and some of the terra cotta. In the 1940s, however, Leon Underwood, a British sculptor, discovered that the head Frobenius had returned was a sand casting, whereas all the other Ife heads were lost-wax castings. No African artists had ever done sand casting. The assumption is unavoidable either that Frobenius had not returned the original or else that be was not the true discoverer, and discovered only the copy. Except for that original piece and one other (which is in the British Museum) the complete set of brass heads (but not of terra cotta heads) is now in the possession of the Oni of Ife and housed in his small but magnificent museum.

Another ancient art that deserves attention is from the Kingdom of Benin (not to be confused with the present-day Republic of Benin west of Nigeria), some 110 miles southeast of Ife. Benin art flooded Great Britain, and indeed the Western European museums, at the very end of the nineteenth century. At that time (1897) the consolidation of European power in Africa was being carried on most furiously, as the colonial powers, in accordance with the Berlin Conference, busily occupied the territories they had claimed. The Ashanti in the Gold Coast fought and held out for some years. The people of the Kingdom of Benin—who call themselves Bini—also fought.

The content of the Bini religion embraced safety, salvation, fertility or increase; a royally sponsored art, made by highly organized craft guilds, was a major component. Sacrifice at altars played a major part. The art was based on altarpiece heads of cast bronze, each of which supported, on its top, a carved elephant tusk. The tusk swept back and up from the head. An altar might have more than a dozen such pieces, each magnificently wrought. Most of these pieces are, today, still in the British Museum, although a small number of them were returned to Nigeria, where they are to be found in the Benin branch of the Nigerian Museum, as well as in several other Nigerian museums.

The other major component of Benin art was bronze plaques which were set into the adobe walls and pillars of the houses. There are a large number of such plaques known. Some of them show the Portuguese in medieval European armor, armed with arquebuses and crossbows. We know from other sources that these are accurate depictions. Thus, we can reasonably assume that other aspects of African culture shown on the plaques—for which we have no other direct contemporary evidence—are as accurate.

The African art that is best known in the West and best represented in African museums stems from the late nineteenth and early twentieth centuries from the era just before the culture and ethnogeography of Africa were frozen in place by the colonial era.

Although scholarship today has created many refined classifications of African art, it is enough here to point out that there are three major geographical "culture areas" of art: the sudan, the Guinea coast, and the Congo basin. Trying to put the elements of style from the three areas into words inevitably erects a screen between the viewer and the artist, but the three can be summarized quickly: Because it is more abstract than other African art, the art of the sudan area has a quality of quietness and inwardness and intensity. The Congo Basin provides a more flamboyant, decorated, exaggerated, extroverted (it has been called) kind of art. The Guinea coast lies stylistically as well as geographically between them.

The Place of Art in African Society

Westerners have tended, in the past, to seek the "origins" of art rather than to perceive its uses. Sometimes religion is the assigned "cause," sometimes something else, yet art can no more have a cause or a single origin than can language. Just as apes did not suddenly one morning awake to find themselves human, so art did not, one day, suddenly spring into being from the fertile mind of some prehistoric genius. Art is a form of communication, and therefore it grows with culture and develops with the human creature.

Decorative and other secular art is to be found in most parts of Africa, but many forms in African art are indeed associated with religion. An equally bona fide claim can be made for its having a political connotation or an economic one or a domestic one.

African masks are usually worn as part of a costume. In court proceedings or in ritual, the symbolized forces of politics and religion can be made carnate, so that the drama of justice or of myth can be reenacted. The myth is not assumed in most African societies, as it is in our own, to be pseudohistorical and about the past. It is rather used to explain—indeed, to communicate—the here and now. Much African masked drama is a reincarnation of the basic myths of creation, the myths of the power structure of the society, the myths of history and religion, and even the myths of settlement patterns. One of the best ways to assure the efficacy of the myth is to sanctify the objects which Westerners call art. Then it is possible for the priests or the kings (or simply the public) to loan their human vitality to the mythical principles that are symbolized.

Figurines are not "worshiped" any more than saints' symbols in our own society are worshiped. They may be used as symbols of forces, ideas, historical events, or myths—which are very real in society and held sacred. That is a grave difference—the symbols stand for something important and holy. Giving living reality to the myth through drama and art is the most vivid way of making people recognize their dependence upon the myth and upon the society whose members live more or less by it.

Sometimes, too, African art is for fun. We would even say that some "art" may be no more than playful decoration added to the basic ideas for producing something that is "needed." Art fills a "need" that is felt or expressed. It is art, in one sense, if it is decorated so that it goes beyond the mere need. If we omit taste (criticism within a culture cannot omit taste, but comprehension across cultures probably must), art is decorated, needed objects. The communication is greater if it is great art; so is the mystery. As with the Jefferson Memorial in Washington D.C., the image draws attention to the principle.

Art permeates African culture—which in turn permeates African art. Art is not set aside from "real life"—it cannot be among a people who do not traditionally make distinctions between art and life.

The Aesthetics of African Art

It is critics and scholars rather than artists who create aesthetics. Only in a hopelessly intellectualizing culture such as that of the modern West do artists become their own aestheticians. It is the critics and the consumers of art who relate art to the rest of culture; it is from the critics that the greatest knowledge is to be gained.

The screen between the viewer and the artist has been intellectualized and nurtured among Westerners. We should be made aware of it. The screen becomes readily apparent if one compares a "primitive" with a "modern" piece. The earliest piece in an exhibition of Portuguese art in London some years ago was a fourteenth-century crucifix about eighteen feet high, done in wood, magnificently displayed so that the visitor, coming in the door, was grabbed by the vision. It was immediately evident that the sculptor had had absolutely no set of principles between him and the wood. There it was—indeed, there *he* was, immersed in the idea. The communication was immediate.

Around the corner in Cavendish Square, Sir Jacob Epstein's madonna is perched high on a convent wall. The Epstein intensity is of a completely different nature from the intensity achieved by the unknown Portuguese artist of the fourteenth century. Sir Jacob had to create an overt, intellectual aesthetic. For the Portuguese artist, such intellectualization or verbalization was not necessary. What he was saying about his belief and his convictions and his vision was a direct representation—almost a union between him and the wood. Epstein may have achieved something greater, but he has not achieved that union. The achievements of the two artists may, indeed, be all but incomparable, joined only by the word "art."

It is such direct union that can be discerned, felt, in the greatest pieces of African art: there is no intellectualized aesthetic or verbalized purpose between artist and art. There is, however, a screen of "aesthetic" between a piece of art and the viewer, probably in all situations. There is certainly such a "screen" between African art and European or North American viewers—and probably for most modern African viewers.

Until recent years, the aesthetics behind African art were seldom verbalized. The study of African aesthetics done by most European and American scholars warped the subject to one degree or another—a translation difficulty from which there was no escape.

There has been a great deal of discussion among students of African art about whether African sculpture is "portraiture," but comparatively little sensible discussion of what might define a portrait. In Western portraiture the point is to capture the personality—likeness, even the caricature of individuality, is prized. It is individuality that our religion—and, of course, our art—tries to recapture. Small figurines in the Côte d'Ivoire, on the other hand, are said to be portraits in the sense that they provide a place or site into which the spirits of the portrayed ancestors can settle. The Ivoiriens are seeking something quite different from us—they are after a principle that lies behind both the religion and the kinship system: strip the personality, and the principles of humanity and of ancestorhood remain.

One reason that some educated Africans do not like African art is not merely that it is associated with "backwardness" and therefore injurious to their *amour propre* but also that they have lost the culture which allows them to see immediately the relevance of much of this art, to respond to it. They have the same problems Europeans have in looking at it. Yet, to appreciate African art fully, there is no better experience than to attend one of the fine African museums and to note the rapt attention of the local Africans, some of them directly from the farthest villages.

African taste in art, like taste in art everywhere else, is created ultimately by consumers. In all art there is an exchange of views between the artist and the critic-consumer. Realization of this point makes us see that most of the comment about "preserving" African art is the grossest sentimentality. Unless art conforms to the cultural patterns and values of the people who make it and use it, it is meaningless. Even if it represents a previous culture, the meanings have changed—what used to mean specific religious ideas now stands for things that are old-fashioned. Thus, art made by African craftsmen for sale to Europeans is sometimes said to be cheapened. The reason is simple: the only "feedback" is that of the market place. There is a widespread and mistaken belief that only the bad taste of Europeans has "spoiled" African art. Actually, the demands of African consumers have also changed. African art—or any other art—has no glorious future if that future is measured solely by its historical tradition.

Today African artists want to be recognized as artists, not just African artists. Their subject matter is drawn from the world in which they live—which is the present-day world, not nineteenth century Africa. They do not sculpt like traditional Africans any more than Pollack or Warhol painted like Whistler. For African artists to do "authentic" African art, in the sense of replicating the nineteenth century forms, would be equivalent to the most distressingly precious folkloring. Folk song in our own society can be made viable only when it is modified and recast into the current idiom of performance. The same is true of today's African art.

If there were no African artists we might decry the "death of African art." Yet the continent is full of them, as it is of writers and musicians. As everywhere else, artists in Africa are regarded as eccentric. Everywhere they are specialists, given a different set of moral demands by the public. Artists are special people—that is as true in Africa as in Paris or London. African artists are trained today, and they always have been. The training may be formal, as it is among the Côte d'Ivoir people where an apprenticeship may last up to five years. During that time the apprentice is made to copy the master's work and to live in the master's household. In such a way, style is handed on: yet individual styles are immediately distinguishable to the aware eye. Today artists are trained in universities and art schools as well as by traditional means.

African Art in the Western World

Although African art had been present in Europe for centuries— the first piece of carving made by African hands to reach modern Europe arrived in the early 1500s on Portuguese trading ships— European artists did not look at it seriously until the late nineteenth and early twentieth centuries. At that time, African art burst upon the awareness of the Western world. Army men like Pitt-Rivers and Torday had brought back large collections of art along with good ethnographic description—in fact, Pitt-Rivers built two fine museums (one in Oxford and the other on his estate in Dorset) to house his collections. The Musée de l'Homme in Paris and the Royal Belgian Museum at Tervueren also acquired large collections.

Several painters and sculptors working in Paris in 1904 and 1905 began to notice African sculptures: Maurice de Vlaminck, Derain, Picasso, Matisse, Vollard, and Maillol were only some of the artists who were greatly affected by African art in the early twentieth century.

No one should jump to the idea that Picasso's women who look two ways at once, or anything else about his work, is a copy of something he discovered in African art. There was little direct stylistic influence (although some can be discovered by latter-day critics). Rather, what happened was that along with the discovery of African and other exotic art, a way was discovered for breaking out of the confines that had been imposed on European art by tradition—perspective, measured naturalism, and anti-intellectual sentimentality. African figurines could give the "modern" artist courage to foreshorten, to emphasize by changes of scale, to adjust scale to message. Looking at African art made such artists know what some of the earlier great painters (for example, El Greco, who stretched his human figures) had already known—that one sees passionately quite differently from the way one sees measuredly. To get inside the vision, it was necessary to get outside the inherited canons of art, and African art was one of the means of getting out.

Americans coming now to the study of African art should know that an interesting process has been occurring during the last twenty years. When the first edition of this book was published in 1963, the finest collections, almost without exception, were in anthropological museums. During the last twenty years, art museums have begun to collect and display African pieces. The Chicago Art Institute and the Museum of Primitive Art in New York are examples. In September, 1987, the new National Museum of African Art was opened in Washington, D.C., as a permanent part of the Smithsonian Institution.

Looking at plastic art is no substitute for handling it—and unfortunately, museums cannot allow their specimens to be handled. Tactile sensations are as important in learning about African sculptures as are visual sensations. The memory of it, in the hands, like the sensation of it, comes through the muscles and the sense of touch as well as through the eyes. Dahomean brass sculpture (from the present-day Republic of Benin) is tactilely sinewy and tough and not at all delicate as it appears to the eyes; actually, of course, the combination tells one a great deal about Dahomean culture. Some African wood carving is in heavy, earthbound wood; other is in wood so porous and so light as to seem almost spiritual. To make remarks like that is not so much to interpret African art (which they do not) as to prepare one for the fact that there is more in it than the artists put there and that the something more is derivative of the cultural image of the human condition. The more we know of the human condition, and the specific picture of it which lies undelineated behind the pieces in question, the more the art can be made to mean.

African art speaks both for African culture and for itself. Like all art, speaking for one human culture allows it, in some degree, to speak for all.

5

AFRICAN FAMILIES

E verywhere there are people, there are families. Family life is to human beings what the herd is to cattle or deer, the school to fish, or the flock to ducks and geese. The family is an efficient organization for controlling and satisfying fundamental needs of the human animal: the need for companions you can trust, for food gathering and preparation, for sexual expression and regulation, for reproduction, for teaching and training the young. And everywhere the family takes a great deal of effort, energy, attention, and imagination. The image of the family underlies many other social relationships.

The family is, actually, a simple business. The central task of the family, everywhere, is to rear a successful younger generation. Its central organizing feature, everywhere, is the ties that come from the mammalian mode of reproduction: the "facts of life" are the same everywhere. A man and a woman, in a sexual relationship, beget and bear children.

The relationship of the man and the woman is very changeable from one society to another. The relationship between father and children is also variable. Sibling relationships between the children who share at least one parent are recognized everywhere. The mother-child relationships are the least variable, but here too exact expression of the relationship varies widely.

In order to understand family relationships in Africa, we have first to get our own ideas about family clear in our heads. Americans traditionally tell themselves that a family is made up of a mother, a father, and their children. However, census data and other data tell us not only that this is merely an ideal, but that it always has been only an ideal. Family structure in the real world is more variable. Seen analytically, we can say that the most fundamental family unit is a woman and her children. That unit is then, in many cases, hooked to an adult male who, people assume even if it is not true, is the children's father.

In the United States, many families are "one-parent families." Either as a result of desertion or divorce (or because no marriage ever occurred) there is no father present with the family. A small percentage of one-parent households are composed of a father and one or more children. The step-family has also "always" existed. Although before World War II the majority of step-families were formed after the death of a spouse/parent, today a proportion result from divorce and remarriage. Indeed, as Americans divorce, the children are most likely to live with their mother. When she remarries, a strange man (called a stepfather) comes into the household and takes over the fathering roles. The stepfather may himself have children who live with his ex-wife and are fathered by *their* step-father. With our own background, therefore, we are not entitled to call *any* other family system "weird." We have, in the course of these changes, however, learned to value family in a different way. Family is to be cherished and supported no matter what form it takes. Although Americans still claim to prefer a simple nuclear family, they are nevertheless learning to support the variations.

The discussion here will focus on those aspects of the African family most at odds with Western tradition: polygyny and bride-wealth. We will then look at the way kinship relationships are used in Africa for purposes that supersede the family as we know it. We must remember, however, that the love and concern and trust of family members for one another is species-wide, and that our job is to understand the variations, not to condemn them.

Some form of marriage is valued in all human societies. Indeed, marriage may be deemed so important a part of the family that it seems, from time to time, to take precedence over child-rearing. In all cultures, it is necessary to know what husbands are supposed to do, as husbands; what wives are supposed to do, as wives; what fathers are supposed to do, and what children are supposed to do. Then, on the basis of these understandings, people can act more or less comfortably as they make their compromises between reality and the ideal.

What, then, is polygyny? It hinges on a basic premise: although married women cannot remarry without a divorce, married men can. When a man marries a second or third wife, the content of each husband-wife relationship will be altered. Moreover, some new relationships have been added: those between co-wives and those between half-siblings. We can now see a major difference between monogamy and polygyny: in monogamy it is possible, even where it is not usual, to create a uniquely deep intense relationship between husband and wife. Such a relationship is probably not possible if the man has two wives. If such an intense and unique quality in the relationship is considered to be the most important thing about it, then polygyny will be opposed. However, if something else—say security of position and/or many children—is the most highly valued element, polygyny is not a contradiction.

The added relationship of co-wives may provide some of the very cultural content and psychic satisfaction among adults which modern Americans try to cram solely into the husband-wife relationship. And it is no more fair to say that a rewarding husband-wife relationship cannot develop in polygyny than it would be to say that intense community of interest among women who share a husband cannot develop alongside monogamy.

The birth rate in a polygynous situation is never higher than the birth rate in a monogamous situation—indeed, it is usually lower. Although some specific man may beget many more children in polygyny than he could in monogamy, no woman in polygyny can bear any more than in monogamy. Indeed, wherever in Africa monogamy has replaced polygyny, the birth rate has always soared (monogamy is not the only factor—enforced monogamy is always accompanied by many other factors which change the way people live).

African women do not, in their indigenous cultures, bear more than one child every two and a half or three years. They achieve this spacing by the only sure means—abstinence during the time they are nursing a child. When the situation changes so as to favor monogamy, their inclination and opportunity to shun their husbands for such a long period of time are usually reduced. In the indigenous cultures, polygyny gives security to both husbands and wives during the time when a mother withdraws from cohabitation with her husband during a nursing period. The number of men in any society who are willing to undergo such a long period of celibacy is small. If you are a wife in a polygynous society, would you rather have your husband at home with your co-wife or gallivanting around the countryside?

Africans say that each wife should have her own hut for herself and her children—husbands usually have a separate sphere of their own, apart from any of their wives. They say that each wife should have a place to cook that is not shared with other wives. Difficulties about cooking space are rare because the problem has been recognized and solved. But polygynists—particularly the women—note that such disputes are one of the fundamental difficulties in polygyny. In some societies, women married after the first three wives (or so), are assigned to one of the more senior wives. The senior wife is always in charge of such groups. Such small groups of linked wives form a cooperating unit—they do not compete with one another.

Obviously, to make polygyny work it is necessary constantly to re-create a situation in which the rewards and obligations among co-wives are as neatly and precisely stated as are the obligations and rules among parents and children, husbands and wives. There are some things that a co-wife must do if she is to be a good co-wife. There are others that she must not do if she is to be a good co-wife. If she does the one cheerfully and well and refrains from the other, she is by definition a good co-wife, whatever her husband's other wives may do, or whatever her husband may think of her.

Examining divorces in Africa shows that some women leave their husbands not because they do not like their husbands but because they do not like their co-wives. Living in an impossible situation, whether that impossibility is created by husband or co-wife, leads in some societies and under some conditions to divorce. There are African women who divorce their husbands because they can't stand their co-wives; there are others who stay with impossible husbands because the co-wives are congenial. A good senior wife or mother-in-law may be as important in providing security, pleasant surroundings, and a rewarding place for a woman to bring up her children as is her husband.

If each has separate quarters and an established code of behavior known to everybody, it is possible for co-wives to live next door, share their husband, and even become quite fond of one another. They have a great deal in common. The ideals of polygyny always are such that harmony among co-wives is possible. At the same time, in many African languages, the word for co-wife springs from the same root as the word for jealousy. The situation is fraught with difficulty—but surely all family relationships are fraught with difficulty, including the husband-wife relationship in monogamy and the parent-child relationship everywhere.

The polygynous family is more complex than the monogamous family, and there are certain difficulties built into it. However, the rewards involved may be great. It is possible in a polygynous family to spread your regard, your love, and your dependence over a wider range of people. You don't put all your emotional eggs in one basket. For this reason alone it can be seen to have rewards. A large group of people has the welfare of each member at heart. Even under more selfish conditions, sheer numbers may dilute the hate pointed at each one.

Women in polygyny have their greatest trouble not in their marital relationships but rather when a woman finds (or imagines) that her children's father is favoring another set of his children over her own. That woman, as a co-wife, can learn to accept all sorts of real or fancied slights; the same woman, as a mother, may have great difficulty in accepting either real or fancied slights to her children.

Westerners sometimes, mistakenly, equate polygyny with a low social status for women. There would seem to be three issues: first, what disabilities do women suffer? Second, what are men's attitudes toward women? Third, does polygyny as an institution increase their disabilities or increase men's disfavor and bad behavior?

Women in Africa are not a deprived group in the sense that women were deprived in the nineteenth century Western world. African women in most areas cannot own land, but all have inalienable rights to farms as daughters, mothers or wives. In most places, they usually cannot hold political office, but in some kingdoms, special offices for women are an integral part of the government—some of these women, particularly queen-mothers, play important political roles. As widows, the rights of women are, in most places, greatly reduced.

African men's attitudes toward women are complex. African men ritualize rather than deny their basic dependence on women. For example, the innermost secret of every religious club barred to women is the male's ultimate dependence on women. Women are often excluded from rituals, but there are two things that initiation into religion and society involve. First, initiation is a ritual teaching to the novitiates that they embody, in themselves personally and in their relationships collectively, the moral force of society—they are themselves the gods (not God) and the sanctions. Second, initiation is a ritualized teaching to the initiates that women must stand behind and support men. In the Côte d'Ivoir, for example, initiation has two denouements: one when the masked dancers who have represented the gods and the social forces suddenly take the masks off and put them on the initiates themselves; the other when the innermost hidden secret of the men's religious societies is exposed to the initiates—and turns out to be a woman.

Polygyny is never a mechanism for reducing the importance or the power of women. Senior wives may have more power than junior wives—but then, senior men have more power than junior men. This is a matter of age and experience, not gender. Certainly, polygyny has nothing to do with male sexual appetite. It is a state into which most African men enter with a certain trepidation. They know that they are in a double-bind: if their wives do not get along, they have unceasing hassle. If they do get along, the women may well cooperate to run the man's life the way they think it should be run, ignoring his opinions. Any man who has a strong senior wife is a fortunate individual, because she will run the household and will straighten out the fusses among the co-wives. He will not have to bother. If he does not have such a wife, two-thirds of his energy goes into administration.

Polygynous men must treat their wives in accordance with the station of the wives—not necessarily with absolute equality, unless the particular society dictates that their stations are those of absolute equals. A greater number of societies lay down quite precise obligations on the part of the husband, but others insist that the obligation is to make the personal adjustments necessary to keep all the parties contented.

It is all but inevitable, in all probability, that polygynists have favorite wives. It should never, however, show up in the way the husband carries out his obligations: clothing them, feeding them, giving them children. Occasionally romantic love enters into this situation. There was an old Tiv chief with seventeen wives who loved them all, but loved one of them in the sense given that term by the troubadours and adapted by latter-day American marriage counselors. The senior ones had given him families and had comforted his years. Unfortunately—and even he considered it unfortunate—he "fell in love" with one of the younger ones. It kept him from being a good family man; it kept him from being a good chief. Romantic love occurs in an African familial situation about as commonly as it does in a European or American one. The difference is that Westerners have a series of myths which make them simulate romantic love to see them over the time between initial attraction and the regard that sensitive and sensible living together, breeding, and growing together can foster. The myth makes it possible for Westerners to select their spouses on something besides random choice—indeed, under it they can arrange their own marriages.

Old-fashioned Africans may select their spouses by "giving in to their parents' wishes," but in most cases in which the parents' wishes do not correspond with their own, they elope. Seldom do Africans make their children marry someone they do not like, although they sometimes (by refusing to refund bridewealth) make their daughters stay with husbands they no longer like.

Bridewealth

The other aspect of African family life that is most likely to be misunderstood is the institution of bridewealth. Initially, the European observers who went to Africa said that Africans bought their wives. In a sense, that is true. It is not true that wives enter the market place or that they were commercialized in any way. It is easiest to explain by noting that part of the marriage contract in any society is that the wife gets certain rights in the husband

and he gets certain rights in her. The rights of each are the obligations of the other.

Initially an African husband has to make a bridewealth payment
that is tantamount to posting a bond that he will carry out his
obligations, thus guarding his new wife's rights. The analogy can
be carried too far, because the nature of the bond and the purpose
of the bridewealth changes, and ultimately its nature is in the
sphere of filiating the children. But, in return for his "bond" and
his obligations, the husband gets certain rights.

To sum them up quickly, a man may get in his wife domestic
rights—the right to establish a domestic unit with her and to her
domestic work and time and care. He may get rights to her
extradomestic economic substance or labor; such was the case in
the late nineteenth-century West, but is seldom so in Africa. He gets
sexual rights in her and obligations toward her. Finally, he may or
may not get the right to filiate that woman's children to his kinship
group. In most African societies, traditionally, a man acquired such
rights in exchange for cattle or ceremonial currency such as spears
or pieces of iron, or else for bride service of the sort Jacob performed
for his two wives in the Book of Genesis—working for the father of
the bride for specific periods, perhaps doing specific tasks. The
difference between matriliny and patriliny can be summed up by
determining whether it is common to transfer the rights to filiate
the children.

It is these rights that the bridewealth purchases, these obligations
that it symbolizes. If a woman "has cows on her back," as the East
African idiom has it, then her children belong to the man and the
social group that paid the cows. This is a matter of legitimation.
It is, indeed, a symbol of legitimation. If the marriage breaks up,
the bridewealth must be returned— except for that portion of it that
in fact filiates to their father's group those children who are already
born.

Polygyny does not necessarily mean that some men do not have
wives, but only that men marry later than women (although it is
also true that women beyond the age of menopause seldom
remarry, whereas men never grow out of the marriageable
population). Polygyny must also be distinguished from concubinage. Concubines are not wives, for all that in some places they
have legal rights. In many societies there are, besides concubinage,
several "degrees" of marriage, and in some there are allowable
sexual and other relationships which may not be granted the status
of full marriage. Indeed, in the Roman Republic there were two
forms of marriage—heiresses would not marry by the ritual that
gave their husbands control of their property but rather formed a

recognized, common-law union in which this economic right was not transferred. There were, thus, two "types" of "marriage": one involved the acquisition by the husband of all the rights; the other of only part of them. Many—probably most—African societies exhibit just such variation in the possible marriage arrangements.

Widow Inheritance

Rights in women are considered, in most African societies, to be heritable. If my father or my older brother dies, leaving a couple of wives, I may inherit his rights in those who are not my mother. Since all rights involve obligations, it would be more accurate to say that I inherit my father's obligations to his wives. If the widow has several children and her children are members of her late husband's kinship group, she has an important position within that kinship group, even though she is not a member of it. Her position in life, indeed, may depend upon her children—thus underscoring the hard fate of a barren woman. Her natal group has little obligation to her after her initial marriage—ultimately none. As some Africans put it, "your wife of long-standing becomes your sister." A woman's status derives from her being a mother of lineage members. Therefore, it is only sensible for her to remarry into that group. Most widows are women of maturity (which may, of course, begin before twenty); they do not expect from a second marriage what they expect from a first.

The result is the institution of inheritance of rights in widows. In one situation the widow is inherited as a wife; there is another, quite different, situation in which (to use the Old Testament term) the brother of the dead husband raises up seed, which is to say that the widow moves in as his "wife," but that the dead husband remains the legal father of any children that she bears. Such an arrangement is called the true levirate. The new husband acquires domestic and sexual rights in the widow; he does not acquire rights to affiliate her children, which are thought to be part of the "spiritual property" of the dead husband.

It is possible, in most African societies, for a widow to decide not to remain with her deceased husband's people. If she marries outside her late husband's group, the bridewealth has to be adjusted.

American and Western European societies do not cope very well with widows. They are an anomaly. They occupy an insecure position and are to be pitied, particularly if they have young children; they are not quite to be trusted, although the divorcee has in the twentieth century taken over the role assigned to the widow in the nineteenth. African societies try to get both divorcees and widows back into families quickly and simply. Loneliness is not an indigenous African problem.

Non-Familial Kinship Groups

In addition to families, there are other sorts of kinship groups in Africa based on a more limited range of relationships than are families. Extended families can attain only a certain size—after that, the members cannot know all their kinsmen, or respond equally to them all. Since the functions of the family are usually associated largely with households, the household limit—certainly the neighborhood limit—is, in most cases, the effective limit of the family. Kinship relationships can also link neighborhoods, and certain types of kinship groups can gear their purposes to other ends, still using kinship amity as the sanction for getting cooperation and achieving its purposes.

There are two sorts of descent groups: patrilineal descent groups include the father-son and father-daughter relationships and the three sibling relationships. The matrilineal descent group includes the mother-son and mother-daughter and the three sibling relationships. Within the descent group, these relations are more limited than they are within a family. Within the descent group, they have nothing to do with bearing and rearing children. However, the goodwill that comes from the kinship can be brilliantly adapted to political and economic ends.

Descent groups may contain several million people and use the sanction of kinship obligations—"blood is thicker than water"—to reward their members and bind them to "right" courses of action. These groups can be called lineages; some types are called "clans." The word "clan" in the anthropological literature is used broadly—it may cover any kinship group that is not a family, and even some extended families (the Chinese *tsu*, usually called a "clan" in English, is in fact a type of extended family). It is not indicative of anything "primitive"—in the early 1990s, the warring factions in Somali were called "clans" in the press, implying the primitive and the alien.

Unilineal descent groups (whose members trace their descent either through maternal or paternal links but not both) are widespread in Africa and were—indeed, still are—the basis for most of the extrafamilial social organization. They form political groups, religious congregations, and even production and land-owning units. They are still strong. They are strong among the educated as well as among the "bush" people.

The strength of unilineal descent groups wanes only when the tasks they perform can be done by some other means with less emotional and social outlay of energy. Unless they are given other tasks, they become less influential when large-scale political institutions, with effective police systems and contract law, are put in place. The unilineal descent group can do all these political and economic jobs, with the sanctions founded on specialized kinship obligations. However, in the present day, the size of the operation makes it more efficiently done by state and contractual methods.

There are some societies in Africa in which unilineal descent groups are not found, but such groups are overwhelmingly present in many more. It is loyalty to the descent group, as well as to the family, that is under discussion when Africans talk about their obligations to "their" people.

In addition to the economic and political purposes that such groups can be made to serve, they are often central to religious ritual and belief. They are, moreover, often associated with the history and the view of the cosmography. They are, in short, one way in which the small world of the family can be tied to the greater world and ultimately to the supernatural.

African children grow up in an intense situation of kinship, family, and lineage. They continue throughout their lives to learn and to be bound by their family obligations and family histories. Perhaps even more importantly, they learn from a very early age to spread their love and regard, their rewards and their worry and concern, over larger groups of people.

Among the Tiv of eastern central Nigeria, for example, a child when he is about six months old is assigned to an older sister or brother, preferably the same sex as the child; the older becomes the nurse of the younger. For the next three or four years—almost until the younger child is ready to become a nurse, they accompany their nurses everywhere. When they cry, the nurses take them to their mothers. When the nurses go out to play, the babies go with them. The bond between a child and his nurse becomes an enduring bond. Children learn a great deal about the culture from one another and especially from their nurses. In our society, children more and more learn from adults.

Tiv children, as an example, are allowed to go any place, so long as they keep quiet. They can go into the most solemn court proceedings and sit down and listen. The moment one of them makes a noise, out they all go. Children at the age of eight or nine often get interested in court cases or political meetings. When their younger charges will not behave, they all have to go away; therefore older children become very adept in silencing the babies. There is nothing from which children are excluded, unless they misbehave and intrude. As a result, they tend to be well-behaved children, aware from an early age of what goes on in adult culture. The abrupt break such as Westerners know, between children's culture and adult culture, is not to be found.

African children get into their cultures early, and there are no abrupt shifts. After they are twelve or thirteen, and sometimes earlier, boys form groups that range the countryside, hunt, and (where there are cattle and goats) tend the herds. Girls by this time are more closely kept at home and are on the brink of marriage.

At marriage, the vast majority of girls shift homesteads. They leave the households in which they are daughters and join those in which they are wives and in which they will become mothers. Men do not undergo this kind of change, but continue to live imbedded in a group of their own kinsmen.

It is probably impossible for anyone who has never lived in a kinship-dominated society to realize the combination of security and bondedness that it implies. In discussion, Africans always emphasize the positive factors: a group of their own, on which they can depend totally and to which they owe allegiance, a group which transcends them and gives them position in society and in history—importance and status as well as physical necessities or even wealth. Nevertheless, they do, to some extent, chafe under the demands of their kinsmen.

Until the present century, there was no "way out" of the kinship situation. There was no place to go if you were exiled. The kinship sanction was enough to control all of your behavior. Modern Westerners would see such a fate in terms of the lack of individuality and freedom. Africans do not. Although today many of them do leave when faced with choices in which they consider that they must give more than they get, few intend to stay away for good.

Parenthood is important everywhere. It is trebly so in a society in which rights to the most important parts of all aspects of life are dependent upon kinship and when most of one's status derives from kinship factors. Only on the birth of a child does a woman become truly a kinsman in her husband's group. Only on the birth of a child is a man assured of the "immortality" of a position in the genealogy of his lineage, or even of security of esteem among the important people of his community. Only on the birth of a grandchild is a man in a position to be truly sure that his name and spirit will live in the history and genealogy of his people. This factor (combined with that other factor that is so true everywhere—that grandparenthood allows a perfect and rewarding position for summing up the meaning of the life cycle), makes grandparenthood enviable, and elderhood the finest estate.

Many Africans express concern lest the kinship groups to which they are bound will wither and perish in the course of industrialization and mechanization of the new Africa. They are determined that, if possible, no such fate will befall them. It will be an interesting experiment. From it we may learn whether or not it is truly modern technology and the development of contract which destroys a ramified kinship system. Can you work an industrial society and retain the importance of descent groups? Westerners distrust all kinship groups save the nuclear family—but then Western European societies never in their history had large kinship groups.

6

LAND AND LABOR

Polity and economy are of a piece. We are used to separating them for analysis, as political science and economics, or as political and economic history or anthropology. Traditional Africans were less likely to make such separations. They see exploiting their territory for their nutritional needs and the political order that ensures security as part of the same thing.

Space and Territoriality

The African view of geographical space tends (with few exceptions) to be based on premises about social relationships. The Western view of space, on the other hand, is based more often on ideas about use and exploitation of the area. In order to understand the African idea, it is important to underline the dominant outlines of the Western concept—one we scarcely know we hold.

Terrestrial space—pieces of "land"—is a "thing" modern Westerners cut into pieces they call parcels. Those pieces can be bought and sold on the same market as their labor or as raw materials or the products they grow and build. This set of ideas is rare in other societies (and it used to be rare in our own). Our neighborhoods are the result of buying and selling, renting and leasing homesites. Our local communities are the long-term result of choices and decisions that had, at some time, to be expressed through market purchase or lease.

Such was never the case in traditional Africa. It is rare even in the Africa of today, outside the cities. In the older Africa, a community was built fundamentally on relationships within social groups based on some principle other than purchase or lease. That community had a territorial aspect. It was the social relationships among the members, not "ownership," that established a person's legal and economic rights to use a particular plot of ground.

The map of the world that Westerners have created is a strange one to most other peoples of the world. Western maps are records, first of astrally determined points on the earth (using the same kind of locating devices that are used, or once were, to determine geographical location at sea). The lines are then extended on the surface of the earth, using precise measuring equipment. The results can then be represented by a grid on a flat piece of paper, with an arbitrary but commonly understood scale. Thus, a surveyor takes a sextant and "shoots the stars." That place can be designated on a map. Measuring from that point, we can dissect the earth, no matter what its physical characteristics. We are the only people in the world who use seafaring instruments to determine our position on the ground.

After the position on the earth is astrally determined, measurements are made of the plot by other surveyors' instruments such as transits and plane tables. These measurements are also translated to the paper. It is whatever corresponds to the representation on the paper that you "own." In this system, a piece of property is determined by its position in relation to the stars, not its location between North Salt Creek and Squaw Butte or its position between the Joneses and the Smiths.

The Western map is, as a matter of fact, a strange kind of map. All the peoples of the world have maps of one sort or another—usually they are not written, but the raw material is there for a "map": a view or image of the terrestrial world. None save modern technical civilization have maps in which precision is so essential. There are some peoples who divide up the world by boundaries such as rivers and hills. Most, however, see it in terms of social relations and the juxtaposition of social groups.

In order to understand the way such peoples are associated with the land and with one another in terms of land—and hence the way the political power system and the economic system of exploitation work—it is first necessary to understand the way they see themselves in relation to the earth.

Here we shall mention two methods by which an area can be made into a socially recognizable "map." One of these is by a series of specific terrestrial points which are given particular recognition and either economic or ritual meaning by the people concerned. The Plateau Tonga of Zambia traditionally hooked their social organization to the earth not by means of anything we would ourselves consider land tenure but by means of a set of rain shrines, each of which is associated with surrounding villages, and each of which is specifically placed on the earth—possibly but rarely subject to being moved on ritual authority. Opportunity for individuals to move from one village to another is great, and one's acceptance as a resident in a village automatically carries with it not only fealty to the shrine but a right to make a farm nearby on any land not farmed at the moment nor claimed as fallow by another resident. Tonga farms can be cultivated for five or six years before the soil is exhausted. Tonga can be seen to have short-term "farm tenure," as it were, in the village area near the shrine.

The Bedouin Arabs of Cyrenaica are another well-documented example in which community lands were attached to points—in this case to saints' graves and wells—or so it was before their grazing lands turned into oil leases and they themselves sought employment in the Libyan oil industry. Many remaining pastoral societies, and most of those that practice shifting cultivation, nevertheless see the land in this sort of association with society. The pastoral Fulani, with their long, sweeping cycles of movement across the sahel, and the slash-and-burn peoples of the Congo forests, with their relatively short moves, can all be included here.

In the other mode of connecting society to space, the social organization is conceived in terms of pure space and is only incidentally linked with the physical environment by farming or other land uses for short periods of time. The Tiv of central Nigeria provide an example. They see geography in the same image as they see social organization. The idiom of descent and genealogy provides not only the basis for lineage grouping, but also of territorial grouping. Every "minimal lineage" is associated with a territory. This minimal lineage (two or three hundred males derived from a single ancestor, whose wives and daughters live with them) is located spatially beside another lineage of precisely the same sort—that is, descended from the brother of the ancestor of the first group. In reference to the father of the two apical ancestors of the minimal lineages, they form an inclusive lineage, and their territories form a single spatial unit. This process continues backward genealogically for several generations, until all Tiv are included; it continues spatially until the entirety of Tivland—some two hundred miles in diameter—is seen as a lineage area, segmenting into increasingly smaller lineage areas.

This "genealogical map" of Tivland moves about the surface of the earth in sensitive response to the demands of individual farmers as those demands change from year to year. The "map" in terms of which Tiv see their land is a genealogical map, and its association with specific pieces of ground is of only very brief duration—a man or woman has precise rights to a farm during the time it is in cultivation, but once the farm returns to fallow, the rights lapse. However, a man always has rights in the "genealogical map" of his agnatic (that is, patrilineal) lineage, wherever that lineage may happen to be in space. These rights, which are part of his birthright, can never lapse. A mathematician friend has suggested that whereas the Western map, based on surveys, resembles geometry, the Tiv notions resemble topology, which has been described as "geometry on a rubber sheet." The Western map is necessarily rigid and precise if the principle of contract is to work; the Tiv map is constantly changing both in reference to itself and in its correlation with the earth, thus allowing the principle of kinship grouping to work. For the Tiv, the position of a man's farm varies from one crop rotation to the next, but neither his juxtaposition with his agnatic kinsmen nor his rights change in the least. Tiv, like Tonga, might be said to have "farm tenure" but they do not have "land tenure."

Thus, instead of seeing their maps primarily in terms of "property," Africans see something like a map in terms of social relationships in space. They emphasize the spatial aspect of their social groups and provide themselves with a social map, so that they are left free to question the ways in which they attach either social groups or individuals to exploitational rights in the earth. In the past they were usually imprecise, because group membership was the valued quality. Westerners, on the other hand, think about their map in terms of property and values, and see the social system which results as fundamentally a series of contracts and hence open to variation. As a result, in any situation of change, Westerners question the social system that lies behind land usage, while Africans question the property ideas associated with the systems of land usage.

Westerners have great difficulty in questioning whether or not a land system is in fact a property system—they always assume that it is, even if land does not enter the market. In order to adjust to at least some of the data on the ground, they made up an astonishing term, "communal ownership." In a technologically developed, contractually oriented society like Europe and America, communal ownership can and does exist—the commune, whatever its nature, can be viewed as a jural person, a "corporation aggregate" capable of owning property under the law. A real difficulty arose when the idea was applied in Africa: the social group was turned into something it had never been before—a legal entity capable of "owning" land.

Property, in the Western sense, and its resultant contractual relationships are the fundamental basis of grouping in the Western type of national state. In a developed market economy, a land market emerges—with whatever agony to the people who must see it to fruition. Therefore, as African societies came to have more fully evolved market economies, the problem before them was how to preserve certain of their valued kinship institutions at the same time they became "modern societies," based on contract and on the market. The Yoruba people of Nigeria turned their extended-family compounds into landholding units before the law, under the

"Communal Land Rights (Vesting in Trustees) Law" of 1958.

This law, in brief, makes the change in the nature of the Yoruba lineage group called the *ebi* a matter of legal record (though the legal language does not mention the term ebi). The ebi in traditional terms was an agnatic descent group which shared a common residence. Every quarter of every Yoruba town had several ebi; an ebi could split into two or more ebi. This body of agnatic kinsmen, with their wives, also had an estate—an area within which they traditionally farmed and which they protected from encroachment by others. Within the ebi, the members farmed not in specific places which they considered their own; rather, the group moved its farms about within the area so that they could remain as a unit to take advantage of the best soils and to control the system of fallowing. The ebi had a head and a council which ran the agricultural affairs of the ebi in a kind of committee. Nobody "owned" anything, formally, but every member had a right to a farm sufficient to support his immediate dependents. These rights to a farm were inalienable.

As the new kind of society developed under colonialism, problems appeared. In the first place, this arrangement granted a man land rights only insofar as he was a part of a lineage, and a woman rights to a farm as long as she was her husband's wife. The moment he ceased to be a resident member of his lineage, his specific land rights were lost until he again came to live there. Under modern conditions, some Yoruba often wanted to remain members of their lineages, but also to have land rights of a different sort. Sale of land was impossible in the old system because land was the spatial dimension of the ebi rather than a commodity which could be considered "property" and sold in the market. As the new social and economic system emerged, sale of land became desirable. A sort of conflict was set up between the ebi land unit and the individual. Either a man had to cease being an individual in the new system, or the ebi land unit, as an institution, had to go.

"The Communal Land Rights (Vesting in Trustees) Law" is the legal mechanism by means of which this particular difficulty was solved. European analysis of Yoruba land tenure had, from the beginning, classed the ebi's spatial dimension as "land owned in communal tenure." The European notion of "tenure" was automatically applied without question as to whether it fit or not. The result was that the ebi, in European eyes, was a "corporation aggregate" before the law. The European legal system gave the ebi a legal reality which it had formerly not possessed. Yoruba were late in recognizing what had happened. However, having recognized it, they and their legislators saw in it a means of preserving the ebi as a social group fulfilling some of the basic needs of what we would call social insurance and community center, at the same time that they have strengthened the institution of private property.

The ebi, now turned into a legal entity before the laws of Nigeria, could "own" land. "Communal land ownership" had in fact been achieved.

Labor

If land provides the fundamental dimensions of society, work provides its gyroscope. If one's work is changed, the balance of one's life is changed in the process.

Economists view labor as one of the "factors of production," along with land and capital. Yet labor is more than that, if only because it is done by human beings who are parts of complex social systems. People at work create not merely products; they also create a web of social relationships. They fraternize with one another in terms of quite specific sets of rules; they take home to their families at least some residue of these relationships with their pay envelopes.

During the Industrial Revolution in Europe and America, work (with all its social ramifications) underwent a profound change—it entered the market place. The dictum "He who does not work does not eat" became "He who does not sell his labor or his brains on the market does not acquire the means to buy the wherewithal to support himself and his family."

Like the Europeans before the eighteenth century, Africans before the early twentieth century did their work in groups, and by arrangements that were not fundamentally geared to the market. Traditional forms of labor in Africa took place within the sphere of the family, the local government, the age-set, and other such organizations. They specifically did *not* take place in the form of buying labor (and the other factors of production) on the market, in order to turn out goods to be sold on the same market.

Before the colonial revolution, work in Africa was an integral part of a person's obligations within family and kinship groups. People helped one another so they would themselves be helped in turn. The men of a local community, however defined, got together for community work such as road and path construction and bridge building, clearing the market place, or putting up a new shrine. One way to get sizable working groups together was for members of an age-set to work together. The age-set in many African communities could furnish from twenty to one hundred men. Organization within the set was already established so that few or no new lines of authority, based primarily on the job at hand and the purpose in mind, had to be established.

There have been, from so-called time immemorial, a few people in Africa who sold their labor on the market. To overlook this point would be to report falsely and—more serious—to ignore the most sensible explanation of why the Africans took to market labor with such alacrity when the opportunity came for them to do so. Traders have existed for centuries. Although they usually depended on slave labor, it was nevertheless possible to hire labor. Thus, most Africans "always" knew that it was possible to hire themselves out and to sell their labor at a going market rate; but only an infinitesimal proportion ever did so. Their work, like their land and like the other factors of production, was organized by non-market principles.

In the West, and in the technologically advanced parts of modern Africa, one still works for the sake of one's family, for the sake of one's citizenship, as well as for the sake of one's sanity. However, in the West, and in the new Africa, one works in a different social context: that of the "firm." The firm is a type of social organization put together on the basis of the principle of contract—a principle that was little developed in most parts of Africa, even by the colonial governments who imposed it on their African colonies.

Perhaps the most important point of this discussion is that Africans have always worked—like all other people, but in this century the spread of market forces has changed them into "labor." Labor in this sense not only means work, it also becomes the collective term for that sector of the population that sells its work. As some Africans became labor in this new sense, they took on new identities and obligations. Sometimes these obligations included movement to find a job—sometimes movement away from the village into a new and rapidly evolving urban culture.

Europeans who came to Africa to establish mines or plantations regarded Africans as labor—a commodity to be purchased when wanted and then ignored when no longer needed. They also reckoned that African labor was cheap labor—and wanted to keep it that way as long as they could. One rationalization for paying low wages was the argument that Africans were not willing or able to work steadily. The African (it was always in the singular) was a "target worker," who would come to work only until he had enough money to buy a bicycle (it was always a bicycle). Then he went home until he needed another bicycle. If this was the motive for employment, then raising wages would only make it easier to attain the target sum, thus reducing labor supply. What employers failed to realize was that unskilled workers, temporarily away from home, might earn low wages yet still be expensive "labor"—measured by the work done for a given sum of pay.

In the 1920s, however, some of the mining firms in the southern Belgian Congo (now Zaire), decided to experiment with what they called "stabilized labor." Instead of trying to lure men in for brief periods, they began encouraging them to stay as a permanent work force, bringing their families with them. Sometimes they even offered to pay the bridewealth for a worker who would agree to become a permanent employee. By such devices the Union Miniere du Haut Katanga, the largest Belgian mining company, reduced its labor turnover from an annual 96 percent in the early 1920s to 7 percent in the early 1930s. By the 1930s, the mining companies of the Zambian copper belt also began the changeover to stabilized labor.

In southern Africa, however, the South African and Rhodesian governments (before Rhodesia became the independent Zimbabwe in 1980) discouraged people settling down in the economically developed parts of the country. Whites took the skilled jobs, reserved for them by law. After a time, they discovered their interest in preventing Africans from acquiring those skills. Forcing Africans into a pattern of migratory labor was one way to accomplish this. As far back as 1912, the South African government passed a Lands Act that laid out a small part of the country as "reserves" for Africans. On the surface, this looked like the American policy of Indian reservations, but Native Americans have a right to buy land off the reservations if they can afford to do so. The corollary of the reserves policy in South Africa was that all the rest of the country— the vast majority and all the most valuable parts—was reserved for the white minority.

After the 1950s, the theory was extended, so that people of African descent had no right even to become a permanent resident of the developed parts of the country, now declared to be "white" areas. They were "white" not because they were mainly occupied by whites, since black people there did most of the physical labor on a migratory basis. They were declared to be "white" because government wanted economic benefits reserved for whites.

The labor pattern that emerged has been called oscillating labor. Workers would leave the "Native Reserves," where they were forced to live, to work for a time in the cities or at the mines. Once there, they were supposed to be short-term residents only and were confined to separate "locations" or urban ghettoes, while their "real" homes were officially in one of the Native Reserves. After a year or two of absence, they could make enough to go home again, only to be forced out by economic necessity after two, three, or five years. These policies made it possible to keep African incomes at about one-tenth the incomes of white workers. Though they preserved aspects of the old culture in the reserve, most African males became conscious of the greater world beyond the "Native Reserve" and of their own relative deprivations.

The size of these population movements was very large indeed, in line with the massive population movements elsewhere in the world in this century. The oscillating pattern was very large even by mid-century. In 1951, a South African government commission estimated that at any moment, 40 percent of all males between ages 15 and 65 would be absent from the "Reserves" on labor contracts. By 1960, for the whole of sub-Saharan Africa, it is estimated that a quarter of the wage-labor force were migrants from beyond the national or colonial frontiers. This did not mean a quarter of all workers—since most labor was still set in the community, not for wages—but it was nevertheless a major change.

The absence of so many men on a temporary basis brought enormous changes to southern Africa. It imposed an element of social disorder on the all-male societies of the mining camps. It imposed new burdens on the heavily-female society left behind in the "Reserves" in South Africa or in the villages of Mozambique. In effect, the system of oscillating labor forced the women in the reserves to provide much of the family's support, thus subsidizing the low wages paid at the mines.

After the Second World War, even some of the mining companies came to realize that low-wage labor was not necessarily cheap labor, but the South African government was unwilling to give up the fiction that a "white" South Africa could be kept a racial monopoly area with black labor present only as a temporary expedient. After 1975, the pressure against the whole of the apartheid system began to rise, and oscillating labor became one of the key points to attack—and, for the white minority, to defend. With the end of apartheid in the 1990s, all this is changing, but we cannot yet see where these changes may lead.

7

AFRICAN POLITICS
AND COURTS

African political life has undergone many profound changes in the last hundred years. Africans first had to adapt their institutions when they were forcibly made parts of several colonial states. Then they had to adapt while the policies of those states were constantly changing in response to pressures in the metropolitan centers of Europe rather than to conditions in Africa itself. Then, during 1960 and the years just following, they had to create, from their own traditions and from whatever cultural residue was left by the colonial powers, viable states that could take up positions in the United Nations. For the formerly-British colonies, the political model at first was the "Westminster model," so called after the home city of the British Parliament. The chief executive, usually a prime minister, is responsible to the majority of the elected parliament. In the formerly-French states, the model was usually that of the French republic, with an elected president, but also with a prime minister, responsible to the majority in the national assembly.

The institutions of the new states stayed in place only a short time. Two common alternatives emerged. One was an out-and-out military dictatorship, with no pretence at parliamentary institutions of any kind. The second was a one-party state: a political party—usually the one that brought the country to independence—became the only official party. One-party states are under the executive control of a strong president who is also head of the party. Elections may be held, but they are more or less openly controlled, and contesting candidates are all members of the same party. Real outsiders cannot run at all, but the one-party electoral system does provide voters with some small element of choice.

The objective of this chapter is to explain the underlying traditions of African political life—ideas that remain the basis on which Africans conduct political affairs. African politics, like any other, must deal with problems of internal welfare and international relations in terms of geographical space, however that may be conceived. First, how did Africans maintain law and welfare among their peoples? Then, how did they maintain cultural integrity and keep other societies and peoples from overrunning them? Again, in order to understand traditional African answers to these problems, we must at the same time liberate ourselves from our own traditional ideas.

There were two basic types of indigenous political systems in Africa (with some intermediary types and a few small societies that fall outside the classification). One of the basic types is the state, familiar to Europeans and Americans because they too now utilize it and have done so for long enough that many of them seem to believe that it is synonymous with order and civilization. A state is a bureaucracy organized specifically to carry out political activities. Every state exhibits an interlocked system of offices or positions that must be filled by officials. Authority is then made inherent in these interlocking positions, which both reinforce and act as a check on one another. In a successful state, the centralized bureaucracy must have the responsibility but also the authority to carry out public policy.

States are, with occasional exceptions, multiethnic groups. To be successful, they must foster the idea of citizenship and provide a way by which people can identify with the state organization. Such an idea of citizenship must not come into too great conflict with membership in families, localities, and ethnic groups, with which people identify.

The state is a political form that was broadly spread throughout Africa. States were found at the edge of the Sahara, at the southern edge of the forests, and in the eastern highlands. The maps accompanying Part Three of this book show the locations of some of the most important of them.

The state, however, is not the only kind of organization that can carry out the political tasks. A second type of political organization in traditional Africa is called a "stateless society" or "non-centralized society." Both terms have the disadvantage that they are residual categories, but their variety makes it difficult to characterize them by any positive shared characteristic.

Many kinds of non-centralized societies are possible. A feudal kingdom of Medieval Europe was non-centralized to a degree— political power of the kind we associate with a state was the private property of feudal lords, towns, and even segments of the Church such as abbeys or bishoprics. The stateless societies in Africa were very different from this, being based on ideas of kinship. Colonial officials had a particularly difficult time molding them to Western norms so that they could serve as a part of the colonial structure of authority.

On the other hand, the state form easily fitted into the political structures of the colonial administrations. The British in particular, under a doctrine called Indirect Rule, used the existing African authorities to underpin the colonial government. Other colonial administrations also ruled through existing African authorities—there were too few Europeans to do otherwise.

States

"State" implies an organization with a monopoly on the use of force—a bureaucratic organization capable of giving orders and seeing that they are carried out. It has territorial limits. Both European and African states were built on an idea of ranked families: the king was a member of a high ranking family or lineage. Yet, also in both places, the state showed weaknesses, particularly that the power of the king over subordinate individuals or groups was always a matter of contest: underlings had either to agree, or be forced, to obey the king.

Most African states were superimposed on older and more intimate forms of social organization. The lineage, and secondarily the local group, provided the royal family. However, lineages often spread beyond the local group, so that the recognition of kin in other villages provided a wider unit of membership.

At the top of the structure, the king often held office because he was a member of a particular royal lineage. Many subordinate officers, such as provincial governors, also held their right to office by virtue of lineage membership. In some West African kingdoms, the kingship rotated through a number of different royal lineages, each taking its turn in furnishing the king.

The powers of the king were considerable, but rival lineages usually found ways to limit the king's powers to protect their own interests. Kings usually had to consult some kind of council, or a group of councils, each with its own sphere of jurisdiction. Other building blocks of political authority cut across the lines of lineage membership. In many African societies, men and women separately belonged to age-sets, or groups born at approximately the same time. Such age-sets held specific duties within the village and within the state, such as military service. As they became older, they gained the authority of age, and their representatives sometimes had to be consulted before an important decision could be taken.

Kingdoms in Africa came in many different sizes. Some covered immense areas, often ruling through smaller kingdoms that had formerly been independent; such "empires" figure largely in African history. Other kingdoms were micro-states, with authority over only a few dozen villages. In West Africa in particular, where micro-states were common, secret societies acted as arbiters of what was, in effect, international relations.

Kingship was often held to be a sacred office. Sacredness resided either in the royal insignia or in the body of the king. If the king himself was the physical symbol of the kingdom, his person was surrounded by taboos and restrictions. In some places if he became old or sick, he was put to death and replaced by a younger, healthier man said to be a more fitting symbol of the kingdom's health and well-being.

The web of government below the level of the king himself could pass through as many as five different levels of chiefs and deputies, each with delegated authority. At every level, the chief was the delegate of the king to the people and representative of the people to the king—typically the chief had to be acceptable to both. In the central and southern Bantu kingdoms, people could move from one chiefship to another almost at will, and the chiefs and those deputies usually called headmen were in considerable competition for subjects. Movement, while not impossible, was much more restricted in the kingdoms of the Guinea coast, mainly because local communities were more consistently organized by kinship.

Tribute passed from the lower official to higher officials in this ladder of delegation—in fact its presentation and acceptance symbolized the delegation of authority. A king would not accept tribute from a person who was not, in his view, a legitimate chief. A chief would not give it to one who was not a recognized king. Tribute was generally of small economic value, and sometimes was purely symbolic.

All African kingdoms used some form of "taxation" in the form of tribute, labor, and calls upon the subjects for sacrificial animals, feasts, or celebrations within the kingdom. Tribute collected at one level of the system of authority was handed up, in part, to the next higher level so that ultimately a part of it from everywhere reached the top.

This hierarchy of authority also acted as a hierarchy of appeal courts. In some cases, the chiefs and kings had oracles as well as courts, and a hierarchy of oracles was established for settling whatever disputes could not be settled judicially. The state was one of the most notable features of pre-conquest Africa. But scattered among the states and within the states were other, stateless societies, which also have added much to the political character of the continent.

Stateless Societies

Whereas most members of stateless societies can understand the notion of the state—indeed, their attitude may be that they understand it only too well—most members of states (even African states) confuse stateless societies with chaos. Even those who understand the non-state forms of political organization are aware that without the idea of citizenship that attaches people to a state, modernization is more difficult.

"State" is, to repeat, a simple idea, even though its manifestations may be terribly complex. Westerners use the state to avoid tyranny (knowing from experience that a bad state may impose tyranny). Africans who live in stateless societies tend to see the state as unavoidably tyrannical. They seek and find order in other institutions. They use several organizations as alternatives to the state. A few—less than half of one percent, and falling very fast—live in small hunting and gathering bands. The San and Pygmies are the best known of these people, but their situation is changing very rapidly. Another political form is the maintenance of justice and territorial integrity through extended family organizations and kinship values.

The classic form of the stateless society—although recent research and analysis indicate that it may be rare in its pure classic form—is a system of checks and balances based on a lineage system. In such a system, there is no single center of power or authority. In fact, there is no authority system at all. The power system is based on two centers in opposition or cooperation rather than on a single center with authority. Since there are two centers of power, no bureaucracy can arise.

The band, the extended family, and the lineage forms of stateless organization all use kinship as the idiom of their system of sanctions. They must not, on that account, be confused with one another. The band solution is perhaps more a solution to economic problems than to political ones, and it disappears when the economy is no longer primarily based on subsistence hunting and gathering. The familial solution works with larger, but still strictly limited, sizes of groups; it has never worked well when the society is faced with more efficient modes of production or with larger groups of technologically more advanced peoples. The lineage solution works better because it can accommodate several million people and can frustrate—indeed, baffle—technologically advanced groups. The family solution is easy for foreigners to understand—and easy for them to demolish. The lineage system is neither.

The lineage system as a solution to political problems at the local level depends on an arrangement of power reminiscent of what used to be called the "balance" of power. It is most often (but certainly by no means necessarily) expressed in terms of kinship with brothers and their groups of descendants balanced against one another—and, at a more distant ancestral remove, large groups of descendants of brothers or other "equivalent" ancestors balanced against one another.

It is a postulate of most of the societies of the world that brothers fight with one another, but that when somebody steps in to stop their fighting, they are likely to join together to oppose that person. Furthermore, though brothers may fight, they must because of their very brotherhood ultimately reach a *modus vivendi*. If we examine the diagram below, it becomes quite obvious that if Brother h fights with Brother g, then anybody who steps in will be regarded as an interloper. If, on the other hand, h fights with f, g will come to the aid of h, and e will come to the aid of f. If the dispute lies between h and d, then everybody who is a descendant of B will come to the aid of h, and everybody who is a descendant of A will come to the assistance of d. In the same way, I and II are equivalent segments.

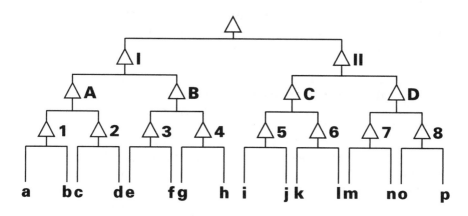

When we discover that each of the units may contain several hundred men with their wives and children—all the sons and the unmarried daughters—it becomes obvious that a certain narrow band of kinship norms can be used to control warfare and to carry out the legal proceedings. Warfare is in fact stopped automatically by the nature of the system—at the very least it is contained. Outsiders, instead of joining in, are usually peacemakers, especially if they are kinsmen to both warring parties.

Laws are maintained in this situation not through a system of chiefs but through opposed sets or councils of elders. If there is a dispute between the members of Lineage 3 and those of Lineage 4, the elders of each group will meet to hammer out a solution to the problem. After all, they say, they are "brothers."

This kind of system has no bureaucracy and no authority. Rather, all disputes, all solutions, all agreements are worked out between segments whose power is "equivalent" and who are balanced against one another. The rest of the outside world has no basis for taking sides one way or the other. In one sense, every court case, every legal dispute which is decided amounts to a treaty rather than to a court decision.

Formerly, the Tiv of central Nigeria organized almost a million people with this system. The Nuer of the southern Sudan organized well over a quarter of a million. The Bedouin Arabs throughout North Africa and over into the Arabian Peninsula were all organized in this way—indeed, there are remnants of such a system in the royal houses of the various Arab states. In such systems there are no officeholders, there are only representatives of groups. The moment the representatives of Group A finish dealing with Group B, and turn back into their own organization, they are members either of Group 1 or Group 2, and therefore any "authority" is automatically limited. In the same way, within Group 2, they must belong either to c or d. At every level, authority within groups is checked at the same time that power in intergroup relations is given full force.

Early colonial officials from European countries sought responsible officeholders in such societies. Obviously, they did not find them, but they did, of course, find leaders. When these leaders did not turn out to be the "responsible" authorities the government officials wanted to find, the latter tended to underestimate both their intelligence and their actual power. Throughout the colonial period, the inclination on the part of colonial governments was to give such leaders authority—to force it on them. Wittingly or not, colonial officers tried to create some sort of a state organization and bureaucracy. Almost without exception, their attempts were baffled. Even when such peoples clamored for chiefs—and sometimes they did—these chiefs were considered to be only the external representatives of the group. *Within* the group they had little or no authority—what little they had garnered was considered tyrannous by the people under them.

Stateless societies can be seen to be bicentric or multi-centric organizations—organizations in which two or more equivalent centers are activated at any particular time. They reach compromises rather than make decisions. Both sides must concur in any proposed solution—there can be no sanctions from some higher authority. A state, on the other hand, is one type of unicentric organization; because of its single center—no matter how pluralistic that center may appear—it can make decisions, laws can be stated, judgments made, and sanctions brought to bear. The differences between the two ways of seeing "law and order" are so immense that it is sometimes difficult to see that the "other" system does in fact provide them.

Law in African Societies

Africa is one of the homes of advanced legal institutions. The written material on African law is extensive. Most of it, however, was written by Europeans during the colonial period. African law suffers from one of two difficulties: some of the writings are uncomprehending restatements of substantive norms as legal rules—the pigeonholes of common law filled with exotic birds. The other difficulty is that what anthropologists and others observed was in fact the workings of legal institutions that had an African content, but were more or less imposed social forms. Yet the law is an area in which African and European views were sufficiently alike that legal institutions worked quite well during the colonial period and, as far as we know, they were not seen as alien to the extent that many other European demands were.

The courts among the Bantu states of the southern third of the continent were the best studied of African states. At least until the end of the colonial period, the local or provincial chief was one of a number of judges on a large and inclusive bench. The bench included representatives of all the important social groups of the community, whether in any particular case they were seen as territorial segments and communities or as kinship units such as clans. The judges formed a regular and pronounced hierarchy and were seated in a row or an arc. The provincial chief sat in the middle; at his immediate right was the second most senior person (however seniority might be computed locally) and at his left the third most senior. To his right, but farther removed, the fourth most senior, and so on, right and left, until the whole court was deployed more or less in a row.

Then, certain areas were designated where the litigants were to stand or, more often, sit on the ground. There were designated places for witnesses, for the nobility, for the followers and backers of the litigants, and for the community as an audience. These court sessions were often held out of doors, but there might be a building for them—colonial governments preferred them inside so that regular schedules, based on clock and calendar time, could be maintained even in the face of inclement weather.

There was, in all cases, a known, and demanded, decorum and order of proceedings. The "plaintiff" (to use an English term with only a 90 percent fit) made a plea—usually without counsel —and was usually allowed to finish the whole complaint, so long as the plaintiff spoke well and to the point. The "defendant" (another translation that does not fit precisely) then replied, telling his or her version of the story. Witnesses were called—including what we would call expert witnesses and character witnesses. Then, after the principals had each told his or her side of the dispute, and after witnesses had been heard, the most junior member of the bench, down at the far end, gave his opinion. His statements probably included moral lectures and statements of the proper kind of behavior that should have been carried out in the situation. His judgment would be followed by that of the man at the other end of the line, his immediate senior, who might disagree, and who added new views and new opinions. The third most junior man followed, and so on until they arrived at the middle where the head chief pronounced the final sentence. He had heard everything that the representatives of the community had to say. He had a chance to weigh the evidence, the judgments, and the opinions of his junior judges. His word on the decision became final.

In these southern Bantu states, there were also well-known and highly effective means for carrying out the decisions of the court. The community, having been represented in the audience as well as on the bench, brought both sacred and mundane sanctions to bear. The decisions of such courts were obeyed. Indeed, such communities might be reasonably said to have a "body of law" or *corpus juris* in the lawyer's sense.

Law in a stateless society was almost as effective but worked differently. Since there is no monolithic power system in the stateless society, agreement had to be reached by consensus or else by compromise. The two contenders had to be brought together in agreement, or at least concurrence, about what is to take place. The principles on which such concurrence is based are usually not as overt as law is in a state society, although the principles by which compromises and concurrence are reached are well known and overt.

The difference between law and cultural norms is vital here and can best be seen from an examination of Western family law. The norms of family living in modern America are fairly well known and fairly circumscribed. The institutionalization of families is such that these norms are fairly well maintained. Only a very few of the norms, however, are restated for legal purposes: the bases for divorce, the laws against abusing children or spouses, and some others. The largest range of family activity is not made part of a body of *law* in the narrow sense. In African stateless societies, no part of family norms had been turned into formal law, but everybody knew the norm and expected people to live up to it. To assume a formal body of law in an African stateless society is precisely the same mistake as assuming that all of the norms of the American family are part of the law of the land.

In order to comprehend African legal systems fully, then, it is necessary to have a new theoretical framework: one that is inclusive of both the law of a state system and that of stateless societies. Such a framework is particularly necessary when we investigate the ways stateless societies changed first due to demands of the colonial governments and now at the demands of the independent governments. People from stateless societies, who are still in the process of adapting to state forms, often experience great difficulty because they see all formal law tyrannous because elasticity is lost in examining each individual case.

Disputes in stateless societies are usually settled by meetings that can be profitably compared with the old New England town meetings, except that in the case of the African stateless societies, there are always two factions and the actual size of the community may change from case to case depending on the closeness of the relationship of the principals to the dispute.

There is, in Old English, a precise and accurate word to describe these "town meetings" or settlement of disputes by the important members of the village. This word is "moot." Well into the twelfth and thirteenth centuries, Anglo-Saxon communities settled their disputes by meeting outside, under the shade of a tree, in whole communities, in order to discover correct and just solutions to disputes. Such is, in a sense, the origin of the "common law."

Courts, unlike moots, are special organs and require some sort of state organization from which they derive their power. While moots are a mode of the community, courts are special arms of politically organized states. Moots and courts can, and in Africa often do, exist side by side within the same society.

During the colonial era, and down to the present day, such stateless societies as that of the Tiv had a full-blown system of moots which ran side by side with the system of courts. Among these people it is considered to be totally immoral to call one's close kinsman before a government court. However, disputes obviously occur between close kinsmen. These disputes are settled in moots. In colonial Nigeria, moreover, charges of witchcraft could not be brought before the courts, since the colonial powers could not allow the court to admit a *belief* in witchcraft. Only *accusations* of witchcraft could be proved or disproved. In such a situation, if somebody accuses someone else of using witchcraft, that accusation becomes slander. However, for those members of the community that believe in witchcraft, the important charge could not be brought into the courts. Therefore witchcraft disputes, throughout the country, had to be settled in moots.

Africans sometimes settled disputes by devices other than courts and moots. Ordeals and recourse to seers and diviners were both fairly widespread throughout the continent. An ordeal is a means for settling a dispute in the absence of any kind of evidence which can prove or disprove the charge, either because there are no witnesses or because (as in the case of witchcraft) empirical proof is impossible.

Probably no people claims that oracles and ordeals have much to do with justice. However, oracles are said to reveal the will or knowledge of the gods, and they do settle disputes. Ordeals include taking oaths on shrines, the deliberate administration of poisonous substances to animals, and even administering such substances to human beings themselves. These substances are not necessarily lethal, and if the animal or the person does not die, the party is usually considered innocent. In some African societies (the best written descriptions are for the Azande of the Sudan in the 1920s), the oracular mechanisms were checked and counterchecked through the requirement that a second oracle corroborate the first before action could be taken. Ordeals have all but disappeared from modern Euro-American courts. However, the divine sanctions which ordeals symbolize are still a part of such courts because it is still necessary for both witnesses and the principals to take oaths on entering the witness stand.

Africans sometimes resorted to contests to settle disputes. This "game" solution to a dispute is one in which the disputants either are forced to or agree to reduce the field of relevance and determine a winner; they declare the winner in the game to be the winner of the real-life situation. In the early history of Roman law and during the Middle Ages in Europe, gladiatorial contests to settle disputes occupied important places in the legal repertoire.

Perhaps the most important of the sanctions, particularly in the stateless societies, was the institutionalized use of self-help. It is common throughout African stateless societies—and also in some of the states—for a man to collect his own debts by going to the farms or compound of his debtor and removing the property (a goat, for instance) that is owed to him. If he can make a case before the moot, if the debtor calls one, and if both his group and that of the debtor agree that the debt is now adequately discharged, his self-help was successful.

Some degree of self-help is either condoned or required in all legal systems. It becomes even more important in non-state organizations than it is in states because the major sanction, and the power behind it, is to be found in the right and the ability of the groups concerned to carry out the decisions and compromises made by the elders.

If self-help gets out of hand it becomes, of course, akin to lawlessness—in any society. The boundaries have to be fixed and the use of self-help contained if it is to be an adequate judicial mechanism. In states, such limitations can be defined by legislation or by precedent. In non-states, self-help is controlled, but controlled somewhat differently. In our example of the man taking the goat, his own group will come to his defense if the others try to retaliate. However, if he takes the goat unreasonably and in a way that they believe the moot would not approve of—if he has a "bad case," or if he is a criminal—his kinsfolk will not risk the peace of the countryside, their hides, and their reputation for him. In such a case, two centers of judgment and power must be satisfied, and in achieving such a satisfaction, any community whose members overstep the accepted norm will find itself attacked and perhaps routed. Yet such attacks seldom occur, because the moots and the good will of the two communities usually effect a settlement.

Africans in every part of the continent are running complex modern governments. The basic ideas behind the political thinking of many of their citizens, however, are still to be found in the type of situation that has been described here. On the surface, African institutions are changing very rapidly, but the quickening ideas, molded by experience and language, have deep roots in African tradition and history. Because the deep roots of both African and European tradition tap the same prehistoric reserves, and because Africans have passed through most of the cultural revolutions which have, perhaps in other terms, also been the experience of the West, their adaptation has been fast and often successful. For all that, however, the distinct African idiom in many instances remains.

8

AFRICAN TRADE
AND MARKETS

ommercial contact between African and European traders began about 1480. Between about the 1690s and the 1830s, the most economically valuable export from sub-Saharan Africa was certainly slaves. Thus the slave trade was dominant for about a third of the five hundred years during which Africa and Europe had been directly trading.

The trading structure was well established as early as the 1660s. Senegambia alone exported as many as 150,000 cowhides in a single year. The Gold Coast exported an annual average of more than half a ton of gold. A century later, slave exports reached around 50,000 a year. Whatever we may think of the morality of the slave trade (and it has few defenders today), the commercial system necessary to acquire and transport that many slaves for sale on the coasts was far from primitive.

Long-distance trade within sub-Saharan Africa began well before the beginning of maritime contact. When the Portuguese seamen first arrived on the Gulf of Guinea, they found African traders already working the routes from the Sahara fringe right down to the coast. African long-distance trade continued to develop during the era of the slave trade. Yet, even at the height of the slave trade, long-distance caravans in Africa carried far less goods destined for export than they did goods for consumption within Africa.

By the nineteenth century, caravans from the Atlantic coast in Angola or the present-day Congo Republic reached the center of Africa, where they could encounter other caravans coming from the Indian Ocean and still others coming south from the upper Nile. When the European explorers first began to enter Africa in the late eighteenth and early nineteenth centuries, they always travelled with the help and guidance of African long-distance merchants, who often knew more about Europe than the explorers knew about Africa.

Markets and Market Places

The African economy was mainly agricultural and remains so to the present. The long-distance traders were a comparatively small group of professionals who worked the routes between markets.

These markets were periodic meetings at fixed market places in most of Africa from Zaire northward. In other regions, where regular market places were less common, people nevertheless met to exchange goods on the market principle. The market principle is the process in which a multitude of buyers and sellers bargain together until they arrive at a price, fundamentally established by the pull and push of supply and demand for a particular commodity.

But alongside exchanges dominated by the market principle, other exchanges did and still do take place on other bases. It is important here to distinguish between the market place and the market principle. The market place is the specific spot where buyers and sellers meet. It could be used for many purposes other than buying and selling—to meet your girlfriend, settle a legal dispute, get the latest news, or pay your respects to important elders or chiefs. Market places in Africa are almost as important politically and socially as they are economically.

We have two tasks at hand. One is to see what goes on in market places. The other is to see how the market principle has worked or failed to work in African societies. We shall find some societies without market places; some with market places, but where few of the necessities of life pass through them; and finally some parts of the modern African economy where the role of the traditional market place dwindles, but that of the market principle dominates society as it does in Europe or America.

A market-dominated economy such as those of the United States and Western Europe—and the society that goes with it—is one in which not merely products and manufactured items but also factors of production such as land and labor enter into the same market. These markets may be more or less controlled by political authorities. The difference to be emphasized here is not a difference between free and controlled markets, but a difference that stems from the entry of land and labor into the same market in which yams, corn, cocoa, clothing, and beer are exchanged.

In a society dominated by the market principle, at least some member of every primary group must sell either one of the factors of production (usually labor) or else the produce of his work and land. The opposite is usually called a "subsistence economy," which means simply that the basic provisions of the members of the society are gained some way other than through market exchange, and that ultimately the factors of production, particularly land and labor, do not enter the market (although they are no less necessary to production).

The word "subsistence" is tricky in English because it means two things at once. It is associated with the word "level" on the one hand, to indicate poverty and life on the thin edge between existing and perishing—"bare existence." A subsistence economy is different; it must not be confused with subsistence level. The only link between them is the ambiguity in the word subsistence. There is no reason that a subsistence economy must always or even commonly be found to hover at the subsistence level. A subsistence economy means merely that the factors of production do not enter the market.

Poverty, obviously, need not accompany the absence of factors in the market and may, just as obviously, be overwhelming in the presence of markets which include the factors of production. Indeed, given an adequate ecological adjustment and a sufficiently good tool kit, poverty cannot exist except in societies organized on a market basis. Famine may occur—but poverty in any other sense does not.

Except for hunting and gathering economies of the rapidly disappearing San and Pygmies, the subsistence level is usually far exceeded by all the subsistence economies of Africa. Some places have a "hungry season" just before the harvest, but that has to do with the agricultural cycle and the difficulties of storage in a tropical climate. Even in the hungry season, people usually eat. They do not eat as much as they would like; in fact, they may regularly lose weight during it. This period, where it occurs, usually lasts at most six or seven weeks.

In a market society, produce and the products of factories are sold on a market, more or less controlled by government, at prices more or less determined by supply and demand. The result is that the market in produce can and does limit and even control the market in such factors as labor and land, because of the workings of supply and demand. Such a system is to be found in many parts of the world, but it is more dominant in some places than in others. In the modern Western economy it is the primary organizing principle. Even in a subsistence economy, with comparatively little exchange, the scarcity or abundance of any commodity has an influence on the value attributed to it. Some subsistence economies have highly developed markets for export produce.

Yet land, labor, brains or ability, and capital were rarely offered on the market in traditional Africa. Capital was available in only modest amounts—a canoe, a fishing net, bellows and forge, agricultural tools. Labor could be "bought," in the sense that slaves were bought and some of their labor could be diverted to producing goods for the market. The labor of free men, however, was seldom "bought" through contract. Land was allocated in such complex and socially determined ways that it too rarely had a market price.

The force of the market principle was therefore comparatively weak insofar as the basic factors of production were concerned.

The problem for understanding the traditional African rural economy is to find how goods were distributed, when not consumed directly by the producers, and how life was organized when the market principle was comparatively weak.

Marketing and Trading

An important distinction can be made between marketing and trading. Marketing is the activity of producers who take some of their products to the market place to exchange for other products. Trade, on the other hand, is the activity where an entrepreneur buys in one market with the intention of selling in another. The fact that marketing and trading go hand-in-hand does not make them inseparable. If produce markets had disappeared in pre-colonial Africa, the society would not have perished or even changed its structure very much. If the market principle stopped working in present-day America, on the other hand, not only the economy but all of society would collapse. Even farmers sell most of what they grow on the market, and buy most of what they consume. The rest of us sell our labor for a salary and buy almost everything we use.

Trading over long distance has been part of the African scene for a very long time. The old traders' traditions and practices have survived in a somewhat altered form. All over the world, pre-industrial long-distance trade tended to be carried on by merchants organized as a trade diaspora. One of the problems encountered in trade across cultural divisions was the vast differences in language and culture, often over quite short distances. One way to surmount this difficulty was to send out merchants to take up residence in a foreign commercial center. There, over time, they could learn the local language and come to understand the alien way of life. Once accustomed to the foreign setting, these emissaries could set themselves up to act as cross-cultural brokers, helping to smooth the way for traveling merchants from their homeland.

Thousands of different merchant communities have organized trade diasporas, going back in time to ancient Mesopotamia. The most familiar will probably be the Greeks and Phoenicians of the classical Mediterranean, or the north Germans of the Middle Ages whose trade diaspora stretched from London far into Russia and ultimately became the Hanseatic League.

In Africa, some of the oldest trade diasporas were those of North Africa, like that of the Phoenicians. When camels began to be used in the Sahara after about the fifth century A.D., North African merchants began to reach across the desert, setting up small merchant communities at the desert edge to the south. From there, sub-Saharan merchant communities brought in goods from the savanna and forest country, including minerals like gold or agricultural products like kola nuts. Many of these early sub-Saharan trade diasporas were originally Soninke in culture, since the Soninke were a major group near the desert edge, but their diasporas spread off to the south under a number of different ethnic names, Wangarawa, Jahaanke, or Juula (Dioula in French) among others. These diaspora communities were so specialized in commerce that the name, Juula, simply means merchant.

Later on, many other ethnic groups began to enter trade as a specialized occupation, most notably the Hausa from Northern Nigeria and the Republic of Niger, who have settled in trade enclaves within many African cities. These enclaves are now called Zongos, where Hausa is still the language of commerce. Others, mainly in the twentieth century, have become trade specialists, like Wolof-speaking Senegalese, whose commercial communities can be found scattered in the market places from their home country around Dakar, through West Africa to Brazzaville in Congo and Kinshasa in Zaire. Today, significant communities of Senegalese traders are street-corner peddlers in Paris and in New York.

In the pre-colonial past, the traders travelled in armed caravans for mutual protection, sometimes as many as a thousand people together. Their goods were carried by porters where the tse-tse fly prevented animal transport, by donkey in much of the savanna, and by camel or pack-ox near the desert edge. Today, they use trucks on the highways, telegraph and telephone for communication, and often travel by air with their trade goods as part of their baggage. Some, whose families had been members of trade diasporas for centuries, have gained a Western education and moved over into the Western-style sector of the economy as members of trading firms.

Nor did all the successful big traders of present-day Africa begin in the trade diasporas. Many worked their way into long- distance trade from a beginning in the local market. Women were the chief retail marketers in much of West Africa. They could slip more easily from marketing into trade where (as with the Yoruba) men produced most of the food. Women marketers and traders have been particularly important in buying and selling food crops and from this base have worked their way over into the import and retail distribution of European manufactures.

Market Places

Market places are primarily regarded as points to do one's marketing and trading. The amount of internal trade in various African countries that goes through the market places is tremendous, but nobody has any idea how much volume or what value of goods may actually be distributed in this way. Weights and measures are more or less absent, although in many parts of the continent standard weights and measures have appeared in the last few decades. The quart beer bottle, the standard-size cigarette tin, the standard-sized four-gallon kerosene tin, and an empty 30-30 shell casing are all used as measures. There are others. There are also many non-standardized units of measurement. Moreover, no formal records are kept by individual marketers. Many West African traders do keep books of one sort or another, although most do not. Marketers, even when they do a little bit of trading along with their marketing, do not separate either their marketing or their trading from their domestic activities. Obviously, acquiring any kind of quantitative ideas about the amount or the value of such goods becomes a task in data acquisition that has scarcely been tackled.

It is true, however, that vast quantities of local produce such as food, craft products, livestock, cloth—everything that is the staff of life and the basis for the provisioning of society—may go through these markets in parts of West Africa and the Congo area. Yet in relatively few places are people dependent on the market places for the basis of their subsistence.

Markets are vital links—the very nodes—in the transportation network. The famous "bush telegraph"—the rapid spread of news by means unknown to Europeans—works in part through the market places. Africa is a country on the move, and it appears that it always has been. However, the peace of the colonial era, and the road building that accompanied it, meant that market places increased in number, that the amount of travel to and from market increased vastly, and therefore the "bush telegraph" worked with greater and greater efficiency.

Market places are, throughout that part of the continent to which they are indigenous, organized under political authority. Indeed, in those parts of East and South Africa to which they have been introduced, it was colonial government that introduced them. In some areas of West Africa, chiefs retained direct control over the market places or appointed special deputies to maintain the market place and keep peace within it. In other areas, committees of elders, representative in whatever way was considered important to the community, took it as one of their most serious civic duties to maintain a market place so that their part of the world would be "kept on the map" and prosperity would reign.

All African market places are policed by someone. In many areas, this task has gone to the policemen of the recognized local government. In others, however, they are policed by special groups designated by the elders to carry out the task. These policemen are always subject to the authority of somebody who is the headman (it may be a committee) to whom they can refer wrongdoers and disputes which occur in the market place. Disputes inevitably arise in market places, because people may cheat each other, and because they may meet their enemies and their debtors. For this reason, ordinary African market places often have a court in session. It may be no more than a place to resolve arguments over shortchanging, quality of goods, and petty theft. In other market places, however, the judges of the local government may set up their courts.

In some parts of Africa, the market authorities enforce quality control. They disallow sale of rotten meat or other unsatisfactory goods. The usual mode of treatment is caveat emptor, but some control is maintained—the degree varying with the personalities and power of the market officials.

Market administrators are usually rewarded. They may be paid salaries by the local government. They may, on the other hand, be allowed to make a levy on the goods sold in the market. Sometimes entry fees are demanded from marketers who intend to sell goods. The amount of the levy or entrance fee is itself subject to what the market will bear. If the levy is too high, traders and marketers will avoid such market places and establish new ones nearby. The only way to avoid such a situation is for governments to demand control and licensing of market places—a situation that was fairly widespread in colonial Africa and is found in some of the new African states.

Market places can "die," which means merely that people cease to come to them. They can also be "stolen," which means that one gains popularity at the expense of another. In short, the location of market places, their organization, and their popularity are all highly volatile and subject to quick change. Since it is to the advantage of individuals and government officials to control large popular market places (by so doing they are able to see and to influence large numbers of people), few petty tyrannies can be kept up for long.

In traditional Africa, almost all market places were associated with religious activities. That is to say, the market places were consecrated in one way or another. To this day, most African market places have shrines associated with them. Such consecration guaranteed that supernatural sanctions would back up the political authorities in their maintenance of peace in the market place. Such supernatural sanctions, and the shrines that were their symbols, varied with the particular religion in question. They may have been no more than a bundle of "medicine." In many areas they were specially consecrated trees. In some, there were special small huts with carved figurines in them. The purpose of these shrines was the maintenance of the market peace. It is well recognized that it is impossible, in even the best-policed market place, to be sure that all who cheat or steal or water their beer or sell bad meat will be caught by the authorities. Therefore, it is best to reinforce their vigilance with supernatural sanctions.

Finally, markets are fun. Each displays an element of the fair or the carnival. In West Africa and the Congo Basin they are major centers of entertainment. Dancers come to the market and display their skill. Work parties, wedding parties, christening parties, and spur-of-the-moment parties come to the market to dance and sing and to announce their good news to enlarged audiences.

In all these regards African market places are reminiscent of those in Europe from the Middle Ages up into the eighteenth century. Market places in Europe were also fairs that were held in the shadow of the church and were policed by the bishop and the market master and their officials. They were religious centers as well as important centers of trade and distribution. Market places may be extremely important institutions in almost every phase of human activity. Yet for all that, the fact remains that their raison d'être is channeling trade and providing an outlet for those who want to trade subsistence wares.

Systems of Market Places

Different market places specialize in different goods and in different activities. One market is a good place to buy X and sell Y. The next one is a good place to buy Y and sell Z. Another may be well known for its beer-drink, and the one after that for its wise counselors and judges. Such specialization, when combined with another fact— that markets do not meet every day—leads to two vital points about the marketing system of Africa, particularly West Africa and the Congo Basin. First of all, every community is at the center of a group of markets which meets every fourth, fifth, or seventh day, depending on the area. There is, therefore, an association of market places with time as well as with special products. In a neighborhood with markets that meet every five days, each community is likely to be either at or near the center of a cycle or a ring of five markets, each of which meets one day of the five-day "market week." These market neighborhoods, or rings, overlap in a chain-mail fashion, and spread across the countryside. Such overlapping rings, with a few gaps, run from Dakar almost to the Nile, and south well into the Congo Basin.

The other major characteristic of the market system is that goods can move through market places and traverse very much greater distances than people themselves. Every different African product that goes through market places follows a route determined by specialization of market places. A large number of "middlemen" add to the price, but the markup is very small, considering the number of intermediary links that may separate a producer from a consumer.

Market places, thus, provide another "map," based on a different institution, by means of which space, time, and social structure are coordinated. This trade map or market map permeates different cultures and crosses national and language barriers. If a market place is commonly used by several ethnic groups, the consecrated shrines and the ritual that surrounds them contain the elements from each religion which make it workable in all the cultures. There may be, indeed, highly original rituals consciously created and especially performed in order to include the vital elements from several religious systems. Violence can still occur, however. Today weapons are forbidden—and usually were so even before colonial governments made the practice general. Moreover, throughout the indigenous market area of Africa, people sit in the position in the market place closest to the path leading to their homes—this is particularly true of women marketers. Such seating arrangements keep the escape routes open. Yet, market places are, at the same time, often legal sanctuaries, because of their position of political neutrality and their consecrated shrines.

The Spread of the Market Principle

One of the first reactions to colonial control was the vast expansion in the number of market places in Africa and of the goods that went through them. Only later did the market places themselves begin to dwindle, as their tasks were taken over by modern transport systems, expanding firms, and thousands of entrepreneurs—some small-scale, others handling large volumes.

In the process of the enlargement of the importance of market places, the importance of the market principle also became magnified. The "market" in both its senses was spreading.

To Westerners, money, trade, and market are more or less inseparable—they need not be separated to be understood. European governments therefore encouraged the growth of market places, and by introducing coinage and demanding that taxes be paid in it (and abetting importation of goods that could be bought with it), they actively hastened the enlargement of the social scope for the market principle.

Money is probably the most important single item in changing an economy. A monetized economy is, by that very fact, different from a nonmonetized economy. Money is a cultural trait that has been discovered several times in the history of the world, including several places in Africa. It is, indeed, a term that may change meanings from one culture to another. Money is said by economists to do at least three things: (1) it is a method for evaluating and comparing goods of different kinds; (2) it is a means of payment; (3) it is a means for facilitating exchange.

The three uses of money must not be confused simply because coinage—a single cultural item—carries out all three tasks in our own society. Money is used in the West to pay fines (although people insist that a fine is not exactly a "price" because crimes cannot be evaluated) and money is used to pay taxes (which is only by the furthest stretch of analogy an exchange). We have a general purpose money. However, we must *not* therefore assume that a money item used for *one* of these purposes in other cultures is automatically used for the other purposes.

Africa had some examples of general purpose money—cowrie shells in a few places in West Africa and the Congo Basin, and again on the East Coast where Indian rupees, Spanish and American money, and Austrian "Maria-Theresa" dollars all circulated long before the colonial period began. Throughout West Africa, the most common kind of currency for ordinary marketing was cloth of particular styles and qualities. Many, if not most, African societies had other forms of currency that could be used for only one purpose. These are called "special purpose money." Metal "hoes" in Guinea and Liberia were used principally for paying bridewealth, while ordinary food in the market place required other forms of currency. Western societies have had special purpose currencies in the recent past. During the Second World War, people had the general-purpose money they earned, but they had to have ration coupons as well to buy gasoline, sugar, coffee, shoes, and some other items. In this way, the government could assure itself that gasoline went mainly to those with a need to drive, or that food and other scarce items were shared equably. In much the same way, special purpose currencies in Africa control the distribution of particular goods— chiefly brides.

Other, social factors also lie behind these specialized monetary systems. Three, or perhaps more, economic principles can serve to organize exchange: they are the market principle, the principle of redistribution, and the principle of reciprocity. Taking the American economy as a model, we can think quite correctly that we live in a market economy. Most of the transactions that take place are transactions according to market principles of price determined by supply and demand, with more or less government "interference." However, we pay taxes, which is a form of redistribution: wealth moves toward a political center and is redistributed from it.

Redistribution may be (but in our own case is not) the dominant mode of institutionalizing an economy. In some African societies until quite recently, much of the allocation of goods took place within a pattern of redistribution. Large family groups or even whole societies paid much of their produce to the family head or higher authority, who then redistributed it according to political principles.

Sometimes in traditional Africa, a gift that was expected to be matched by gifts or favors was given in a particular ritual manner. On the Senegambia coast, for example, traders made ritual gifts that included the widest possible variety of goods; some gifts were sometimes called "one of everything," meaning everything under the sun, though in practice it simply meant one of every kind of trade good. Such gifts were designed to reassure opposing traders of one's good intent. When it came to actual exchange of commodities, however, hard bargaining on the basis of supply and demand was clearly the prime concern. Of course, both sides considered the value and cost of the preliminary gifts as part of their profit and loss accounts.

The other allocative principle can be called reciprocity—exchange of goods and services between people who are permanently in relationship with one another, but in which the precise values are not overtly computed, in spite of the fact that they may work out fairly evenly. Mid-twentieth-century Americans have a sort of vestigial reciprocity, confused easily with market because we acquire on the market most of the goods that enter the institutions of reciprocal allocation. Gifts we give at Christmas are an example. It is still bad taste to compute market price on the gifts that are exchanged.

In the American economy today, the market is central; redistribution has an important part, but is purposely underplayed. In pre-colonial Africa, the emphasis was different. Redistribution and reciprocity were supposed to be more important. Goods were often supposed to be sold at prices that changed very little over time; they had a semi-official exchange value imbedded in tradition. One ox equalled ten cloths of a certain type; so many oxen were the proper bride price; so many measures of millet were equal to a measure of milk. In fact, goods rarely changed hands at these traditional values, simply because people knew that an ox or a measure of millet was scarce or plentiful at that time. The market principle thus slipped in by the back door, so that, when millet was scarce a half-measure would "count" as a whole. When it was plentiful, perhaps two measures were necessary to "count" as one.

Through the past century, the market economy has gradually triumphed, first through convenient fictions, then more and more openly through the spread of general-purpose money. Though special-purpose moneys continued to be used for such payments as bridewealth, it became increasingly easy to transfer from one kind of money to another—like buying ration coupons on the black market in wartime. Finally, even that fiction has disappeared and most bridewealth passes openly in the form of general purpose money—bank-notes and coins issued by the African governments. However, the spread of the market principle into new spheres, here as in other aspects of life, has created tremendous moral problems that are not entirely resolved.

In rural Africa, the noisy, colorful market place is a growing phenomenon. In urban centers, open market places of the old style still function as vital institutions, operating on the market principle. Western-style firms are also present alongside them—dealing in manufactures, imports, exports, and retail sales. The market place and the supermarket exist side by side.

9

AFRICAN RELIGION

A ll African religions are monotheistic in the sense that there is a single high God. He is said to have created the world and humankind; he is a central source of order. Many African religions are also polytheistic in that either pantheons of gods or large numbers of spirits or ancestors or some other kind of divinities may stand between human beings and the ultimate God.

African religions tend to have a precise, one-to-one association with a particular form of social group. In this characteristic they are unlike the international religions, which are supple enough to subserve many forms of social structure. African religion and African society are different ways of viewing the same universe, for God and the spirits are, even to the skeptical, members of the same society as living human beings.

Prayer and sacrifice are found in all the religions on the continent. Prayers, however, are likely to be generalized requests for health and well-being. They include statements of innocence of evil intention. Sacrifices are used not so much for purposes of cleansing (although such may be dominant, as in Kikuyu religion) as to provide paths of communication between the human beings and divinity. To oversimplify, life is the supreme value; sacrifice takes life (usually goats or chickens) as a means of getting in touch with the source of life and enhancing human life.

Perhaps the most characteristic quality of African religion is that there are many strings to the bow. For each purpose to be achieved, there are several ritual and moral ways of doing it. African religion does not in most places have undeniable orthodoxy (the exceptions are those such as traditional Dahomey in which an established priesthood existed). Therefore it has no heterodoxy. It is to be understood rather as a set of goals, a dogma of the nature of God and man, and a more or less experimental (and therefore constantly and rapidly changing) set of rituals for achieving those goals within the conceptual framework of the dogma. To study African religion means to study the ritual, the dogma behind it, and the goals to be achieved by it.

Ritual occupies an important place in Africa. Passage through the life cycle tends to be marked with religious ritual—at least, it should be, and if a person gets ill the reason may be found in the fact that a vital rite was omitted. Naming ceremonies, initiations, weddings,

116

burials—as well as the seasons and the annual schedule—are usually marked by religious rites. The world must be constantly renewed by the ritual activities of people, so that humanity may prosper as the world prospers. Most importantly, perhaps, ritual occurs in association with medicine as means of curing the infirm and postponing death.

Africans have, however, a tendency to neglect ritual until it is demanded by the divinities. Demands take the form, they say, of crop failure or illness among the living members of the societies. The immediate reaction to misfortune is always to ask "Why?" and to consult a diviner about those aspects which are beyond the reach of the human senses. Until you discover the source of the difficulty and repair the ritual breach, you cannot effectively treat the difficulty.

Perhaps most impressive of all to a European visitor is the casualness of African religious activities. This casualness does not mean that Africans do not take their religions seriously, but only that they do not consider the divinities either prudish or unsolicitous.

A Rubric for African Religion

The absence of orthodoxy in African religion means that many versions of the substantiating myths can be collected. The "truth" lies in the common motifs of the many versions. In Dahomey, priests can give fairly congruent versions of views concerning the nature of human beings and divinity and the establishment of the social and divine order. In stateless societies such as the Tiv, every person is his own expert—in religious matters as in everything else. What specialists there are maintain their position by social criteria and not by priestly ones, even as they use ritual knowledge for political ends.

Underneath the wild diversity of African religious practice runs a common set of themes and occurrences which an investigator can pick out and turn into a story. Careful investigators know that if they read such a story as a connected version of African statements, they will be wrong. Rather, a story is the most economical means to interrelate beliefs and practices. Unlike the myths that we have tried so far to expose—untrue but widely stated—this story is true but never stated.

In the beginning (the story behind African religion might run) God created the Heavens and the Earth. And he created them without regard for good and evil. They existed and, like God himself, were morally neutral. God, having accomplished his task, withdrew. The extent of his withdrawal varies from one society to the next—from the truly "otiose" or removed God, who is not available to human beings, to a God almost as personalized as the Judeo-Christian divinity. In all places, however, the created universe was a mechanically or organically perfect system (both analogies misinterpret the African view to some extent, but allow Westerners to see the interconnectedness in it). It lacked only one thing: energy (again, to use a non-African metaphor). The power had to be supplied by the human creatures and their ancestors and the lower spirits that God had created. Human effort and spiritual energy (which often had to be primed by human effort) were the driving forces.

The nature of the beings that lie between men and God is everywhere said to be unknown, but everywhere described by local people. There are usually at least two levels in the hierarchy—in the "channels," to use a bureaucratic analogy. One is the ancestors, the other is a set of aspects of God or more straightforward, personalized godlings. The will of God (which may be fixed, and therefore unwilled in any specific instance) is made known down through the channels; it is satisfied by ritual, sacrifice, and the protestations of prayer, which go up through the same channels.

Good and evil enter such a system by two possible routes, and African religions may use either or both: evil is inherent in human selfishness, which leads human beings to pervert the ritual that is the means for supplying the force. This (one might almost say "Protestant") notion is commonly found among peoples who live in stateless societies; here it is human selfishness in its individual manifestations that creates misfortune and causes death. Human weakness and selfishness throw a monkey wrench into the works.

The other source of evil is the "joker," played wild. The joker is a widespread religious phenomenon—the Judeo-Christian devil is, in fact, a joker who perverts all the rules and hence accounts for evil. Legba of Dahomean religion can be seen as the archetype of the joker whose ineptitudes, carelessness, and malice have allowed misfortune, death, and the threat of dissolution of society to enter the firmament. "Fate," as the joker is often called, must be invoked to explain catastrophe in the absence of human selfishness and weakness.

The human task is, through worship and sacrifice, to hold up the human end of the process by supplying the motive force for the universe. Even more important, it is up to human beings, through right and generous living, to avoid creating the antisocial and anticosmic situations that bring about disaster. Whoever says that African religion has no moral content (and it has often been said) does not know an African religion—or else is saying that African religion does not much concern itself with people's sexual conduct and does not set forth its moral precepts as ten imperatives.

The line between myth and theory is still vague in the study of comparative religion. A myth organizes data as narrative in order to condense mountains of facts or beliefs into recognizable form; a theory, while it is not exactly a story, does the same thing. Myths and theories are also subject to different canons of proof: theories must stand up to experiment and ratiocination. Myths must stand up to the abrasions of social life. In that sense, this organization of the data is a theory—it allows the exposition of the concepts, but it cannot be gathered, in this form, from any informant.

Dogma

Like most religious practitioners, Africans start at the opposite end of the chain of events from theologians or social scientists. They begin with the situation that calls for explanation and perhaps intervention between God and his emissaries. In Africa, that situation is most commonly individual or community misfortune: disease or sterility, misgovernment or plague.

Today's Westerners often fail to remember that it is only about three hundred years ago that William Harvey discovered the circulation of the blood, and that little more than a century has passed since bacteria were discovered to be the carriers of some diseases; that only a few decades have passed since we discovered viruses, and only a few years since we discovered the first hints about the etiology of diseases created by chromosomal malformation or the immune system. Scientific information of this sort filters, via the press and the educational system, so rapidly into the general knowledge of the educated public that it becomes difficult to appreciate ideas about the nature of disease and its causation held by peoples who lack such scientific knowledge.

Most traditional African religions postulate that were it not for the workings of the forces of evil, human beings would live forever in health and happiness. Therefore, when disease and misery strike, the source must be rooted out. That source contains two elements. On the one hand is the cause of the difficulty. Africans, within their knowledge, are as sensible about cause as anyone else, and most of them know that some diseases are communicable, and that droughts appear in recurring cycles. Cause in this sense, however, leaves certain questions unanswered—all the "why" questions. Therefore, misfortune must have not only a cause but it must have a source of motivation (like the running of the world itself must have motive energy).

Therefore the very fact that misfortune strikes is in itself an indication that all is not well in the world and in the cosmos. Both cause and motivation must be discovered. We can see (from a Western point of view) that motivation cannot be determined by what we would consider rational means. Westerners have, in fact, been rigorously trained not to ask "why" questions about misfortune. When a doctor tells us that we have a rare disease we do not immediately say "Why me?"—at least we do not say it to the doctor. We have become a statistic, for better or for worse. It is, however, exactly the "Why me?" question that Africans ask, and to which they seek an answer. In answer, they link social problems to divine action. In so doing, they air and often solve the social problems in the course of seeking to counter the divine manifestations.

When misfortune strikes, the first thing one must do is go to a diviner to discover the device which was used to bring it about and perhaps also to discern the author of it. That author may be a spirit to whom insufficient attention has been paid. It may be an ancestor who is punishing a descendant—perhaps an innocent one—for social, moral, or spiritual shortcomings of the group of descendants. Or it may, indeed, be a "witch"—a human author of evil—venting anger, envy, or selfishness.

African diviners use many modes of carrying out their task. They may throw palm nuts and read answers to their queries in the juxtaposition of the fallen kernels. They may toss chains of snake bones. They may rub carved oracle boards together. They may become possessed and receive their answers through a spiritual intermediary. They may administer to chickens a poison that is sometimes lethal and sometimes not, and then judge by the results. They may examine the entrails of sacrificed beasts. In short, when one is seeking to establish a connection which is in scientific fact a *non sequitur*, any means save a scientific one can be brought into play.

Divination in African religion is vital because it tells priests, patients, and the entire community what ritual they must perform. Successful diviners are highly intelligent and often high-strung men or (occasionally) women. Divination is one of the specialties most likely to attract the person with an intellectual bent. Diviners must have an excellent knowledge of the societies in which they live; they sometimes make excellent informants for anthropologists. They must also have courage. It is they who are putting their fingers on, and bringing into the open, the inadequacies and the sore spots in day-to-day living. Unless they are strong and forceful, they can be cowed. Many diviners who complete their training never practice, specifically because they cannot stand the heat in the kitchen.

Once divination has been carried out, two steps remain. One of these is ritual, the other medical (or in the case of community misfortune, legal). Indigenous African practice was first to carry out the ritual so that the motivation for the misfortune could be counteracted. Only then could medical curing be undertaken, for to do so before ritual counteraction of the motive force would be fruitless.

Ritual

All African ritual—perhaps, indeed, all ritual—involves putting a person, or the representatives of a community, into touch with God or his representatives. The person must then also be safely returned from the state of sacred contact. There are two main components of most African rituals: sacrifice and prayer. There are many lesser elements: magical gesture, a social demand that ritual must be carried out by certain people in the presence of certain other people; prayers must be supported by communities—the congregation— and the sacrifices must be consumed by the beneficiaries, past and present, of such ritual.

Most sacrifices in African religion involve the taking of life—there are a few offerings of food, tobacco, or kola nuts that are of a different nature and are sometimes called sacrifice by Westerners. For major purposes, however, sacrifice takes life. The common sacrificial animal is the chicken, although every kind of domesticated animal that one can think of has probably been sacrificed. In West Africa, and indeed throughout most of the continent, the blood of the sacrificed animals is smeared onto the beneficiary of the sacrifice and onto the emblems of divinity, whatever they may be. There are, however, some areas in East Africa in which the cheam of cattle or goats—that substance contained in their first stomach—replaces blood. The point is that the taking of life and the smearing of the symbol of life onto the person and the divine emblems establishes a contact between the two. While thus exposed, one is in a state of extreme jeopardy. However, only through such exposure is curing possible.

Either as a part of the ritual, or at the completion of the ritual, the sacrificial animal is eaten. It is cooked and consumed by the congregation of the persons who have benefitted from the specific ritual in question. The ingestion of the ritual animal redoubles the solidarity of the community and also provides symbols of status.

A good deal of nonsense has been written about human sacrifice in Africa. Human sacrifice was witnessed and reported by European travelers in several parts of the continent during the nineteenth century; it has occurred secretly (occasionally exposed by police and courts) on a small scale in the twentieth. Human sacrifice is, in almost all cases (but there may have been a few exceptions), an act of desperation: since human life is the dearest life, it is therefore the most powerful when taken in sacrifice. The idea of human sacrifice is not unknown in modern international religions—it is merely that most of them have devised symbolic means by which the sacrifice, once made, can have permanent effect and need never be repeated. Africans too have devised many means of maintaining the idiom of human sacrifice while not actually carrying it out. One is outright symbolic association of an animal (commonly the dog) with the human being; another is to treat the corpses of those that died natural deaths in such a way that they count as sacrifices and hence death comes to represent the greatest good of the community.

Although there are vast quantities of texts of prayers from African religious services preserved in the literature, there has not been as yet any extensive and systematic comparative examination of them. Only very broad generalizations can be made. Prayers often protest the innocence from evil of all those present, particularly the ritual participants. Such protests often involve oaths: "May I die if . . ." or some equivalent form. The request is usually uttered in very broad terms: for health, welfare, and fertility of entire communities. There are also private prayers in African religion, but it is difficult to say whether the general opinion that they are of considerably lesser importance than the prayers uttered in public ritual is the actual case, or whether it is just that the public prayers are overwhelmingly easier to observe and discuss.

Witchcraft: The Parasite of Religion

Witchcraft has to a greater or lesser extent been a parasite on religion in widely scattered areas of the world for the simple reason that it answers many of the same questions about misfortune that religious dogma sets out to answer. There are deep psychic bases for setting the cause of one's troubles outside one's self—the defense mechanism called "projection." Western history is rife with witchcraft: accusations, trials, and executions of people who were necessarily innocent of the charges made against them for the simple reason that there were no human means to perform such acts. African history displays the same phenomenon; the same subject/object confusion, the same charges, trials, and executions. Witch hunts go in waves, whether in Calvin's Geneva, seventeenth-century Massachusetts, or Zaire today.

Most telling of all, witchcraft is a faulty logical device. Its fault lies in its premise. The premise is that human disease and death can be caused by the ill will of other human beings. Often a vast lore surrounds the necessarily secret devices (because they are non-existent) by means of which malice is converted into misfortune. It may be the "evil eye"; so that even a glance can be lethal. There may be mysterious ways of introducing foreign substances beneath the surface of the skin. "Black magic," even black masses, may be said or performed in order that good can by inversion be turned to evil. In this realm of imaginative activity there can be no limit on the ways in which people think that evil can be done. Somebody, evil through and through, can always invent a new way.

Witchcraft under some conditions has some positive benefits, although such a view can be quickly overworked. It is a means in most places by which the tensions in families and within communities can be brought into the open and relieved. It is nevertheless also true that witchcraft is usually more upsetting than it is soothing to a community. Africans are not, however, constantly afraid of witches, nor do they lead their lives in terror of black magic, as some nineteenth-century writers would have us believe. To a community that believes in it, the occurrence of witchcraft is rather like an accident rate to a community that uses automobiles. One deplores both accident rate and witchcraft, but learns to live with them. One is not ever convinced that misfortune will strike one's self as long as one conducts one's own affairs sensibly, morally, and with caution.

It takes a very high degree of education and training to stamp out witchcraft from a community that has known it. It also takes good government and good welfare. The reason is that witchcraft is one of the most suitable answers to the question "Why me?" "Those nasty people" have brought about my misfortune. The world is always full of nasty people and misfortunes. The *non sequitur* is apparent only to the most sophisticated and to those who lack a dogmatic faith that evil spirits may indeed possess persons and turn them into evil instruments.

Islam and Christianity

Christianity has impinged on Africa for centuries. Ethiopia is largely Christian, and has long been so. The Coptic Church there and in

Egypt is one of the basic forms of Christianity. Christianity in northeast Africa, however, has lost ground to Islam, which has spread widely across the sudanic lands and down the eastern coast of the continent. Many African nations today regard themselves as Muslim; and most others regard themselves as Christian.

Islam and Christianity, although in one sense they have divided the continent between them, in another sense are both only marginally in control. It is the opinion of both Muslims and Christians that both religions will continue to spread in Africa during the coming decades. They are probably right. Many Muslims and some Christians believe that Islam demands less culture change of African converts than does Christianity—that it will therefore expand more rapidly. On the other hand, Christianity is offered in present-day Africa in many shades of deviation from the original missionary teaching. The immensely popular Aladura or "praying churches" of Nigeria are evidence of the vitality of new religion mixing the older African beliefs with the Christian message.

Christianity, however, has a pronounced lead in another respect: it is the Christians who created, manned, and financed most of the schools in Africa. Therefore the elites have, with few exceptions, been educated primarily in Christian schools. Thus, in much of the continent, the new national leaders profess Christianity.

One thing can be certain. With development and industrialization, African religions will dwindle in importance. It is unlikely, however, that they will disappear for many decades to come. The reason is that they are both tough-minded and have been found to work well in the social situations of small groups; they also answer that nagging question, "Why me?" Christians and Muslims fall back on a doctrine of the will of God—or else back on the explanations garnered from traditional religions.

On most other points, however, there is an amazingly close overlap between the basic ideas of Islam and Christianity, and of the African religions. Neither Islam nor Christianity is foreign in its essence to African religious ideas. And once they are stripped of some of their specific modes of expression, African religious ideas are not foreign to the Christian or the Muslim either.

It is impossible to overemphasize the influence that Christian missionaries have had in Africa. It should at the same time be pointed out and recognized that much of their influence was of a cultural nature rather than merely of a theological nature. They have indeed taught new theologies, but they have also taught literacy, new ways of expressing basic theological notions, new moral precepts, and the principles of bureaucracy. Christianity and Islam both bring the morality of the individual into religion in a way that is not done in African religion itself. In the past, that has often led Christian and Muslim observers to say that African religion had no moral dimension. The great debt that Africa owes to missionaries is that when the forces of trade, colonial government, and the missions themselves were creating cultural havoc, only the missions began to build a culture for the new era. Whatever any individual Westerner may think of the missionary edifice, every African knows that it is to missionaries that they owe the beginning of the African educational system.

Part III

AFRICAN HISTORY

10

THE PEOPLING OF AFRICA

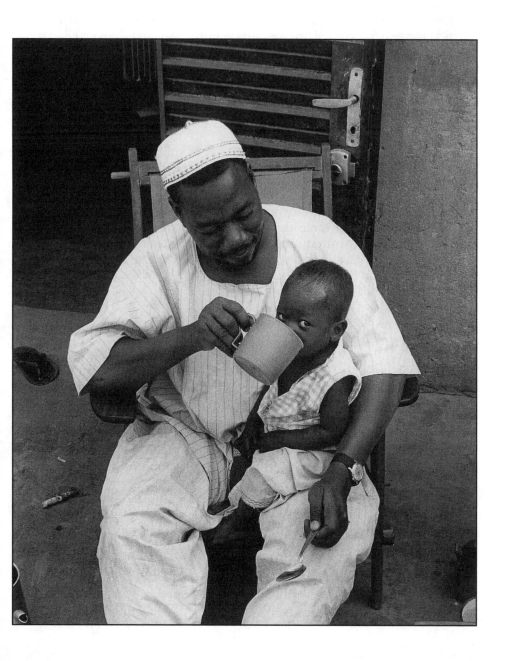

H uman beings originated in Africa. Africa, although it was the last continent to be "explored"—which means that it remained longest unknown to Western civilization—has nevertheless yielded the oldest human remains and artifacts yet discovered. However, to say that Africa is the "home" of humankind does *not* mean that the first human beings were like Africans as we know them today. Indeed, all modern human beings are fairly recent arrivals, and most of today's Africans are recent immigrants into their continent.

It was long considered (and has been corrected only recently) that humankind first evolved in Asia, spreading from there to populate the rest of the world. Most major civilizations were committed to that view either because they themselves were located in Asia or because their myths of origin made that assumption comfortable. Today, however, we have far more facts. Almost all authorities agree that the earliest human-like creatures first appeared in Africa. It would seem that culture-bearing human beings emigrated out of Africa, filled up the rest of the world, and then moved back and forth into and out of Africa until present times.

When Is A Human Being Human?

In any discussion of our ancestors before two million years ago— which is more vivid if you realize that that's at least four hundred thousand generations of parents, each bringing up the kids—a knotty question emerges: when did human beings become human? Professor Raymond Dart, the first to recognize the immense age of some of the fossil skulls being found in South Africa, said it best: these earliest anthropoid forms were "trembling on the verge of humanity."

The question of when they toppled over into humanity has traditionally been answered on the basis of what we can discern of their behavior rather than of their anatomy and physiology. For many decades, anthropologists defined humankind as tool-making animals. The assumptions were "obvious": if the animal made tools, it was human. If it did not, it wasn't. However, the unexamined corollaries of that definition cast long shadows—assumptions that could only recently be stated, let alone questioned: is every ape that can make a tool a human being? Today we know that if the tool-making definition is maintained, both chimpanzees and gorillas are "trembling on the verge of humanity"—both make tools of a crude sort. Elephants, however, do not. Elephants do indeed break branches off trees and use them to swish flies—but the branch is not considered to be a tool because it was not "manufactured." That is, it has not specifically been changed to do the jobs better. One usual way of putting the idea is to say that the branches have not been "worked," and therefore are not tools. Obviously, this kind of distinction can rapidly deteriorate into a quibble. Chimpanzees, however, *do* "work" the simple tools they create (and so do some woodpeckers in the Galapagos Islands).

The opposite derivative from the definition of human beings as tool-making animals was the false idea that since apes were not human they could not make tools. Today it seems futile to define humanity on the basis of tools it produces—and then to reject all the evidence of other creatures' using tools.

With advances in the science of genetics (and many other sciences), our definitions of humanity have had to change yet again. Humankind shares about 98 percent of its genes with the chimpanzee, a slightly smaller portion with the gorilla, and an even smaller portion with the Asian ape, the orangutan. The differences in body musculature between human beings and the apes arise from a few distinctive human features, the most telling of which is that human beings are truly bipedal—that is, they walk on two legs, leaving the hands and arms free to do something else. As a result, the human head is balanced on the spine so that it needs fewer heavy muscles to hold it up. Walking on two feet and carrying loads has led to a knot of muscle in the buttocks, which none of the great apes share with humankind.

However, there is more to this issue than physical differences in the bodies of apes and human beings. When we ask "Were they human?" we usually mean "Were they like us?" That question brings up a lot of problems. First of all, the only remains so far found (or ever likely to be found) of very early human beings are fossils of their bones. Their flesh and external appearance can only be guessed at. What was the color of their skin? What was their hair texture? We do not know. Early people may be cast in the image of those we most admire (usually ourselves) so that we can claim that our admired type is the oldest and the original; just as readily, they can be cast in the image of the people we least admire so we can say that "we" (whoever "we" may be) have come a long way from the disadmired type. The only way to deal with these riddles is to think of ourselves as part of a continuum of all living beings, and not merely to compare ourselves with our nearest relatives.

What is true, however, is that humankind and culture evolved together. Human beings did not first evolve a large brain and then discover culture (as the counterfeiter of the Piltdown man hoax would have had us believe). Neither did pre-humans first discover culture and then evolve the large brain because of the benefits it conferred. Rather, the development of culture and the evolutionary changes in the physical traits of the creature counteraffected one another.

We have far more information about our earliest ancestors than we did even a few years ago. Little, however, is yet known; with every major fossil discovery, both the scientific theories and the reconstructed history have to be changed. Moreover, as new sciences develop and are brought to bear on the problem of human origins, the sources of our information grow more and more complex. Once limited to skeletal anatomy and archaeology, we can now call on such sciences as biochemistry, the chemistry of isotopes, radiometry, the study of pollens, and evolutionary biology—and most important of all, on advances in genetics. Molecular and chemical evidence has, in short, been added to fossil evidence.

Another set of questions centers around dates—how old are these human or protohuman fossils? The skull of Neanderthal Man, which started it all, was found in Germany in 1856 and turns out not to be very old—no more than forty to sixty thousand years. The first really old skull was found in 1926, in Africa—its exact age was long disputed.

When we first began to study them, these fossils could be dated only by their association with geological phenomena. Geologists provided the "stratigraphy"—by analyzing the layers of rock or debris that were associated with the fossils. In the 1940s, a new technique was added—dating with radioactive carbon. Carbon is present in all living things. The element carbon has a radioactive isotope, called carbon-14. After death, no more carbon-14 is added to the chemical composition of the plant or animal. By measuring the degree of radioactivity still exhibited by the carbon-14 in a specimen, it is possible to determine the age of the specimen. However, carbon-14 works only on specimens younger than 50,000 years, by which time the radioactivity of the carbon-14 has totally decayed.

Later, it was discovered that a radioactive isotope of potassium, potassium-40, could provide dates over much longer periods of time. Potassium forms about two and a half percent of the earth's crust, but because it reacts very fast with water or air, it is found only in compounds. Potassium-40 in those compounds is radioactive; it decays by emitting the gas argon into the air. The processes of its decay can help archaeologists date the approximate time of a particular volcanic formation. Fossils found in association with such formations can then be dated. Volcanic deposits in East Africa show a marked "chemical fingerprint" that differentiates them from other deposits laid down at other times or in other places.

Paleomagnetic evidence also helps in dating. The earth's magnetic field shifts through time. The magnetic fields that were present at the time a layer of rock was deposited leaves a permanent magnetic record. The differences between present and past magnetism can show the passage of time.

Apes and Hominids in Ancient Africa

Although ape-like creatures are found earlier, in the Miocene Period, the relevant geological ages for studying human origins are the Pliocene, between about 5 and 1.9 million years ago, and the Pleistocene, now considered to begin about 1.9 million years ago. The Hominidae form a family of living and fossil forms that somewhat resemble modern human beings but also resemble monkeys or apes. The oldest hominidae are found in Africa.

Skeletal material discovered in both Tanzania and Ethiopia attest to the presence of a relatively small-brained hominid who walked on two feet and lived between about four million and three million years ago. The Ethiopian version of this species has been called *Australopithecus afarensis* (southern ape from Afar). Some authorities believe that A. *afarensis* is actually a sub-type of a more widely scattered species, *Australopithecus africanus*, known at somewhat later dates. The significant fact is that at least one human-like species had come into existence at this distant time.

Other hominids soon evolved—if we accept "soon" as a measure of time on the geological scale. Between about three million and two million years ago, two new species of australopithecines appeared, A. *boisei* and A. *robustus*, along with a larger-brained species called *Homo habilis*. The earliest securely dated, manufactured stone tools are associated with *Homo habilis*. It is unfortunate that this period of time is still one of the least known in East African prehistory.

The picture clears somewhat about a million and a half years ago. A new hominid appeared on the scene—*Homo erectus*. This new species had a considerably larger brain than its predecessors. Some authorities consider it to have been the first "real" human, although not yet the same as our present species, *Homo sapiens*. *Homo erectus* not merely joined the existing hominid types; it ultimately replaced them, including its presumed immediate progenitor, *Homo habilis*. The australopithecines also disappeared, though *A. boisei* lasted until about one million years ago.

Well before this time, the hominids had begun to move out of Africa. Remains of *Homo erectus*, known as "Peking Man" and "Java Man," dated about 700,000 years ago, have been discovered in China and Indonesia. At roughly the same time, *Homo erectus* seems to have moved into Europe as well, where characteristic tools dated about 800,000 years ago have been discovered in central France. Similar discoveries have been made in southern Italy. The earliest skeletal remains in central Europe are those of Heidelberg man, dated about 500,000 years ago.

This combination of evidence leads to a secure conclusion that *Homo erectus* began its migration from Africa about a million years ago—and some recent evidence suggests that the migrations might have taken place even earlier. Stone tools found on the shore of the Sea of Galilee are datable to about 1.3 million years ago. The spread out of Africa may have been even earlier than that, because it is unlikely that archaeologists will find the *very* earliest evidence. Other finds of tools in Pakistan can be dated, a little less securely, to about two million years ago. The mere fact of an earlier date, two million instead of one million years, is hardly important at this distance in time. What counts, however, is the evidence that *Homo erectus* was more able, inventive, and adaptable to different environments than many had previously thought.

Finally, about 300,000 years ago, early varieties of *Homo sapiens* appeared, also in Africa. This species in its turn soon replaced *Homo erectus*, not only in Africa but everywhere in the world.

This general scheme was given quite a shake-up in 1987 when a scientific paper offered data which some specialists claimed showed that all living human beings were descended from one woman, in Africa, who lived about 200,000 years ago (an earlier 1983 paper which provided that data, but not the straightforward claim, had gone unnoticed by all by specialists). This data derives from a particular fact about human reproduction: although when the egg is fertilized by sperm, half the genetic material comes from the mother and half from the father, there is a molecule of "mitochondrial" DNA that comes only from the mother. It contains only 37 genes (compared to the perhaps 100,000 genes in the nucleus), and is therefore comparatively easy to work with. This "mother of us all" has been called "mitochondrial Eve."

Sides on this issue have been continuously forming and re-forming.[1] It is still too early to say what the ultimate result will be. This dispute within the scientific community, however, does give a vivid example of how complex the issues involved with human origins have become.

Stone Age Cultures in Africa

Archaeologists are in the middle of a process of decoupling the bio-physical features of ancient human beings from their cultural creations. The sailing isn't always smooth, because the behavior of the animal has to be inferred from tools and other artifacts, together with a few animal bones and (in comparatively recent times) pollen associated with living sites or burial sites. Chipped stone began to appear about two million years ago, at the beginning of the Paleolithic Period (that is Greek for Old Stone Age). This chipped stone culture is called the Acheulian, and it was astonishingly long-lived.

The earliest Acheulian tools occur while *Homo habilis* and *A. bosei* were still around, but they are more clearly associated with *Homo erectus*. Indeed, the time-span for Acheulian culture is so long that it extends from the time of *Homo habilis* to the earliest period of *Homo sapiens*. In southern Africa, the sub-species called *H. sapiens rhodesiensis* was not only present in the late part of the Acheulian period, but continued to be the dominant human type in the Middle Stone Age that followed.

Cultural complications appeared about a quarter of a million years ago. Two terms are important here: Mousterian culture, which was associated primarily with Neanderthal people, and Lavalloisian (these names, like Acheulian, come from the villages in France where the assemblages were first discovered by archaeologists).

Then, about eight thousand years ago, immense new variation suddenly appeared. The big argument among archaeologists is whether or not these changes indicate development of a mentally modern humanity. Such arguments stem from the fact that archaeologists can work with only half of culture. They can study the artifacts created by ancient people, but they cannot discover from the artifacts themselves what meanings those ancient peoples associated with the artifacts. They therefore argue about whether or not there was a change in the capacity of the human brain and

[1] A good, and readable, description of the processes and of the factions that have formed, and their changing experiments and theories, is to be found in Lewin, Roger, *The Origin of Modern Humans*, Scientific American Library, 1993.

further argue about possible meanings and uses of the artifacts they discover. It is from just such informed argument that our knowledge proceeds.

Acheulian culture disappeared from North Africa about the time that the desert began to encroach as a result of the climatic change, and in Cyrenaica and Morocco there are new cultures that look like general Mediterranean cultures. They are known as Lavallois-Mousterian, and in places where the physical type is known, it is Neanderthal. We do not know whether the Neanderthal people were intrusive into Africa or originated in Africa, but it seems more likely that both they and the Mousterian-type culture originated elsewhere and moved into Africa.

From this time on, the cultural remains of the northern and southern edges of the Sahara are different. Lavalloisian-Mousterian is approximately contemporary with what is called Sangoan culture in the savannas south of the Sahara. Most authorities think that Neanderthals were dominant north of the Sahara, while *Homo sapiens rhodesiensis* was the more important type in the south.

People of a fully modern time, *Homo sapiens sapiens*, began to appear in southern Africa about 100,000 years ago, and human skeletons begin to be really numerous beginning about 20,000 years ago. From that time onward, we can begin thinking of people in Africa as the distant ancestors of present-day populations.

At the end of the Pleistocene, about 8000 B.C., the climate (which had been cool) began to change. Two immigrations took place, one of the tall, modern-type species called Cro-Magnon, and the other of a shorter type species—probably like today's Mediterranean peoples. Each brought a specific type of culture into northern Africa, extending up the Nile. The result was such cultural items as tanged projectile points appearing in the Congo Basin in association with Middle Stone Age cultures, and new forms of tools appearing in South Africa and Rhodesia. As recently as about 2500 B.C. the Sahara was still moist enough that both Mediterranean and Negroid populations were moving about in it. In that period, fishing and the use of water resources became increasingly more important. The physical type known as Khoisan, and represented by today's San in southern Africa, made its appearance toward the end of the Pleistocene. The other modern types have their earliest fossils associated with the Middle and Late Stone Age.

The Late Stone Age was a period of great adaptive specialization. A large number of different cultures can, by this time, be found throughout the continent. Savanna cultures are quite different from those of the forest, and those of the Rift Valley are different from either of the other two.

Neolithic or New Stone Age culture, marked by complexity and reduced size of the stone weapons, spread throughout the Sahara by 3000 B.C. but did not proceed south of the Sahara; there it never did replace Middle Stone Age food gathering as a way of life. The security of the hunting-and-gathering way of life was not threatened farther south as it was in the north, with desiccation and other changes. Hence there was no pressure demanding the changes toward agriculture and stockkeeping.

After 2500 B.C., when the Sahara was getting drier and drier, many of the Neolithic populations were forced south, and new food crops had to be developed—rice in Guinea, sorghums in the sudan areas, and the indigenous grains called teff and eleusine in parts of Ethiopia. It may have been at this time that the domestication of indigenous African yams occurred.

Not very many years ago, the "races of Africa" were the subject of most books about the continent. We knew nothing else to talk about. As we have learned more, the "races of Africa" has receded as a topic for discussion. Race, as we know it, is a set of processes in which geographically isolated "types" develop, only to change into other types as they re-meet, re-breed, and as time goes on. Races are, in terms of geological time, very short-lived, and the races we know today are all quite recent developments.

11

FARMS AND IRON

There have been many occasions in the history of human development when cultural steps were taken from which there was no return. These steps were intrinsically simple, yet they so improved the processes of living that to go without them thereafter would have been literally unthinkable. Tool manufacture was such a step. Once the idea of a tool is present, people will make tools—particular techniques may be lost; whole cultures may wither; but tools will be made—and the general direction of development will be toward efficiency. The discovery of uses for fire was another such irreversible revolution. The comforts it provides—both for heating and for cooking—are so apparent that people put vast ingenuity into acquiring and maintaining fire. To revert to fireless living would be quite unthinkable.

Such shatteringly simple discoveries make cultural evolution more than a mere analogy to biological evolution (which it nevertheless remains). We are used to thinking of evolution as complication—going from the simple to the complex. In one sense, particularly if we examine the technological development of humankind, that proposition is correct. In another sense, complication and simplification can take place simultaneously. It is easier to live with fire than without it. The increasing complexity of cultural evolution is material and usually superficial; underneath the complexity lies a growing simplicity.

Although the use of stone tools and fire are in the distant background of African history (and all human history), two other simplifying discoveries bring us to the borderland where history and pre-history meet. The discovery of agriculture and animal husbandry made vast new amounts of energy available. The discovery of metallurgy made the use of that new energy more efficient.

The Agricultural Revolution

As far as present-day archaeologists are aware, fixed agriculture and urban living developed together in the Middle East about 10,000 B.C. In most parts of the world, societies which depend on hunting and gathering for their subsistence were necessarily limited to a

140

few hundred people. Because these groups traveled over a wide enough area to find sufficient sustenance, fixed villages or other dwellings were impractical. One exception was fishing communities which were sometimes quite large and fairly permanent over long periods of time.

The shift from hunting to agriculture was revolutionary in the long range of human history, but it may not have taken place as rapidly as the word "revolution" implies. People who lived by gathering wild crops did not settle down all at once to grow crops. Changing from gathering food to producing food was probably a very gradual development. Cultivation may have been practiced sporadically or haphazardly when soil and water conditions happened to be right, using crops that required little care. Experimental plant cultivation might have supplemented traditional hunting and gathering. Extensive cultivation requires not only knowledge about crops and how to grow them but also customs that support an agricultural rather than nomadic lifestyle. Peoples with a long history of traveling to new sources of game, grain, or water probably adapted to sedentary existence only when outside forces, such as environmental changes, forced them to consider alternatives. Agriculture both requires and allows larger populations.

Early steps toward agriculture had a profound influence on the movement of people in early Africa. About 15,000 years ago, people who lived in what is now the southeastern Sudan Republic discovered new, more intensive ways to collect wild grains. They gradually moved north into the Middle East and west across North Africa. It is fair to assume that the superior technology of the new gathering techniques made possible population growth and migration into more sparsely-settled territory. For lack of good evidence, it seems safe to assume that the existing sparse population was absorbed into that of the newcomers in most cases. Geneticists may soon provide better answers than we have today.

The evidence for this migration is both archaeological and linguistic. The linguistic part of the hypotheses goes back to "the rule of least moves." If a large number of similar languages, about equally distant from one another linguistically, exist in a fairly confined region (as many different varieties of Afro-Asiatic languages do in the Horn of Africa) and one language group is found to spread outward from a corner of the cluster, it is easier to conclude that the one language within the cluster originated with the others in the cluster, rather than to assume that the whole group of clustered languages arrived from somewhere else. (Similar reasoning is used in biology to study the origin and diffusion of plant or animal species.) The language spoken by the migrating grain gatherers was an ancestor of the large family of Afro-Asiatic languages which includes Hebrew, Arabic, and Ancient Egyptian as well as scores of African languages.

Somewhat later, by about 5000 B.C., agricultural technology began to remake the society of the Nile valley in Egypt, and that innovation clearly came from the Middle East. The crops and animals—wheat and barley, sheep and goats—were the same in the two places. Whereas an African discovery of how to gather grain efficiently had earlier spread into the Middle East, Middle Eastern discoveries now spread into Africa.

As we learn more about the cultures and civilizations of Africa, we realize that Egypt lay culturally as well as geographically between Africa and Asia. Egyptian religion can be best understood by reference to African religion; many other aspects of Egyptian history and polity are illuminated by African ethnography. It was stylish in the past to assume that all social and cultural forms were invented in Egypt and spread to other parts of Africa. Today we know that was an oversimplification. Egypt was basically an African culture, with intrusions of Asian culture.

In order to see the picture most clearly, it is necessary to go back several millennia. Some twelve thousand years ago the Sahara was habitable, but dry—not as dry as today, but drier than a wet phase that came later. People hunted across the territory that was later to become Egypt.

The Sahara subsequently went through a wet phase, when people encroached upon it from both north and south. During the wet phase of the Sahara, the hunting-and-gathering subsistence economies seemed to include considerable fishing, which, as we have seen, can support comparatively large populations. Increased numbers of inhabitants allowed considerable gene flow through large areas and diverse populations. Then, some six or seven thousand years ago, the desiccation of the Sahara began again, which was eventually to bring it to the state that we know today. With progressive drought, people withdrew from the desert in all directions.

It seems likely that the peoples who left the Sahara and went north were swallowed up into the greater populations of the Mediterranean. Those who went south were the progenitors of a people with physical traits that today are classified as negroid. Both genes and culture spread north and south of the Sahara.

The story can be summed up this way: As people withdrew from the Sahara to the south, they brought with them the genes of the Sahara population and consolidated them into a racial "type." They also carried with them the cultural background that underlies both Europe and Africa and is the basis of what has been called the "Old World Culture Area."

The people who moved south presumably continued as fishermen. The agricultural revolution reached them in two waves, both depending on the finding of satisfactory crops for the areas in which they lived. Near Eastern grain crops do not thrive in the sudanic areas of Africa, and they will not grow at all in the forested regions. The first phase of the agricultural revolution in Africa south of the Sahara came with the domestication and spread of millets and sorghums and a species of rice. *Oryza glaberrima*, or African rice, was first domesticated in the western sudan and developed there independently of Asian rice (*O. sativa*). The second phase came with the introduction of root crops and bananas that could thrive in the forest. Some of the crops that are basic to African agriculture today were either developed from indigenous roots or came from Southeast Asia, long after agriculture had been established in the sudan. Others came still later—indeed since the fifteenth century A.D.—from the Americas, including maize, manioc, and peanuts. The result was to give African farmers the ability to support increasingly dense populations over a very long period of time. In this sense the agricultural "revolution" was not a rapid process. The first advances south of the Sahara were almost certainly made before 3000 B.C., but the latest, depending on the inland diffusion of American crops, introduced here and there on the coast during the sixteenth century, reached more isolated areas only in the eighteenth or even the nineteenth century.

Many unanswered questions remain, and pre-historians of Africa are undecided how the agricultural revolution actually reached the population of Africa south of the Sahara. Most agree, however, that one early center was in the western sudan, while another was the Ethiopian highlands. Ethiopia and the Horn of Africa have always been a little separate from the rest of sub-Saharan Africa. They have close cultural and botanical ties to the neighboring highlands of southern Arabia. Some crops that originated in Ethiopia diffused very slowly to other parts of Africa. Coffee—the name comes from the Ethiopian province of Kaffa—spread to many parts of Asia before it reached some parts of Africa that now depend on it as an export crop. Other African crops also diffused outward to the rest of the world. Sesame, which originated in the western sudan, had reached the Middle East before 2000 B.C.

The question of crop diffusion is further complicated by a process anthropologists call "stimulus diffusion." That is, the idea of planting crops may have entered sub-Saharan Africa from the outside, while the development of crops appropriate to a particular region had to wait for the domestication of species that could thrive there. The picture that begins to emerge is therefore one of many crosscurrents, not a simple introduction of agriculture as a ready-made system of food production.

Yet, at a slightly more abstract level, a general picture can be drawn. We know that the idea of metalworking went from Southwest Asia into Africa, both north and south of the Sahara. The idea of agriculture may well have followed a similar course, even though the use of specific crops followed a more complex pattern. The millets, for example, appear to have been domesticated in the western sudan, and afterward to have diffused eastward to the Nile Valley and on into Asia, while the idea of agriculture may well have moved in the opposite direction. Further botanical and archaeological research will undoubtedly provide a more complete answer.

What is obvious is that fishing and hunting communities of prehistoric sub-Saharan Africa could grow very rapidly when they acquired agriculture. They could grow still more rapidly as they found or imported crops better suited to their environment, and that presumably did occur. People of predominantly Negro type first filled the savannas of the sudanic belt just south of the Sahara. Some undoubtedly moved into the forests as fishermen and hunters, even before the coming of agriculture. As the range of crops increased and techniques improved, they moved in still greater numbers into and across the forest until they ultimately came to occupy most of Africa.

The Coming of the Iron Age

The spread of peoples of sudanic origin into and beyond the forest is not only associated with early agriculture; archaeological evidence indicates that iron smelting and the manufacture of tools moved south with much the same timing as agriculture itself. However, the two did not necessarily move together, and the beginning of the Iron Age was, in most places, a slow process, passing through several stages of improving techniques.

The use of iron was probably discovered in several parts of the world, since meteors contain usable iron that can be fashioned into tools or decorations. Iron smelting from terrestrial iron ore, on the other hand, requires special furnaces. Iron smelting may have been invented only once, in Anatolia where a few iron objects have turned up that seem to date from about 2000 B.C. By that time, the Middle

East was already about a thousand years into the Bronze Age. Bronze was satisfactory for many purposes, and at first iron remained rare and expensive. It was only about the eleventh century B.C. that iron became common enough to replace bronze tools in ordinary use. This improvement in techniques for manufacturing iron marks the real beginning of the Iron Age.

The secret to producing relatively malleable, low-carbon wrought iron—or steel which is both malleable and will hold an edge—was to heat charcoal and iron ore together in the confined space of a furnace, but at temperature well below the melting point of iron. Combustion with oxygen gave off carbon monoxide which then picked up a second molecule from the ferrous oxide of the iron ore to leave comparatively impure but perfectly usable iron, as the carbon monoxide became carbon dioxide. The process was time-consuming and produced only a little iron with each smelt, but the product was much superior to the brittle high-carbon pig iron the Chinese and Europeans finally learned to produce in large quantities with blast furnaces—but that development did not take place until well into the Christian era.

Iron technology diffused as rapidly into sub-Saharan Africa as it did into Europe. It reached Italy about 750 B.C. and central Europe about 650 B.C. By 800 B.C. it had already reached southern Arabia and Carthage in North Africa. From there it diffused into sub-Saharan Africa—across the Red Sea to Ethiopia, across the Sahara to West Africa, and perhaps by other routes as well. By 600 to 700 B.C. it had already reached present-day Nigeria and Rwanda and Burundi in central Africa. Its spread from these centers into other parts of Africa was so complex it is hard to trace with precision. Archaeologists find, however, that iron working did not diffuse alone. Its remains are found with an assortment of tools and other evidence. They often divide evidence into two groups, an Early Iron Age Industrial Complex and a Later Iron Age, which was considerably more sophisticated technologically.

As in other parts of the world, metallurgy improved by borrowing inventions made elsewhere and by local inventions that spread abroad—just as agriculture changed and improved with new techniques and new crops. But the coming of farms and iron to Africa followed a different pattern from that of the Mediterranean world, where farming was practiced for several millennia before the Bronze Age, and bronze was known for centuries before iron. For all practical purposes, Africa skipped the Bronze Age altogether, and the time lag between the first farming and the first iron work was much shorter everywhere south of the Sahara. To the south of the equatorial forest, they may have come nearly at the same time.

The Expansion of Bantu-Speaking Peoples

Who carried iron and agriculture from the fringes of the Sahara to most of Africa? It now seems clear that some of the carriers were Negro peoples who came originally from northeastern Nigeria. They spoke a language related to the present-day Bantu languages in much the same way Latin is related to present-day Romance languages like French or Italian. Bantu languages are now spoken throughout Africa south of a line that can be drawn from the base of the West African bulge across to Kenya. They are so closely related, they must have been a single language only a very few thousand years ago. Furthermore, the Bantu language family belongs to a larger group of language families, all of them found today in northern or eastern Nigeria This suggests that people who spoke the original Bantu language must have left northeastern Nigeria and spread quite rapidly throughout most of central and southern Africa.

Almost all linguists and historians accept this hypothesis as the best explanation for the spread of Bantu languages. But there agreement ends. Some authorities go further, linking the languages, the people who spoke them, ironworking, and agriculture to a single movement. Following this hypothesis, the original speakers of proto-Bantu expanded into central and southern Africa because they had iron weapons to conquer the aboriginal hunters and fishermen they found there and because they had agriculture to support a growing population on the new land.

Unfortunately, present evidence will not support such a simple hypothesis. A language, or farming, or iron metallurgy are all culture traits. They can be learned and passed from one people to another, and each can be passed on independently of the others. We know that Bantu languages were passed to new people; the Pygmies of the Congo forest and the Tutsi of Rwanda and Burundi are a different physical type from the people of the Bantu homeland, yet today they speak Bantu languages. This kind of transmission to others was even more likely to happen with useful techniques like ironworking and agriculture. What we actually know, then, is that Negroid people moved into Africa south of the forest zone over a period of one to two millennia. At nearly the same time, a new language, metallurgy, and agriculture moved into the same region.

We can also assume from our meager evidence (and what we know of human history elsewhere) that these movements must have been related in a very complex combination of currents and countercurrents. We know, for example, that some techniques for working iron diffused inland from the East African coast, but the original knowledge of how to work iron may well have come by some other route. We also know that certain styles or inventions could spread widely from their place of origin. Some of these can be traced; peculiar forms of flanged iron bells (and the techniques for making them) diffused from the Niger Valley in Nigeria to central Africa on two separate occasions, long after the dispersal of the Bantu-speaking peoples and their languages.

Some of the crops that were important in Bantu-speaking areas of Africa were probably domesticated on the forest fringes in West Africa. Others, with somewhat greater certainty originated in Southeast Asia, and were probably brought across the Indian Ocean in the early centuries of Indian Ocean maritime trade—just as people from Indonesia came to settle on the island of Madagascar, where their descendants still speak a language related to Indonesian. However, there is no evidence that people from Southeast Asia actually settled on the African mainland. It is possible that the Asian crops diffused across Africa north of the forest and were then picked up by the Bantu-speaking peoples and carried southward. It is equally possible that the Bantu-speakers simply began using these crops in their new homes, having found them in use by others when they arrived.

Domestication of Animals

Whatever the diffusion pattern of the Southeast Asian crops, the use of cattle came into sub-Saharan Africa in still another way. Cattle and cattle keeping (but not the custom of milking them) apparently came from the Middle East at a very early time. In West Africa, they appear along with the early development of agriculture. Because of tsetse fly in the equatorial forest, they could hardly have been brought directly from West Africa to the southern savanna. They apparently diffused southward down the ridge of highlands in east central Africa and from there into the southern savanna. The names for cattle in various eastern and central African languages suggest that they were already in use before the introduction of Bantu languages, but the practice of milking came after the Bantu languages were already spoken to the south and west of present-day Tanzania.

Cattle were a very important supplement for the diet of a farming population, but they could be even more important in regions too arid for agriculture. Cattle can live where crops cannot grow, as long as they have a source of drinking water and plenty of land. After the best land was already occupied, specialized communities that wandered with their cattle in search of grazing land began to develop on the fringes of the agricultural world. Little is known of their earliest history in Africa, but they were present long before the Christian era in steppe and desert country that stretched from the Horn of Africa, around the Ethiopian highlands, and westward to the Atlantic.

Then, about the time of Christ, camels were introduced from Asia. They spread very rapidly along the southern fringes of the Sahara, introducing still another fundamental change in the pattern of African history. From the sub-Saharan fringe of the desert, they diffused northward to North Africa, where they soon became the dominant form of transportation. Camels do not do well in humid climates, but, in arid and semi-arid climates, they are the most efficient form of animal transportation humans have discovered. They can carry far more than mules or pack oxen, more rapidly, and over longer distances without water. The labor cost for their human attendants is lower than it is for any other pack animals. Camels also fit into an ecological niche that was barely occupied, being able to find food in regions with rainfall as low as five inches a year. The Romans had developed a complex system of paved roads in North Africa, as elsewhere in their empire. With the introduction of the camel, the high capital cost of road construction was no longer necessary. The pack animals could follow unpaved tracks just as well.

After about A.D. 500, when camels became familiar in North Africa, their use intersected with another import from southwest Asia. The date palm had been domesticated in Mesopotamia several millennia earlier, and it had gradually spread along the desert fringes toward the west. Dates need a peculiar environment, with little rainfall, but with irrigation water available to their roots. In proper conditions, they could produce more food per acre than almost any other crop, but dates are too rich in sugar to be a staple food crop for human populations. Their value was greatest when they could be traded to others in return for grains, meat, and milk products. For camels, the dry pasture near date-growing oases was ideal. This means that transport was available to carry away the dates in exchange for other products.

From this beginning, the combination of oasis and desert suited to dates and camels made possible the creation of long-distance trade networks that could reach southward across the Sahara. After about A.D. 800, the Sahara was no longer a barrier to sub-Saharran contact with the outer world; camels provided cheap transport between the two shores, just as the seaways provided cheaper transport than inland caravans in most other societies.

Because they could live longer away from sources of drinking water than cattle could, camels increased the range of pastoral nomadism and increased the numbers of nomads that could support themselves beyond the frontiers of agriculture. In the process, they shifted the balance in an ancient conflict between people who lived a settled village life and those who were locked into a pattern of continuous or periodic movement in search of fresh grazing land.

It should be clear by now that "traditional" Africa was far from static. In the longer run of history, no society can fail to change over time, but some kinds of societies change more rapidly than others. We know of two decisive breaks in the rate of change in human history. One was the coming of agriculture with its increased population density. Human contacts became more frequent and new technologies could diffuse more rapidly from one part of the world to another. The second acceleration in the rate of historical change came with the industrial age, which began for Western civilization at the end of the eighteenth and the beginning of the nineteenth century. Africa is only now beginning to enter that phase.

12

AFRICA IN WORLD HISTORY

The position of sub-Saharan Africa compared to other world civilizations is one of the most sensitive historical problems of the present day. The fact that Africans were brought to the New World as slaves and the fact that Europeans conquered nearly all of Africa and dominated it for half a century were at one time irrationally interpreted to imply some degree of African inferiority. Such attitudes were spelled out in elaborate theoretical works, and they permeated the whole fabric of historical and anthropological "knowledge." As modern Africa emerged from the colonial era and African-Americans demanded an equal share in their own society, historians of all races and nationalities began to readjust their view of Africa and its place in world history.

The racism and cultural arrogance of the old view are now discredited in respectable intellectual circles. However, some of the interpretations that grew out of them are still in the textbooks. Given the racism that still exists in the culture of Europe and America, these old, distorted views of Africa persist. Perhaps as a result of such persistent misrepresentation, African and African-American historians have been tempted to overreact with exaggerated claims as to the greatness of the civilizations of the African past. The problem is to assess the true nature and meaning of events in African development. But such assessment is doubly difficult because it carries strong political and emotional implications that stretch out in every direction.

Culture and Value Judgments

There is a basic problem inherent in making rational judgments about the comparative quality of different human cultures. Scholars once talked in terms of "high" cultures and "low" cultures, but these judgments were based on Western values. Many aspects of culture cannot be judged rationally outside the context of a particular culture or style. Western music critics may agree in believing that one eighteenth-century string quartet sounds better than another one does, but the judgment is made within the framework of a particular style and by people who share present-day musical culture. (Even within this framework, the only "proof" of the superiority of one composition over the other is the consensus of trained judges.) Once the framework of common style and common culture is left behind, judgment is even more difficult. A particular piece of African music may sound "better" or "worse" than a particular Western composition to one individual, but there is no way of convincing someone else of that "fact" by rational argument. Even though a symphony orchestra has more participants playing a more complex score on technologically advanced instruments than an African ensemble has, the sound produced by each will be preferred by some but not by others. Similar considerations apply to the whole range of possible aesthetic judgments.

In other matters, such as ethics and morality, many cultures share certain ideas about right and wrong. Needless killing of human beings is generally considered to be wrong, but the key word is "needless." A few African societies used to practice human sacrifice, because they believed it was necessary to the well-being of society as a whole. In the West, criminals are executed for the same reason. Even if the ethical standard is universal, the interpretation is often culture-bound.

A few aspects of culture, however, may be subject to rational judgment. Technology is one of these. A technique is a means of doing something, and its value can be measured by its effectiveness in serving the desired end. An iron ax is demonstrably better than a stone ax—though some cultures may still prefer stone axes for ethical or aesthetic reasons. A phonetic alphabet is demonstrably more efficient than a system of ideographs, but aesthetic considerations make Chinese ideographs endure. In technology, then—and perhaps in that field alone—it is possible to make estimates of the degree of advancement of particular cultures at particular times, keeping in mind that such judgments apply *only* to technology and *not* to the whole culture.

Comparative Technological Progress

Taking only technology into account, it is clear that Africa of the nineteenth century—the period of its major confrontation with the West—was the less advanced of the two societies. In the longer run of history, however, it is equally clear that northwestern Europe has not always been ahead. In the first millennium before Christ, the western sudan and northwestern Europe were nearly on a par. Both had acquired iron and agriculture from the Middle East, but neither had yet moved on to evolve an urban civilization. The differences that stood out in the nineteenth and twentieth centuries were therefore the product of historical change over the past twenty-five hundred years or so. During those centuries, Europe developed the most efficient technology in the world, while Africa changed more slowly. It was a dual process requiring a dual explanation—partly from African history and partly from European. In fact, the explanation has to be sought in a broader view of world history, since the rise of barbarian Europe to world dominance was a process that involved the whole of the Afro-Eurasian land mass.

From this perspective, it is clear that neither Europeans nor Africans invented civilization. The combination of metallurgy, writing, agriculture, and cities first developed in only a few places, thousands of miles apart—lower Egypt and the eastern Mediterranean, Mesopotamia, the Indus Valley, and the north Chinese river valleys. In each case the technological base was similar, but early development led them down divergent paths. By about 1000 B.C., all of these small foci of technological progress were in indirect communication with one another; an invention or discovery in any one of them could be borrowed sooner or later by the others. As communication improved, the range of mutual borrowing and the rate of technological progress increased.

In the millennium before our era, each of these foci of civilization began to expand. The east Mediterranean center spread westward, taking in the whole of the Mediterranean basin and parts of Europe north of the Alps. By the time of Christ, the Roman Empire had organized the culture area politically. Indian Ocean trade and land routes across central Asia to China gave a new intensity to contacts between the Mediterranean basin and the other centers. These culture areas had also expanded, each in its own neighborhood. By this period, the Afro-Eurasian land mass was divided into two distinct technological zones. One was the region of intercommunication and relatively developed technology. The second was more isolated, a zone of fringe communication with the major centers, where development was often held up by difficult environments.

Both sub-Saharan Africa and northwestern Europe were part of this underdeveloped world of the pre-Christian era, but the Alps were only a small barrier compared to the Sahara. As Roman civilization spread through Roman conquest, part of northwestern Europe joined the intercommunicating zone, at least for a few centuries. The fall of the western Roman Empire in the fifth century ended northwestern Europe's full membership in the "civilized world"; but Byzantium and the Islamic world south of the Mediterranean remained in the core zone, and northwest Europe was close enough to be able to pull itself back over the horizon of literacy, city life, and direct communication with the outside world.

Between the tenth and the thirteenth centuries, Europe rebuilt its civilization through the mediation of Byzantium and Islamic civilization and reentered the intercommunicating zone. Overland trade linked the Baltic and North seas to the Mediterranean, and seaborne traders ventured regularly into the Atlantic.

The sudan, on the other hand, remained cut off behind the barrier of the Sahara. People and ideas and techniques made their way across the Sahara, but only with difficulty. If any regular Roman trade with sub-Saharan lands had existed, it left no record, though iron work and agriculture were already spreading onward toward the southern tip of the continent. A series of states came into existence along the frontier between savanna and desert. Some of these predated the Iron Age itself. The kingdom of Kush had been in existence since the end of the second millennium B.C. Others came much later. In about the first century A.D., settlers from Arabia founded the kingdom of Aksum in the Ethiopian highlands, which later conquered part of southern Arabia as well. In about A.D. 350, Aksum invaded the Nilotic sudan to the west and destroyed the city of Meroe. With that, the kingdom of Kush disappeared from history, but sedentary civilization continued on the upper Nile. Kush was succeeded by a group of Nubian states, contemporaries of the Roman Empire. Before the year A.D. 600, both the Nubian states and Aksum responded to their contacts with Rome. Missionaries from Roman Egypt converted both to the Monophysite variety of Christianity.

Meanwhile, and farther west, other new states emerged in response to the new camel traffic. Takrur or Fuuta Tooro came into existence along the middle valley of the Senegal River. Between the Senegal and the Niger bend, the Soninke state of Ghana was also founded before A.D. 600. Still another center of state formation emerged in the Lake Chad basin in the central sudan, and we can assume that still other states probably existed, even though we lack direct evidence.

Unlike Aksum and Kush, where contact with the north was easier by way of the Nile or the Red Sea, state formation in the central and western sudan owed comparatively little to its fragile communication with the Roman world. In the western sudan, political organization had long taken the form of more or less self-sufficient villages, politically independent of one another. In many parts of West Africa, this pattern lasted until the end of the nineteenth century. In the absence of dangerous enemies or extensive trade, these small units were probably considered preferable to the economic drain of tribute payments to a distant capital. The growth of trade and the need to protect the trade routes and organize markets made a larger political unit necessary. The earliest states all appeared on the desert-savanna frontier, where differences in ecology favored the exchange of goods—salt from the desert and animals from the steppe for millet and other grains from the savanna. It is possible, in fact, that local trade of this kind had led to state formation long before extensive trade across the Sahara made the existence of those states known to the Mediterranean world.

Nomads and Sedentaries

Still another reason why people living on the savanna side of the desert-savanna fringe needed a large political unit was a danger implicit in their location. In the steppe to the north, too dry for farming, were the nomadic pastoralists—Berber, Tuareg, and others. The very fact that they had to move in search of pasture gave them a military advantage; they could concentrate their forces for raids against their richer sedentary neighbors. If the sedentary peoples failed to organize large populations and large territories for mutual defense, they might become tribute-paying dependents of the nomads. Well organized sedentary states could not only protect their desert frontier from nomadic raids; they could also reach out and control the desert trade routes themselves. Less well organized peoples living on the fringes and in the Sahara oases became their tributaries.

This ancient opposition between nomadic and sedentary peoples was not peculiar to the Sahara and its fringes. It was a regular and constant part of human experience in similar environments over very long periods of time—from the emergence of pastoral nomads to the Industrial Revolution. The recurrence of similar patterns of events is sometimes called a "style of history." A "style" of this kind falls short of the necessary requirements of a scientific "law," but it is a useful concept—the degree of observed regularity is great enough to permit generalization. Generalization about "styles" of history is a convenient analytical device for understanding how human societies change through time.

This particular style of nomadic-sedentary relations was common to much of the Afro-Eurasian land mass. The Sahara is simply the western end of a wide belt of arid and semi-arid lands stretching eastward from the Atlantic coast in Mauritania, across Africa, across the Red Sea to Arabia, on beyond the Persian Gulf into central Asia, finally across the Gobi Desert and along the northwest frontier of China to reach the Pacific at the Sea of Okhotsk. From the beginning of recorded history, a pattern of nomadic raids into sedentary territory is apparent from the Great Wall frontier of China to the steppe frontier of eastern Europe, from the northeast frontier of India to the northern and southern frontiers of the Sahara.

Historical recognition of the nomadic-sedentary conflict is almost as ancient as the conflict itself. In the book of Genesis, it was the mythic origin of violence and murder within the human family. "Abel was a keeper of sheep, and Cain a tiller of the ground." The lord preferred Abel's offering to that of Cain, and his ecological preference led to murder. Much later, in fourteenth-century Tunisia, Ibn Khaldun, one of the founders of analytical history, used the nomadic-sedentary conflict as the theme of his greatest work, the *Muqaddimah*, which analyzed the rise and fall of Islamic dynasties. Still more recently, Owen Lattimore's investigations of ecological tensions along the northwest frontier of China have added still more to our knowledge of historical patterns along the frontier between the desert and the sown.

In Lattimore's terms, the struggle between nomads and sedentary farmers was a struggle for land that was marginal to either form of occupation. Nomads were not content with land that could be used only for grazing. In Lattimore's aphorism, "The pure nomad is a poor nomad." The nomadic ecology could be far more productive if it could be linked to better land—which sedentary farmers could have used equally, or if it could be linked to the agricultural wealth of desert oases easily dominated by nomadic military power. Nomads therefore could be expected to use their advantage in mobility in order to seize control of the oases and the marginal lands.

These same marginal lands and oases were equally important to the sedentary society. Its strength, countering the mobility of the nomads, was its wealth based on the higher yields of sedentary agriculture and greater density of population. But this wealth also had to be organized for frontier defense. Farmers were tied down to their fields, immovable capital, and stores of grain. If these were to be defended, the nomads had to be stopped before they could concentrate for a raid. This in turn required elaborate preparations, which could go as far as building a permanent military line like the Great Wall of China. At the very least, the marginal lands had to be brought under control. The desert oases were also important as strongholds for sedentary control over the steppe. The key was political organization. When a sedentary state was strong and united, it could mobilize its wealth for frontier defense. If organization broke down, it was open to nomadic attack. The oases and marginal lands often went first; larger raids could then penetrate into the heart of sedentary territory.

The nature and outcome of these raids depended on nomadic leadership and intentions. When the raids were led by men who were fully integrated into the nomadic culture, they were destructive and little more. The aim was simply to seize the accumulated wealth of the sedentary society or to exact tribute; the raids rarely led to a permanent military occupation that might tap the sedentary sources of wealth on a long-term basis. From time to time, however, nomadic leaders were able to seize control of the sedentary state and set themselves up as a new dynasty. To do this required a special kind of leadership that was culturally marginal— men who knew enough of nomadic life to gain a nomadic following, yet who also understood the structure and norms of the sedentary state. They could then try to seize control of the state, not destroy it.

As the leaders assimilated the sedentary way of life, they carried some of their original followers with them as subordinate officials. Those who failed to make the adjustment drifted back into the desert. The new dynasty would then find itself in the same position as its predecessors, confronted by a nomad threat. If it could profit by its newness to avert administrative inefficiency, it would again seize the marginal lands and drive the nomads back into the least favorable environment. If the frontier weakened again, the nomads could seize the marginal lands once more, and the process began all over again under new leadership.

Needless to say, a simplistic model of this kind is not intended to be interpreted as an accurate description of specific events, much less a "law of history." However, it can serve as a useful description of a style of history over a very long span of centuries—until the Industrial Revolution finally gave sedentary powers the ability to dominate the desert once and for all.

The Rise of Islam

The rise of Islam in nearby Arabia was immensely important for the future of Africa. The new religious message was spread in circumstances that took on the historical style of nomadic-sedentary conflict. By A.D. 600, the Western Roman Empire had fallen to barbarian infiltration and invasion. The Eastern or Byzantine portion of the Roman Empire was still strong in the Balkan peninsula and Anatolia, and it still controlled Egypt and Syria. At this period it was also changing internally, becoming less universal and Roman in character and more narrowly Greek. These changes affected the loyalty of the Egyptian and Syrian provinces, which followed the Monophysite version of Christianity in opposition to the established Orthodox Church of Constantinople. For Syrians and Egyptians, Byzantine rule came to look more and more like a form of foreign domination combined with religious persecution. Byzantium's neighbor to the east was the Sassanian Empire in Persia and Mesopotamia. It too was weakened by religious controversy, and both empires bad been weakened by a long series of Byzantine-Sassanian wars.

In the Arabian Desert to the south of these sedentary empires lived bedouin nomads, divided among themselves and worshipping many different local gods, although both Jewish and Christian influences were also present. Along the Red Sea coast, however, a number of trading towns like Mecca and Medina were in closer touch with the currents of sedentary civilization to the north. Here then was a setting in which culturally marginal men from the trading towns had enough contact with the nomads to establish links with them and also understood sedentary civilization well enough to lead a dynasty-founding invasion of the crumbling empires that controlled the Fertile Crescent from Egypt to Mesopotamia. Nomadic unity came from the ideological base of a new religion. Muhammad, a young merchant from Mecca, began to preach the new message early in the seventh century, drawing on Christian and Jewish roots but also incorporating some of the cultural traditions of Arabia itself. By the time of Muhammad's death in A.D. 632, his followers controlled the key cities of Mecca and Medina and much of Arabia. By 635, they had united the desert nomads into a mobile force capable of moving north. By 651, they had conquered the whole of the Sassanian Empire and the Byzantine provinces of Syria and Egypt.

Thus, in hardly more than a decade and a half, culturally marginal leaders from the Arabian cities had set themselves up as a new dynasty controlling parts of the former Eastern Roman and Sassanian empires. They moved the capital from Mecca to Damascus and soon lost control of most of Arabia. The principal leader took the title of caliph, or successor to Muhammad, thus claiming religious as well as secular authority. The conquerors took the Arabic language with them, but the Islamic civilization that emerged owed far more to Persian and Roman traditions than it did to Arabian. The new dynasty took over Byzantine administrative forms along with some of the Byzantine administrators. The real base for its later conquests eastward into central Asia and westward to Spain was the Fertile Crescent, not Arabia.

Conversion followed conquest, but it was more than mere conversion to a new religion. The political unity of the caliphate lasted only a short time, but the religious unity of the Islamic world

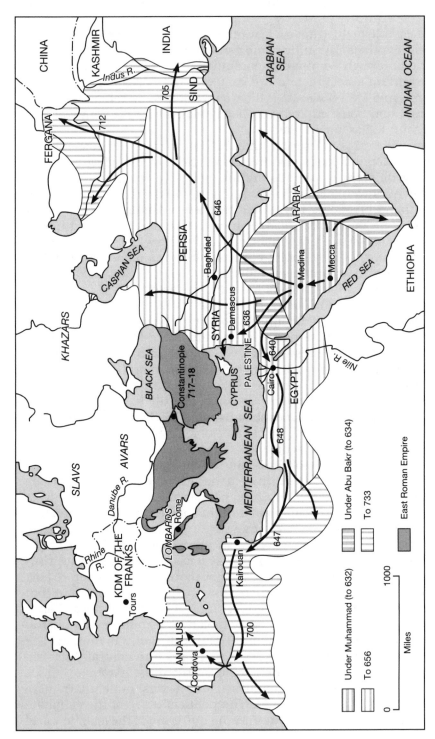

Figure 6. The rise of Islam.

made for a new region of intercommunication. Islamic civilization became heir to the cultural and technological heritage of the zone stretching from the Atlantic to the frontiers of India and China. With Arabic as the universal language of religion, the Islamic world was in a position to act as mediator and transmitting agent, even between culture areas that had not been conquered or converted to Islam. Greek philosophy, for example, was taught to north-western Europe through Muslim transmitters, and the "Arabic" system of positional notation in mathematics was an Indian invention, though it entered Europe as Arabic numbers.

Islam in Africa

From the eighth century to the eighteenth, Islamic civilization was to be Africa's chief contact with the intercommunicating zone. However, Islam was slow to move into sub-Saharan Africa, as though the very success of the Muslim drive to the north had removed the temptation to move in other directions. The Christian kingdoms of the upper Nile and the Ethiopian highlands were left alone for several centuries. As a result, they found themselves more isolated than they had been in Roman times.

Much the same was true of the Indian Ocean network of maritime trade. Roman ships had traded as far south as present-day Tanzania. Sassanian Persia had later dominated the western basin of the Indian Ocean, keeping up communication between the African coast and the civilizations to the north. The rise of Islam and the Muslim conquest of Persia, however, drew Persia into a new orbit of trade, and communication was diverted to within the Islamic world itself.

In place of the Sassanian Empire, the new Abbasid Caliphate moved its capital from Damascus to Baghdad. From about A.D. 750 to 1000, the Abbasid Caliphate dominated sea trade to southern and eastern Asia. For a time, Abbasid ships sailed past the Bay of Bengal and Malaya, and on up the South China Sea to Canton itself. They also took up the old Roman routes southward down the African coast.

Contact between the sudanic states of West Africa and the Islamic states of the north intensified, although more through the possession of camels than due to military superiority. The Muslim conquest drove rapidly across North Africa and into Spain, but the nomadic peoples of the Sahara were hardly touched by that conquest. Nomads, from the Beja of the Red Sea coast to the Berbers of the western Sahara, looked on the sedentary civilization as nomads have usually done—that is, as fair game. The "Arabs" who now ruled North Africa found themselves in charge of a sedentary civilization with a frontier to defend. Aside from defensive operations, they left the desert people alone. In time, most of them became Muslim by voluntary conversion, but rarely before the tenth century and often much later.

Thus, the rise of Islam created a new zone of very intense intercommunication, stretching from Spain to Persia and beyond. Camel caravans brought the sub-Saharan shore of the desert into the Muslim economic sphere. Thus, sub-Saharan Africa was in much the same position as northwestern Europe was during the Dark Ages. It was on the fringes of the Islamic world with some commercial contact but, through religious difference as well as physical barriers, beyond the frontier of "civilization." Europe's return to the inner zone was comparatively easy. Northwestern Europe still retained some of the culture and technology of the Roman Empire, and Islamic civilization was also an heir of Rome. Christendom and Islam also faced one another across military frontiers in northern Spain, Italy, and the Mediterranean islands. For sub-Saharan Africa, the barrier of the desert remained. Sedentary states to the north and south had trouble controlling the nomads between them, but gradually that barrier began to crumble. From the eleventh century onward, Islam began to penetrate south of the desert, bringing knowledge of the alphabet, literacy for some, and at least a distant and tenuous contact with the dominant civilization of the time.

Like earlier influences from the outside, Islam came to sub-Saharan Africa through several different channels. In the far west, the Sanhaja Berbers of the Sahara converted to Islam shortly before A.D. 1000. Commercial contacts and missionary work then carried the religion to the Senegal Valley, just south of the desert. In about 1030, the rulers of Takrur became the first sub-Saharan dynasty to embrace Islam. Other states in the western sudan, however, resisted religious change. Ghana, which reached its greatest power in the ninth and tenth centuries, appears to have kept its traditional religion in spite of its commercial contact with the north.

A second route of Islamic penetration was southward from Libya through Fezzan to Lake Chad. Roman penetration of the desert had followed this direction, and the Fezzani had long dominated the Sahara trade. Their conversion to Islam in the ninth century was a step toward the conversion of Kanem, the most important sub-Saharan state in the Lake Chad basin. The first Kanembu ruler to accept Islam came to power in 1085, though religious conversion of the general population undoubtedly took place only gradually in the centuries that followed.

Conversion came less peacefully to the Nile Valley. In the early centuries after the rise of Islam, commercial contacts across the Red Sea and movement of people from Arabia to Africa brought some degree of Islamic influence, but the Christian Nubian kingdoms still held out—along the desert reaches of the river where the Nile provides irrigation water, as well as in the savanna country farther south. In the 1280s and 1290s, however, attacks from Muslim Egypt destroyed Christian Nubia along the Nile. Even though the savanna kingdom of 'Alwa lived on, it was not strong enough to control the desert. Partly as a result, Arabs began to move into Africa in greater numbers than ever before. During the fourteenth and fifteenth centuries this migration became so large that the Nilotic sudan was permanently Arabized in language and many aspects of culture, though the Arab immigrants also mixed with Africans to create a present-day population that is only partly of Arab descent. This Arab penetration of the sudan resembles other nomadic attacks on a sedentary state, but in this case the marginal leadership was missing. Rather than seizing or re-creating a new state, these Arab invasions destroyed Christian Nubia without putting anything in its place. About A.D. 1500, a Muslim sedentary state, the Funj sultanate, did emerge in the savanna country of the upper Nile, but it was founded by Africans, not by Arab nomads. In Ethiopia and the Horn of Africa, Islam also entered into competition with existing Christian states. Commercial and cultural contact between Ethiopia and Yemen had always been close, and Islam spread first to the port towns on the African side of the Gulf of Aden. By A.D. 1000, peaceful conversion was already well advanced in the eastern highlands of Ethiopia, while Christianity was spreading southward at the same time in the western highlands. By about 1300, the Muslim sultanate of Ifat emerged as a military competitor against Christian Abyssinia for the control of Ethiopia, but this time the Christian state won. By 1415, most of the Muslims had been driven out or forcibly converted to Christianity.

Outside influence came to East Africa by sea, and not merely from the Muslim world. Traders came from India, Indonesia, and even China, but commercial ties with Persia and Arabia became dominant from the thirteenth century onward, and the port towns of East Africa began to enter the intercommunicating zone. Mogadishu in present-day Somalia was the principal center for the northern coast. Farther south, Kilwa came to dominate the trade that flowed from the Rhodesian gold fields to the coast at Sofala. Here and elsewhere along the coast, stone-built towns whose remains can be seen today are evidence of African membership in the greater world of Islam. But Islam was grafted onto an African cultural base. Arabic was used for writing and religion, but a Bantu language ancestral to modern Swahili was the language of ordinary speech.

By 1450 or so, on the eve of maritime contact with Europe, Africa as a whole was still isolated from the main currents of change. In spite of eight centuries in the shadow of Islamic civilization, which Islam had penetrated at many points on the fringes of sub-Saharan Africa, constraints to communication with the outside world remained impressive. In the Nilotic sudan, for example, Islam came through Arab invasion and infiltration—really another case of nomadic attack on a fragile sedentary state. The region became Muslim, but its communications with the Mediterranean world were no more regular or effective than they had been during Roman times.

The obvious prosperity of the East African port towns is deceptive. Although they were African towns, they looked toward the Indian Ocean. Their connection with the interior was almost nonexistent, and the immediate hinterland was sparsely populated. Wide belts were infested with tsetse flies, or were semi-arid. It was not, perhaps, such a formidable barrier as the Sahara, but it was barrier enough. One sign of the isolation of the area is the lack of geographical knowledge available in the Muslim world. Arab geographers were avid for any scrap of information. From the eleventh to the fourteenth century, they were able to give a fair account of the geography and culture of the western sudan, but they knew almost nothing about the interior of East Africa.

Any assessment of African and world development over the period from about A.D. 600 to about 1500 must be one of sharp contrasts. The sweep of Islamic civilization, stretching by the end of this period from Morocco to Malaya, had brought an intensity of intercommunication. One result of this change was the rapid development of northwestern Europe, largely through its ability to borrow and assimilate the technology that was available—from Greek science to Chinese printing and gunpowder, from Indian positional numbers to Muslim ship's rigging and algebra. But most of Africa was still largely isolated, and its technological lag behind the intercommunicating world was greater than ever—not because Africa was unchanging, but because the rest of the world was changing more rapidly than ever before. African achievements up until this point had been considerable, in art, music, jurisprudence, and material technology, but these improvements were mainly based on what Africans could invent for themselves.

13
THE END OF ISOLATION

istorical knowledge about Africa has a curious relationship to African history. Written records are available only for those times and places where literate people were present—either foreign visitors or Africans who kept records. Since literacy is a crucial technique for human societies and it was imported into Africa (as it was into most of the world) after having been invented elsewhere, literate reporting from any part of Africa is a rough marker for the end of African isolation. The timing of the first written records varied greatly from one part of the continent to another. The introduction of Islam always meant the introduction of literacy, since Muslims (like Christians and Jews) were "people of the book." A second great impetus to literate reporting came with the fifteenth-century maritime revolution and the appearance of European travelers on the coasts. Finally, its spread inland took place gradually but with increasing rapidity from the sixteenth century to the twentieth. As each new part of Africa appeared over the horizon of literate reporting, the historical record based on oral tradition and archaeology can be filled out with a third kind of data.

The Western Sudan

For the western sudan, Islam brought both local writing (most of which is now lost) and reports by Arab travelers. It is possible to disentangle much of the web of history after about A.D. 1000, at least to the point of picking up broad patterns of change. We are, however, at the mercy of the few sources. Histories of Africa have much to say about Ghana and Mali and relatively little about Kanem or Takrur—not because Kanem or Takrur were less important, but simply because the Arab geographers whose accounts have survived happened to have more information about Ghana and Mali.

Even for Ghana or Mali, history is difficult to reconstruct. They are often categorized as "great empires," but the phrase can conjure up a whole world of misconceptions—as wrongheaded as those that most educated people carry concerning the "empire" of Charlemagne. At the peak of its power in the ninth century, Ghana was probably not very different from the Carolingian Empire, either in scale or in degree of control over the subordinate territory. That

166

is to say, neither one was really able to keep a constant surveillance over most parts of the empire, even to the extent of knowing in detail what was going on. We often tend to imagine ancient states as though they were run with administrative technology that was only available much later. In fact, both these empires were distant overlordships of multiple self-governing local regions that did what was demanded of them in order to stay out of trouble and otherwise ran their own affairs. Even such an elementary matter as the general enforcement of a single system of law was beyond the power of either Charlemagne or the rulers of Ghana.

Part of Ghana's function as a state is nevertheless clear from the reports of Arab geographers and its position on the edge of the desert. It was the first of a sequence of "empires" in this location. Each in turn grew to power and wealth by controlling the flow of trade across the natural frontier between desert and savanna. This trade was crucial for the western sudan, which lacked a local source of salt. Rock salt from the desert was exchanged for gold, mined well back from the desert's edge in Bambuk, Bouré, and later in Asante. A state that could dominate the desert-savanna frontier over a considerable distance could tax the passing trade, even though it might lack direct control over the salt deposits of the Sahara or the gold deposits of the sudan.

When Ghana's capital was sacked by a nomadic raid in A.D. 1076, the empire fell apart. Its place of preeminence was taken by Mali, not a desert-edge state, but one that manipulated the gold-salt exchanges by controlling Bambuk and Bouré themselves, and by driving a line of expansion westward down the Gambia Valley to the sea, where salt was manufactured from sea water. Mali, in turn, lost some of its power with the fifteenth-century rise of Songhai on the great northern bend of the Niger. In the strategy of trade control, Songhai's power marked a return to the preeminence of the desert edge, and at its peak Songhai's control reached into the desert to the salt mines themselves.

Location on the desert edge had disadvantages. While nomadic attack was a constant danger, the climatic pattern may have been even more telling in the long run. Rainfall was subject to great annual variation, with the possibility of no harvest at all in a bad year. This danger was slightly mitigated by the major rivers that rise farther south in regions of assured annual rainfall—the Senegal, the Niger, and the Shari, which flows into Lake Chad. Many of the people in the northern savanna, however, had to adapt to an uncertain rainfall. In the seventeenth century, for example, the harvest in the Niger bend country failed one year out of every seven to ten; in the eighteenth century it failed one year in every five. If

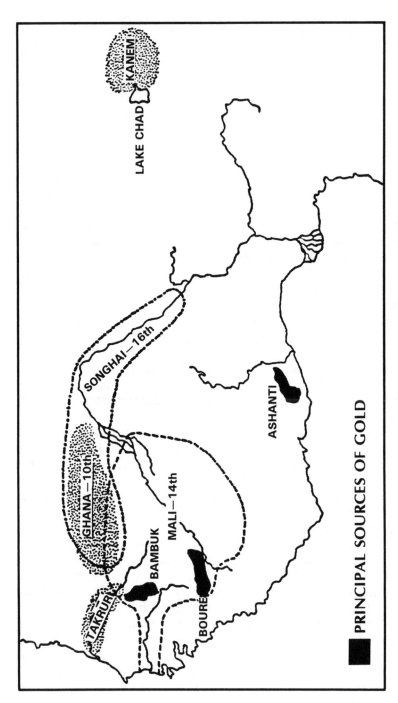

Figure 7. Areas of influence of major West African empires.

KANEM

LAKE CHAD

SONGHAI—16th

GHANA—10th

ASHANTI

TAKRUR

BAMBUK

MALI—14th

BOURÉ

■ PRINCIPAL SOURCES OF GOLD

these failures were well spaced, people could provide for bad years by storing grain, but rain sometimes failed for several years in a row. When this happened, they had to move or die. In recent centuries, at least three periods of general famine and depopulation struck the whole northern savanna belt from the Atlantic to Lake Chad, the first in 1639–43 and the second in 1738–56 and the third was in 1969–73. Oral traditions tell of similar crises in the distant past. The Soninke, the rulers of ancient Ghana, tell of a prolonged dry period that forced them to disperse from a homeland called Wagadu. If Wagadu can be correctly equated with the core area of Ghana, it may be that Ghana fell through famine and depopulation, not merely nomadic attack.

Other states were prominent elsewhere along the desert edge. Kanem to the east in the Lake Chad basin and Takrur in the Senegal Valley both have origins at least as far back as the tenth century, and probably earlier still. But the state was not a universal institution in West Africa. The large incorporative empires existed for centuries alongside smaller states and stateless societies. Historians once assumed that the large states must have been created by conquerors who came across the desert (which also explained why they were so prevalent near the desert's edge). In fact, West African political forms are not like those of North Africa; they have far more in common with states elsewhere south of the Sahara. Historians today believe that African states and stateless societies alike are local developments. They also question the belief that the state is necessarily a sign of human progress. In many respects, such as agricultural technology, the stateless peoples of West Africa were more advanced than those who had the most elaborate political structures. In many circumstances, a minimal political organization lightly unifying a set of virtually independent villages was preferred, even when large states were present in the region and could easily have been copied had there been an inclination to do so.

The large states of the desert fringe nevertheless played an important role in mediating between the Islamic world to the north and the savanna and forest to the south. North African traders stopped at the desert ports, and Africans from the desert fringe, like the Soninke or the Hausa, carried the trade goods throughout West Africa. They were often among the first to convert to Islam because of their commercial connections with North African Muslims, and their trade networks carried Islam, literacy, and a knowledge of the outside world. By A.D. 1500, these networks had led to the creation of Islamic communities scattered throughout West Africa north of the forest, and the trade routes themselves reached down to the Gulf of Guinea.

The Southern Savanna

African contact with the outside world, however, decreased in proportion to the distance from the desert ports. The northern edge of the forest was a breaking point in the pattern of long-distance trade; it is also a breaking point in historical knowledge. While communication undoubtedly passed through the forest, none of the surviving records from the northern savannas tell what happened historically in the similar environment to the south of the equatorial forest. It is safe to assume that contact between the northern and southern savannas before 1500 was indirect at best, and the east coast cities were far away.

In this southern setting, African societies developed in isolation— but they did develop, and they were in contact with one another. Innovation could spread widely, though much of it grew from local roots. One important early change in material culture among some of the Bantu-speaking peoples was to use cattle for specific purposes. The tsetse fly limited the range of cattle keeping, but those who came to live in fly-free zones added cattle keeping to their traditional hoe agriculture, and they came to value cattle for ritual as well as material reasons.

A second crucial change was the development of regional specialization. Salt was found in some places, but not in others. Local trade in salt therefore began at a very early date. Minerals were also concentrated, and a mining complex grew up in Zimbabwe, Zambia, and Zaire, where iron, copper, and gold were mined as early as the ninth century and probably earlier. Trade in metals spread from these centers, and by 1400, foreign products imported by way of the Indian Ocean ports were reaching destinations as far inland as present-day Zambia. Glass beads, textiles, and other manufactures were exchanged for African ivory and gold, but the hookup to intercontinental trade came only after the African interior had already developed its own regional commerce.

By the fifteenth century, a series of states began to take shape in the southern savanna, as they had done in the northern savanna about a thousand years earlier. Little is known of the earliest phases of this development, since the states were already established when the Europeans arrived on the coast. It is evident, however, that these kingdoms owed little or nothing to external influence. One of the most powerful was the kingdom of Kongo on the Atlantic coast south of the Congo mouth, far from any obvious contact with the rest of the world. It lay mainly in present-day Angola, with a total area midway between the size of Maryland and West Virginia. The

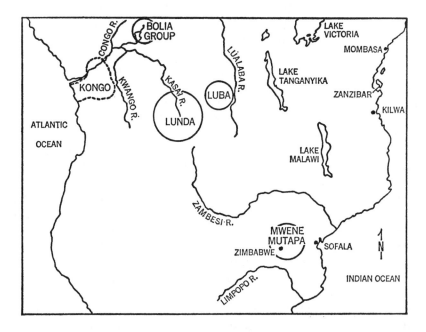

Figure 8. Early states of the southern savana. Boundaries indicated for Kongo only. For the rest, circles locate the core region only.

basic political unit was the village, as it was in West Africa, with higher administration based on districts and provinces. Traditions recorded in the fifteenth century suggest that the institutions of kingship were borrowed from other peoples to the north, but that is all.

Farther inland, other political centers began to develop about the same time. One of these was the Bolia group of states in the dense tropical forest around the northern end of Lake Mai Ndombe. A second in central Shaba was associated at first with the Luba ethnic group, but its institutional forms spread, with modifications, to the Lunda as well, until they finally extended over the whole of the African heartland from Lake Tanganyika a thousand miles west to the Kwango River. A third center of fifteenth-century state building centered in present-day Zimbabwe. The elaborate stone ruins at Great Zimbabwe were so impressive that their name has been used for the ancient kingdom and for the present-day republic, though Great Zimbabwe can be used to distinguish the city from the larger units. This kingdom was founded by the Karanga people, whose power was based on their gold deposits and trade with the Indian Ocean ports. Buildings so impressive they were originally dated to the seventeenth or eighteenth centuries are now believed to have been built late in the fifteenth. That was the period at which the rulers of Great Zimbabwe controlled most of the country between the Limpopo River on the south and the Zambezi on the north, from the Indian Ocean westward to the edges of the Kalahari Desert. The ruler bore the title of Mwenemutapa, which led the first Portuguese travelers to write about the "Monomotapa Empire." But the "empire" barely survived the period of their arrival, and in the early sixteenth century, it broke into two parts. The Mwenemutapa still controlled the north, but a rival dynasty, the Changamire, took over the southern section.

Far to the north, in the East African highlands, similar changes were in progress. Since literate visitors did not reach that part of Africa until the nineteenth century, we are left with only the record of archaeology and oral tradition, but that is enough to indicate a similar process of state-building, beginning perhaps as early as the thirteenth century. A large empire ruled by a dynasty remembered as the Bachwezi was roughly contemporaneous with the height of Great Zimbabwe or the kingdom of Kongo, but it too appears to have broken down into a series of small states in about the year 1500.

The Maritime Revolution

African societies, whatever their relative degree of isolation, were gradually coming to terms with their environment, borrowing or inventing new techniques for dealing with the problems of social life and material existence. Then, quite suddenly a few decades before 1500, Africa's relationship with the intercommunicating zone shifted dramatically. The cause of this change was a major breakthrough in the field of maritime technology.

Before the fifteenth century, reasonably safe long-distance trade by sea was possible only in favorable conditions. The Mediterranean was almost ideal for early shipping, and the Indian Ocean was favored by a pattern of monsoonal winds, which blew from the northeast for about half the year, then turned and blew from the southwest for the other half. Ships were guaranteed a favorable wind from the African coast to the Straits of Melaka and back again, simply by waiting for the appropriate season. These alternating winds made it possible for Arabs to reach China and for Chinese ships to reach the East African coast in the fifteenth century. Indian Ocean trade was so extensive that changing styles in Chinese porcelain are still used today by archaeologists to establish the date of many East African ruins.

The whole western coast of Africa was another matter. It was navigable enough, and Africans maintained some coastwise traffic by sea, but the west coast was cut off from other seas by two major barriers. One of these was the stormy coast of South Africa between southern Natal and Cape Town. Even after the Europeans learned to sail around Africa, this coast saw far more shipwrecks than any other. The second barrier was of a different kind. Along the Atlantic coast of the Sahara, it was easy enough to sail southward with the northeast trade winds, which blew all year long and set up an ocean current flowing in the same direction. The problem was to get back to the north against the combination of contrary wind and contrary currents.

The crucial breakthrough, not only for Africa but for world history, was made off the Saharan coast. The solution to the first problem was to develop a ship that could sail into the wind efficiently enough to overcome the pull of the current. This was accomplished along the Atlantic coasts of Spain and Portugal through the merging of Mediterranean ship design, new forms of hull construction from northern Europe, and lateen sails borrowed from the Arabs of the Indian Ocean. The result was the caravel— an excellent example of the kind of technological advance that was possible within the intercommunicating world.

The second step was even more important. The Portuguese knew that Muslim traders from North Africa went across the Sahara for gold. As Christians, the Portuguese were barred from the overland route, but they began in the fifteenth century to experiment with caravels to make the voyage by sea. Sometime early in the century, they found that they could return to the northward if they tacked back and forth so as to take advantage of the fact that the trade winds blew slightly more onshore in the daylight hours and slightly more offshore at night. But all this was merely a prelude to the crucial discovery. Somehow in the course of voyages down the coast, probably in the 1440s, Portuguese mariners discovered that it was not necessary to sail laboriously north tacking against the wind. A ship that left the coast altogether and made a long tack to the northwest, keeping as close as possible to the trade wind, would sooner or later pass beyond the trade-wind belt. In the vicinity of the Azores, the current flowed toward the Portuguese coast, and the winds were variable but mainly westerly, allowing an easy return home. This discovery not only unlocked the western coasts of Africa for European shipping, it opened the Atlantic as well. It is significant that Columbus made a voyage to the Gold Coast before he went to America. He therefore knew that he could let the trade winds blow his ships to the west, because a zone of prevailing westerlies lay farther north to blow them back to Europe again. In short, what the Europeans learned on the Sahara coast was not simply a good sea route to Guinea; it was their first insight into the worldwide pattern of winds and currents. Within a few decades, European ships could reach virtually any part of any ocean.

Simultaneous with the maritime revolution, a second technological change took place in the intercommunicating world. Gunpowder, invented in China, was joined to improving metallurgy to produce the first effective artillery. By the sixteenth century, cannon were being used not only in Europe but also across the whole belt of countries stretching from Morocco to Japan. As the coasts of Africa therefore emerged from isolation, they were confronted by intruders who were both mobile and well armed. As the use of firearms spread rapidly through the Muslim world, a similar confrontation emerged along the fringes of the desert, from the Senegal River to the Red Sea. Africans thus faced better-armed neighbors on all sides.

Time of Troubles in the Sixteenth Century

It would be a mistake to exaggerate the suddenness of Africa's emergence from isolation or the effectiveness of early firearms. Most African societies, other than the East African port towns, were quite untouched by the first results of the maritime revolution. New currents of trade grew up only gradually. Maize, manioc, and other crops from the Americas diffused inland over decades and even centuries. Some African states, however, felt the direct influence of European power and faced a crisis of forced and rapid readjust ment to the new situation. For most of sub-Saharan Africa, however, it is more accurate to think of a time of troubles, of slow readjust- ment as the European presence on the coast impinged piecemeal and sporadically on inland societies.

Portuguese activity in Africa was intense for two or three decades after about 1480. Portuguese resources for overseas activity concentrated on Africa, and the earliest strategy was to enter the African gold trade. In 1481 the Portuguese began building an elaborate stone castle at Elmina on the Gold Coast to tap the Asante gold fields. They were not interested in conquest or colonization, only in a base from which to defend their trade against other Europeans. They also hoped to convert some of the more important African states to Christianity, using a program of Christian missions and technical assistance to create dependence on Portugal. The target states in West Africa were the three largest and strongest states lying near the coast—Jolof, which then controlled most of present-day western Senegal, Benin in southern Nigeria, and Kongo in central Africa. In the first two, the plan miscarried. An attempt to install a pro-Portuguese pretender as ruler of Jolof failed in 1488. Trade and diplomatic relations with Benin brought a few missionaries from Europe, but they soon died and nothing substantial came of the effort.

The Portuguese effort in Kongo came nearer to success. In 1487 the ruler, Manikongo Mzinga Kuwu, appealed for missionaries and technicians, and the Portuguese obliged. His son and successor was converted to Christianity, had himself baptized Affonso I, and founded a line of Christian kings. At first, the Kongolese drive for modernization brought some success, though it failed in the long run. The missionaries and technicians were too few, and they died too rapidly to be really useful. In addition, the Portuguese seized the offshore island of São Tomé and turned it into a plantation colony in the decades after 1500. The São Tomé planters needed slaves from the nearby shores of Africa, and their interests predominated over the good intentions of the distant government in Lisbon which was opposed to slavery. The growth of the slave trade was disastrous for the whole region, but the Portuguese were not the only problem. In the final third of the sixteenth century, the rains failed more frequently than usual, and a number of different refugee groups turned to marauding. The most notorious of these were the Imbangala, whom the Portuguese called Jaga. At one point they destroyed the capital of Kongo, though later they became allies of the Portuguese, who were powerless against direct attack. Drought continued into the early seventeenth century, and the Portuguese gradually withdrew their principal center from Kongo to the island of Luanda on the Angola coast farther south.

In the western sudan, the time of troubles took a different form. The most important states of the sixteenth century were Songhai on the Niger bend and Borno, successor to Kanem in the Lake Chad basin. Their outside contacts were with North Africa, where important changes were taking place in the second half of the century. The Ottoman Turks became a major naval power in the Mediterranean and began to gain control of a series of North African port towns as far west as Algeria—among others, Tripoli, which served as the northern terminus of the trans-Saharan route northward from Borno. Rather than posing a threat to Borno, the presence of a strong power to the north at a time when Borno was gaining power in the south worked in the interests of both. Borno and Istanbul established diplomatic relations and cooperated in keeping trade routes open, and Borno was able to import firearms and hire Turkish mercenaries. All of this gave a new impetus to the spread of Islamic learning south of the desert.

The fate of Songhai was almost the reverse. After reaching a peak of power and influence during the first decades of the sixteenth century, Songhai's power began to decline. Religious controversies led to a series of disputed successions and brief civil wars. Portuguese trade with the gold fields cut into Songhai's commercial advantage as a desert-edge state. Meanwhile, Morocco was growing in power north of the desert. In the 1590s a Moroccan army crossed the desert and defeated Songhai. Morocco was not strong enough to maintain control over any significant section of the western sudan, but it was strong enough to prevent the rise of a new sudanic state on the desert fringe—one that could again exploit the advantages that had once brought wealth and power to Ghana, Mali, and Songhai. Even without the sporadic Moroccan intervention that continued through the seventeenth and into the eighteenth century, European entry into the gold trade from the coast ruined the possibility of a sudanic state ever again monopolizing that trade as Mali had once done.

The sixteenth-century troubles in East Africa were similar; the Europeans there were strong enough to ruin the older patterns of commerce but too weak to create a viable alternative. The Portuguese effort in the Indian Ocean region was marked by grand designs and too little power to carry them out. The Portuguese hoped to monopolize the spice trade from Indonesia to the west, but their maritime dominance was sporadic at best. By mid-century, Muslim "smugglers" had recaptured much of their former trade.

A standoff between Portugal and the Ottoman Turks at the mouth of the Red Sea was especially damaging. Neither the Turks moving south from Egypt nor the Portuguese moving north from Mozambique were able to control the Red Sea route from the Mediterranean to the Indian Ocean. As a result, trade simply went elsewhere—to the Persian Gulf for the Muslims, or to the round-Africa route for the Portuguese. In addition, both Turks and Portuguese intervened in the political affairs of the Ethiopian highlands. Early in the fifteenth century, the Turks furnished firearms to local Muslim powers, who attacked Christian Abyssinia and almost destroyed it in the 1540s. Portugal then intervened on the other side, saving Abyssinia from extinction but not from a prolonged decline in power and well-being—a decline that lasted into the nineteenth century. But here, as in Kongo, external influences were not alone. The Muslim-Christian struggles opened the way to a long series of invasions by the nomadic Oromo. Originating in southern Ethiopia, the Oromo moved around and into the highlands, seizing whole regions. In time, many of them became sedentary, but meanwhile their invasions and migrations during the seventeenth and eighteenth centuries devastated much of the highland country.

The Portuguese were variable and ambivalent. As of 1500, Kilwa was the dominant power, with control over the coastwise trade as far south as Sofala. A Portuguese fleet attacked Kilwa in 1505. The Portuguese then built a new base on Mozambique island, and they seized Sofala as an entry point into the gold trade. For a short time, they were successful even in the interior, establishing cordial relations with the Mwenemutapa and converting some of his people to Christianity, but the flow of gold soon dropped from its previous levels. By the seventeenth century, the Changamire dynasty rose in power, gained control of the gold fields, and dispossessed Portugal's allies.

In the coastal region that was to become Tanzania and Kenya, Portuguese power was even less substantial. They captured and garrisoned some of the coastal cities, but Turkish raids from the sea came as far south as Mombasa in the late sixteenth century. This activity terminated the old prosperity that had depended on coastal trade with ports in the Red Sea and Persian Gulf. The southern terminus of the African coast was now securely held by the Portuguese, the northern by the Turks. Again, the weakening of the coastal cities may have contributed to their difficulties in the hinterland—raids from the Oromo behind the northern sector in present-day Somalia, and from war bands of Zimba who moved northward just behind the coast in the 1580s, sacking both Kilwa and Mombasa. These raids bear some resemblance to the Jaga invasion of Kongo on the opposite side of Africa, and both may have been connected with major political changes in the Lunda empire of the interior. After 1598 the Portuguese built a major fortress at Mombasa to anchor their power on the northern coast, but it remained insecure. By the eighteenth century, even Mombasa was lost, and Portugal was too weak to prevent a trade revival under the general patronage and protection of Oman, an Arabian sultanate at the entrance of the Persian Gulf.

For the east coast, then, the coming of the Portuguese was not so much a new link with the intercommunicating world as a breach in the well-established pattern of contact that already existed with the world of Islam. In spite of their partial dominance over some of the coastal cities for almost two centuries, the Portuguese cultural contribution was slight. The cities remained Islamic in religion, grafted onto an African base. It may be that Portugal's most important contribution to East African culture history was to increase the Africanization of coastal culture by reducing contact with Arabia.

14

THE ERA OF THE SLAVE TRADE

I t is one of the ironies of African history that the end of isolation led Africa, in hardly more than two centuries, to a new commerce in which its chief export was its own people. Historians have long disputed the causes and consequences of the slave trade—both for Africa and for the world—and the debates are far from finished.

Recent research nevertheless makes it possible to dismiss some of the older myths about the slave trade—myths that originated in the eighteenth- and nineteenth-century European image of Africa, with all its racist overtones. Where the slave trade was once explained by the "primitive" condition of African societies and the "natural docility" of the Africans, it is now clear that Africa was not primitive and African slaves were far from docile. Slave revolts were a standard feature in the American tropics. Not only were the African-Americans of Saint Domingue (now the republic of Haiti) the first non-Europeans to overthrow colonial rule, but other, less known, revolts were also successful. Communities of runaways and rebels were scattered through the back country of South America and in the tangled mountains of the larger Caribbean islands. Several such communities maintained their independence of European control until the abolition of slavery itself ended their need for isolation.

The Origins of African Slavery

Other research helps to explain why Africans came to make up the majority of slaves in the Western world. In southern Europe—unlike northern Europe, where the slavery of the Roman period changed gradually into various forms of inequality generally categorized as serfdom—slavery continued throughout the Middle Ages and down to the eighteenth century in some places. Mediterranean slavery had nothing to do with the race of the slaves. It was a matter of religion; Christians enslaved Muslims, and Muslims enslaved Christians. Black Africans were present among the Mediterranean slaves, but not in large numbers until the fourteenth century. Before that time, the principal external sources of slaves for Christian Europe were the northern and eastern coasts of the Black Sea.

In the fourteenth and fifteenth centuries, slavery in southern

Europe served three purposes—to furnish domestic service, to provide oarsmen for the galleys that were the principal naval craft, and to concentrate people for new enterprises. Wherever mines or plantations were established in places with an insufficient supply of labor, the institution of slavery was a convenient way of mobilizing labor, especially for sugar plantations on the Mediterranean islands, southern Spain, or Portugal.

Even before the discovery of America, Europeans began to set up similar plantations on Atlantic islands like the Canaries or Madeira. By the early sixteenth century, they had moved as far as São Tomé in the Gulf of Guinea, and these moves were followed later in the century by similar establishments in the Caribbean and Brazil. At each step, the existing population was too small to provide enough workers for a labor-intensive crop like sugar, and the previously isolated populations lived in environments which had not been exposed to the common diseases of Africa and Europe. This meant that the people had no immunities derived from childhood infection or inheritance. With the introduction of Afro-European diseases, these regions passed through a series of devastating epidemics of measles, smallpox, typhus, malaria, or yellow fever. The result was a population disaster, sometimes ending in the effective extinction of the original population, especially in the tropical lowlands of the Americas—the region best suited for plantation agriculture. Thus, the Europeans, who already had the institution of slavery as a way of forcing labor mobility, used it in the Atlantic just as they had done in the Mediterranean.

Some form of slavery or forced labor was useful for other reasons as well. The natural conditions of a frontier region, with plenty of land and few people, made for high wage rates. It was tempting in these conditions to use force in order to make people work some of the land more intensively. As the native populations declined in Mexico and Peru, the Spanish turned increasingly to various forms of peonage. On the eastern frontiers of Europe, the landed class tightened the bonds of serfdom, but the solution found for America's tropical lowlands was slavery.

Africans were not the only enforced immigrants to the New World. Convicts, unsuccessful rebels against the government, and indentured workers, who bound themselves more or less voluntarily to serve for a period of years, were shipped off to the Americas in large numbers. Native people were also enslaved and used for plantation agriculture, especially in Brazil. Of the three sources of labor—Africa, America, and Europe—it was soon clear that the Africans survived best in the tropical American environment. At the time, African superiority in this respect was attributed to some special quality of the "Negro race," but modern knowledge of epidemiology shows that early environment rather than race is the true explanation. Europeans died in large numbers in the American tropics, just as they died in even larger numbers in the African tropics. The original inhabitants also died on contact with Afro-European diseases, but Africans had acquired some immunity, both to tropical diseases and to the ordinary range of diseases common on the Afro-Eurasian land mass. Migration from Africa to the Americas brought higher death rates for the first generation, but lower rates than those of Europeans who moved to the American tropics.

Given the choice of slavery as a labor system and the fact that Africans were the most efficient workers, the problem of supply remained. A large-scale slave trade would have been impossible if Africa had been truly primitive. Given the European death rate on the coast, foreigners would probably have been unsuccessful without established practices. Commercial networks were already in existence before the discovery of America, both in West Africa and in the southern savanna. African rulers often enslaved war prisoners, and the prisoners were sold into the slave trade—often for shipment to distant places where escape was less likely. Some were exported across the Sahara to North Africa, and the Portuguese were briefly in the business of buying slaves in one part of Africa and selling them in another, even before the demand from American plantations drew the focus of the slave trade across the Atlantic.

The Slave Trade in Africa

Slavery in Africa, however, was different from slavery on an American plantation. At the moment of capture, slaves could be killed or sold and were without rights. They could be sold to an ultimate master in Africa or to the Europeans for transportation overseas. If they ended up on an American plantation, their rights would be few and they were treated as mere labor units. But in Africa, slavery was not mainly an economic institution. The object in buying a slave was to increase the size of one's own group, often for prestige or military power as well as wealth. Women were therefore more desirable than men, but men and women alike were assimilated into the master's social group. They were inferior members of that group, but they had rights as well as obligations. In many cases, a second-generation slave could no longer be sold, and slaves belonging to important people could often rise to positions of command over free men.

The Atlantic slave trade thus tapped an existing African slave trade, but in doing so it sent people into a very different kind of slavery. Over the centuries, it diverted increasing numbers to the coast for sale to Europeans. The organization of this trade varied greatly from one part of Africa to the next. In some regions, Europeans built trade forts—twenty-seven on the Gold Coast over a distance of only about 220 miles. African authorities allowed the Europeans to run their own affairs within the forts, but they often charged rent for the land. Other trading posts were nothing more than a few unfortified houses on shore for the storage of trade goods and a tightly fenced yard containing a barracks or "barracoon" for slaves awaiting shipment. In that instance, the Europeans who stayed onshore between ships' visits did so with the permission of the African ruler, under his protection. Another form of trade was the "ship trade," in which Europeans sailed down the coast, calling at likely ports, but without leaving European agents permanently stationed onshore.

Whatever the point of trade, elaborate customary procedures had come into existence by the end of the sixteenth century. Trade normally began with a payment to the local authorities—partly a gift to demonstrate good will and partly a tax. Each section of the coast had its own trade currency of account—the "bar" (originally an iron bar), the "ounce" (originally an ounce of gold dust), a form of brass currency called manilas, or cowrie shells from the Indian Ocean. Various European commodities were customarily valued at so many bars or ounces. Bargains were struck in terms of the number of bars or ounces to be paid for a slave and then once more in terms of the "sorting" of different European goods that would be used to make up that value.

The internal trade to the coast was more diverse. Some African kings participated in the slave trade and occasionally tried to monopolize it in their kingdoms. Others, like the ruler of Fuuta Tooro on the Senegal River, sold few slaves themselves but charged heavy tolls for those who shipped slaves through the kingdom on the way to the coast. Still other states expanded by conquest in order to be able to control the passage of slaves. The kingdom of Akwamu followed a pattern of expansion in the late seventeenth century, moving to the east and west of the Volta River in present-day Ghana, but some distance back from the coast. After a period of growing strength based on revenue from the flow of trade across the kingdom, Akwamu was able to reach down to the coast itself in the 1680s and to dictate terms to the coastal trading states and the European garrisons alike.

Other African societies adjusted to the demand for slaves,

changing their own social and political institutions. Along the fringes of the Niger delta, the Ijo for centuries had been fishermen and exporters of salt to the interior, but they eventually participated in the slave trade. Early in the eighteenth century, a series of new city-states like Nembe, Bonny, and Kalabari came into existence, with a commercial and political organization designed expressly to serve the demand for slaves. Each city-state was divided internally into a series of "canoe houses," in effect a commercial firm based on the extended family plus domestic slaves. The houses operated large trading canoes, vessels that might have fifty to a hundred paddlers and a small cannon. Trade was highly competitive between houses. Within a house, command went to the most successful traders. A slave might rise to become head of the house. The Ijo canoes on the creeks of the delta were supplied, in turn, by other trade networks leading to the waterside. The Aro subgroup among the Ibo, for example, had small colonies of Aro settled in towns throughout Iboland. Slaves were passed from one Aro community to another until they were sold to the Ijo and finally to the Europeans. The Aro held their special position partly because they also controlled an important religious shrine, and many of the slaves they collected were originally intended as sacrifices at the shrine, although they in fact were eventually transported to the Americas.

African societies south of the tropical forest also adjusted to the trade in slaves. By the late seventeenth century, the Imbangala, who had first appeared as destructive raiders a century earlier, turned to commerce. Their kingdom, inland from the Portuguese post at Luanda, drew slaves from a wide range of central Africa. A little later, the Ovimbundu in the hinterland of Benguela took the same course. Several Ovimbundu kingdoms became wealthy from their trade networks reaching far into the interior, ultimately as far as the present Shaba province of Zaire. Like the Imbangala to the north, the Ovimbundu states were far too strong to be threatened by Portuguese power on the coast. In time, a rough alliance came into existence, in which the Portuguese acquiesced to the trade monopoly of the inland kingdoms for the sake of having a regular and plentiful supply of slaves delivered to the coast.

Southeastern Africa also contributed to the slave trade, especially present-day Mozambique (and its hinterland) and the large island of Madagascar off shore. The principal African carriers of the trade within southeastern Africa were the Yao from the vicinity of Lake Malawi. They first went into the long-distance ivory trade and then shifted to slaves as demand increased during the eighteenth century. The most important destination for slaves from this area was the Mascarene Islands in the Indian Ocean, where the French developed sugar plantations on the pattern of those in the West Indies. A few thousand slaves also found their way around the Cape of Good Hope into the slave trade of the Atlantic. By the early nineteenth century, Zanzibar and the Swahili coast to the north became an important destination for slaves from Madagascar and Mozambique, with a trickle of slaves passing still farther north to Arabia and the Persian Gulf.

The Growth and Incidence of the Slave Trade

The European demand for slaves grew slowly and steadily; over many decades African institutions adapted to meet the demand. From an annual average of less than 2,000 slaves imported into the Americas each year in the century before 1600, the trade grew to about 55,000 a year for the eighteenth century as a whole. The peak decade for the whole history of the trade was the 1780s, with an annual average of 88,000 slaves arriving in the Americas each year; deliveries reached more than 100,000 in a few individual years. At least for the crucial period from 1701 to 1809, it is possible to estimate the drain of population from various regions of Africa by taking the combined estimates of the exports carried by the three most important carriers England, France, and Portugal. (See Figure 9.) While the map represents the origins of the vast majority of all those carried, it also leaves out some important aspects of the trade. During that century, the sources of the trade shifted dramatically from one part of the coast to another. The Gold Coast, for example, supplied 20 percent of exports in the 1740s, but only about 9 percent in the 1790s. Meanwhile, the Bight of Biafra slave export statistics rose with the development of the Ijo-Aro trade network from about 1 percent in the 1730s to almost a quarter of the whole in the 1790s. Exports from central Africa doubled between the 1770s and the 1780s. In short, while the demand for slaves was relatively steady, it was met by rapid shifts from one source of supply to another, depending on African political conditions or the development of new trade routes from the interior.

People in the United States, with a view of world history that centers on their own country, often think of the slave trade as a flow of people from Africa to the United States. In fact, about one-third of all slaves who landed in the Americas went to Brazil; about a half went to the Caribbean islands and mainland; only about 6 percent of the total came to the United States. Yet the African-American population of the United States today is one of the largest in the

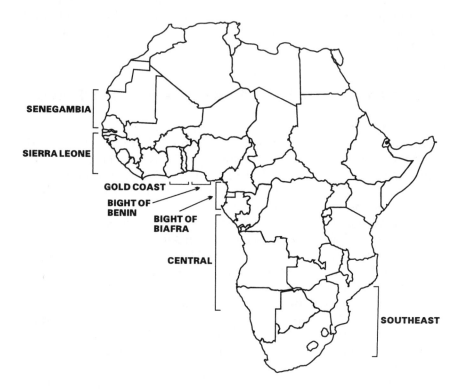

Figure 9. Approximate sources of the eighteenth-century Atlantic slave trade, 1701–1800. (Dutch, British, French, and Portuguese exports.) Totals in thousands.

Region	Slaves Exported	Percent of Total
Senegambia	201	3.6
Sierra Leone	484	8.7
Gold Coast	677	12.3
Bight of Benin	1,279	23.2
Bight of Biafra	814	14.8
Central and Southeast Africa	2,058	37.3
TOTAL	**5,513**	**100.0**

Source: Paul E. Lovejoy, *Transformations in Slavery,* p. 50.

New World. The explanation lies in a sharp and important demographic distinction. While the birth rates of the slave population of the North American colonies began to increase at a very early date, the slave population of the tropical plantations suffered an excess of deaths over births. This meant that in some locations the slave trade could not be a one-shot affair of importing a basic population that could then maintain its own numbers. It had to be continuous merely to maintain the existing level of population; any growth of the plantation economy required still more slaves from Africa.

Several factors help to account for this demographic peculiarity. Morbidity and mortality rates were higher among slaves raised in Africa than they were among the American-born. Planters also imported about two men for every woman, and they worked the women in the fields along with the men, preferring to have the women's labor rather than creating the kind of social setting in which they would be willing to have children.

The planters may have been correct, on strictly economic grounds, in believing that it was cheaper to import new labor from Africa than to allow the leisure, additional rations, and other privileges that might have encouraged a high birth rate among the slaves. The real cost of slaves was very small indeed before the middle of the eighteenth century. In 1695, for example, a slave could be bought in Jamaica for about £ 20 currency—about the same value as six hundred pounds of raw sugar sold on the London market. All things being equal, a new slave could be expected to add more than six hundred pounds of sugar to the plantation's production in a single year. A prime slave on the coast of Africa cost only about eight guns and sold in Europe for sixteen guns allowing a handsome profit on the slave trade itself.

The real price of slaves in Africa rose steadily during the eighteenth century. One result was to make planters think twice about their policy of importing slaves, rather than allowing them to breed naturally. By the 1770s, several Caribbean planters began to readjust by balancing the number of men and women on their estates, granting special privileges to child-rearing mothers and time off for child care. It is uncertain how generally these new policies were applied, but some of the older colonies, such as Barbados, began to achieve a self-perpetuating slave population by about 1800. Even where slaves were still imported, the demand tended to drop as the local birth rate rose, and the total number imported dropped in each decade from 1790 to 1820. When the United States, Great Britain, and Denmark abolished their own part of the slave trade in the first decade of the nineteenth century, the planters complained, but the really serious need for continued slave imports was nearing its end—at least in the older plantation areas.

The slave trade nevertheless continued long into the nineteenth century. In spite of British efforts to halt the trade by a partial blockade of the African coast—and by diplomatic pressure on Portugal, Brazil, and Spain—a sugar boom in Cuba and a coffee boom in southern Brazil brought a new demand for slaves from places where the plantation economy was newly introduced in that century. The slave trade therefore lasted until Brazil decided, in 1850, to enforce its own anti-slave-trade laws and Spain made a similar decision for its Cuban colony in the 1860s.

The Impact of the Slave Trade on Africa

Leaving aside the unanswerable question of what Africa might have become over these centuries without the slave trade, some evidence for assessing the impact of the trade is available. We know that most of the slaves sent to the Americas were captured in war. Some warfare took place in order to supply slaves to the trade, and all warfare produced captives who could be sold. Thus, the rise and fall of African states, contested successions, or periods of chronic warfare between states attracted slave dealers who followed the armies and purchased the prisoners. Famine was another cause of enslavement in the regions of unreliable rainfall, where a series of bad harvests forced people to sell their domestic servants, or even their kin and themselves. Judicial condemnation for crime or political dissent also sent some people on their way to the Americas.

The knowledge that warfare was the principal cause of enslavement in Africa is not as useful for assessing the impact of the trade as one might suppose. If a war took place with the specific and sole aim of capturing slaves, then the slave trade can be blamed for the damage to society at large. When, however, people were enslaved in the course of wars that took place for other reasons, the slave trade was a neutral factor. It might even have been beneficial. All wars are destructive, but a war fought so as to maximize the number of prisoners might well be less destructive than most. Our present knowledge is enough to indicate that both types of warfare took place in Africa, but not enough to tell which type was more common. On one side, historians can point to spectacular events like the collapse of the empire of Oyo in present-day Nigeria, a political change which led to a whole series of wars lasting for many decades in the early nineteenth century. It is clear that these wars were fought over real issues, not merely to supply the slave trade—yet they supplied more slaves to the trade than any other source in their time. In other cases, historians have detected what appears to have been a "gun-slave cycle," where an African state armed itself with guns and used them to capture unarmed neighbors, whom it sold for still more guns. Once caught in this cycle, it was hard to escape. Sooner or later, the neighboring peoples would have guns as well; at that point, slave raiding to buy guns might be necessary for survival. Cases can be found where African states, like Dahomey in the late eighteenth century, reorganized as military machines for the capture of slaves. But the gun-slave cycle may have been limited to certain areas. For example, in the open savanna, cavalry was the dominant military arm far into the nineteenth century, but the long reloading time of the typical eighteenth-century muzzle-loader limited its advantage against rapid-fire bowmen in the forest or wooded savanna.

Still another problem in assessing the impact of the slave trade is the obvious variation from one African society to another. Some societies were completely destroyed, others may have become wealthy by selling their neighbors to the Europeans, still others were never seriously involved in the trade at all—either as sellers or as victims. If we knew more about the level of African populations during the period of the slave trade, we could make some estimates as to the per capita drain of population, enabling us to arrive at a better assessment of the impact of slavery. However, it can still be argued that the underlying influence of the trade was far more profound than any mere drain of population or change in the incidence of warfare. Having been isolated from the intercommunicating zone, the Africans of the western coasts had, as a result of the arrival of seaborne Europeans, both an opportunity and a challenge. If Africans had responded by seeking new products to sell in return for the Indian textiles and European hardware offered by the maritime trade, they might well have discovered new economic institutions, technological innovations, and a more rapid rate of economic development than ever before. As it was, the Europeans wanted slaves, and the challenge of meeting this demand diverted African creativity to an essentially unproductive enterprise. When the slave trade finally ended, African societies took up the challenge of supplying products rather than people, but time was already running out; the European invasions came before the adjustment could be completed. It seems clear from this point of view that, at the very least, the slave trade forestalled some of the positive fruits of more intense contact with the outside world.

On the other hand, it is hard to sustain the view that the slave trade destroyed African civilization or detained Africa on its path to progress. African civilization was not destroyed, and Africa made progress during this period in spite of slave trade. Literacy spread in the western sudan with the spread of Islam. Literacy in English and Portuguese spread along the coast, where African slave dealers learned to read and write and sometimes sent their children to Europe for education. Recent studies of African states like Asante show a continuous development from small-scale, kinship-based political units to the institutions of a large state, capable of assimilating its conquered territories and exercising administrative control that was at least as effective as that of feudal monarchies in western Europe before the thirteenth century. Metallurgy and textile production also improved, and hand-loomed cotton cloths were sold into world trade during the eighteenth century, before the cheaper machine-made cloth from Europe drove them from the market. In short, measured by technology, there is no doubt that African societies advanced during the period of the slave trade, though it is equally certain that the advance was too slow to close the gap between African technology and that of the intercommunicating zone.

15

SECONDARY EMPIRES OF THE PRE-COLONIAL CENTURY

The era of the slave trade and the era of European conquest are unmistakable periods in the history of Africa. They also overlap; the earliest of the major European conquests took place before the last cargo of slaves was shipped to the New World. These two eras did not merge end-to-end like a cinematic "lap dissolve"—where one picture gradually fades away while the other simultaneously brightens. About a century before the European conquests began in earnest (about the 1780s, even before the slave trade reached its peak), new influences and tendencies began to appear. During this "precolonial century," Islamic renovation in West Africa led to the formation of a series of new empires. Political boundaries altered sharply over the whole range of eastern Africa as well, from the Nilotic sudan south to the Cape. Over all these changes hung the shadow of the European Industrial Revolution, which increased Europe's technological lead and brought more intense European activity to all fringes of the continent. Many of the emerging tendencies of the pre-colonial century were cut off abruptly by the European invasions; others were diverted into new channels. The events and developments of that century are important for understanding the direction in which African societies were headed before they were pulled so abruptly into the orbit of European colonial rule.

In eastern Africa, the dominant theme was military innovation. From the beginning of history, people have fought wars and changed the arts of warfare. These changes have always tended to alter the locus and distribution of power within society. In Europe, the security of the private castle helped to fragment political power in the feudal age, just as the better artillery of the fifteenth and sixteenth centuries helped build the centralized monarchies of countries like England and France. In nineteenth-century Africa, a similar change took place, but with an added twist. Major changes in the technology of war came so suddenly that they were seized and used by one state or segment of society before opponents had a chance either to imitate or to counter with new defenses. The result was a total disruption of the old power relations, as some groups were able to win easily and cheaply over others who had been more isolated.

The military changes of nineteenth-century Africa came from two sources. One of these was industrial Europe. Guns and tactics had been improving steadily in Europe itself. By the middle of the eighteenth century, the chief disadvantage of the musket—its long reloading time—had been corrected to some extent by the tactic of volley firing by disciplined infantry units. As early as the 1740s, this new tactic made European-trained armies dominant in distant parts of the world, such as India. Later, in the nineteenth century, the pace of change increased in weaponry itself. First came grapeshot and explosive shells for artillery, then, in the 1860s, breach-loading guns that could be fired several times a minute. In the late 1870s magazine-loading automatic rifles followed, and in the 1880s came the first effective field machine guns. Each of these changes opened the way to cheap military conquest by whatever African state could arm itself with the newest weapons before its neighbors could do the same. The result was a new political phenomenon known as a "secondary empire"—secondary in the sense that it was based on the military technology of Europe, but not controlled directly by a European power in the manner of the primary colonial empires of the period after 1880.

The second source of military innovation was similar in its consequences, but completely African in origin. This was the development of new tactics based on a highly trained and disciplined infantry unit armed with a short stabbing spear in place of the hurled javelin. In this case, it was not the weapon that was crucial, but the discovery (made several times before in other historical circumstances) that infantry trained to act as a body were far more effective, man for man, than a loosely organized mass of part-time soldiers. The result was the famous Zulu age-grade regiment, or *impi*, which made its appearance in southern Africa toward the end of the eighteenth century. At that time, the Nguni peoples of present-day Natal were divided into a number of small chiefdoms, and the new tactic is generally credited to Dingiswayo, chief of the Mthethwa. Dingiswayo took the existing institution of initiation and used it in new ways. All young men passed through a process of education and initiation as they reached puberty, and those who passed through these ceremonies together constituted an "age grade," a continuing social unit. The innovation was to take each age grade in turn and organize it as a permanent military unit of young men who lived together, trained together, and fought together. The ruler thus had a standing army made up of regimental units that cut across kinship and other social ties. Dingiswayo used this new source of power to conquer and incorporate a number of surrounding chiefdoms until he had built a unified state. At his death in 1818, command passed to Shaka, ruler of the Zulu, who began to use the military strength of the new state far more aggressively than Dingiswayo had ever done.

The Mfecane in Southern Africa

Shaka's wars in northern Natal (which themselves lasted only twelve years) led to a long and complex sequence of conquest, forced migrations, and regroupings that are known as the Mfecane in the Nguni languages. While some chiefdoms were incorporated into the Zulu state, others were destroyed and the survivors driven off as refugees. Some of these refugees reorganized and imitated the impi style of social and military organization. Some segments of the Zulu military system broke away and took up their own course of conquest. Some neighbors of the Zulu borrowed the military system and used it to build a state large enough and strong enough to stand off the Zulu attack. The result was a vast movement of political change and migration spreading outward from Zululand, beginning in the early 1820s and lasting into the second half of the nineteenth century.

Neither Shaka's Zulu state nor any of the other new states founded in the course of the Mfecane were secondary empires in the ordinary sense of the term. Their military success, however, depended on a similar monopoly over a military innovation. Once the new tactic was well known in the vicinity of Zululand, it was no longer the guaranteed key to success on the battlefield. This in itself tended to push offshoots of the Mfecane farther and farther from the Nguni homeland. As they moved, social institutions changed and adapted to new situations, but the incorporative feature of the age-grade regiment, coupled with the practice of rewarding successful warriors with wives, made it possible for the moving Nguni not merely to conquer but also to absorb some of the conquered populations. Once embarked on the course of continuous migration and conquest, the emigrant Nguni found themselves with a built-in dynamic that drove them to still further conquest and still further movement.

Sooner or later, however, the offshoots of the Mfecane did settle down. The states they founded, and the states that were founded by others in defense against the Mfecane, gave a new shape to the political geography of southern Africa. Several Nguni groups moved across the Drakensberg mountains, where they completely disrupted the Sotho chiefdoms on the high veld, in the present-day Transvaal and Orange Free State. Some Sotho, however, regrouped under the leadership of Moshweshwe to found the new state of

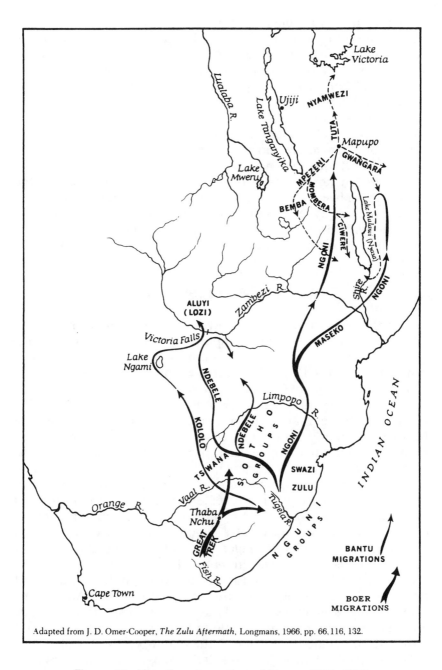

Figure 10. Migrations in southern Africa c. 1815–1850.

Lesotho, which was able to maintain its identity (if not its original frontiers) right through the colonial period to ultimate independence. Other Sotho adopted the Zulu military system and set off on their own conquests; one such group, the Makololo, ended as rulers of Barotseland in present-day western Zambia. To the north of Zululand, the Swazi also adopted the military innovation in self-defense and established the state that became Swaziland, but other Nguni offshoots went still farther north—one to found the empire of Gaza to the north of Swaziland, another settling in present-day Zimbabwe, where they still live as the Ndebele; still others moved north across the Zambezi Valley, destroying the remnants of Mwenemutapa and the Portuguese sphere of influence in the process. By the 1840s and 1850s, some of these northern movements had reached into present-day Malawi and Tanzania, where they broke into a number of separate "Angoni" kingdoms.

The Boer Secondary Empire

During the 1830s and 1840s, the events of the Mfecane intersected with those of a true secondary empire based on European weapons. The origins of this confrontation go back to the mid-seventeenth century, when the Dutch East India Company established a way station at the Cape of Good Hope to serve ships passing between the Netherlands and Southeast Asia. The tip of Africa had a Mediterranean climate and a relatively sparse population of Khoikhoi (formerly Hottentots, though the term is avoided today because of pejorative implications in South African usage). It was an easy environment for Europeans, and a small number of actual immigrants from Europe, perhaps no more than two thousand in all, grew into a white population of ten thousand by the 1770s and forty thousand by 1815. By that time, the whole population of the colony was about twice that size, a quarter being slaves imported from East Africa, India, Madagascar and Indonesia, and the other quarter the descendants of the native Khoikhoi.

Cape society in the eighteenth century was significantly different from the kind of society that later emerged in South Africa. The Khoikhoi had been more isolated than the Bantu-speaking Africans and hence were more susceptible to European diseases. A series of disastrous epidemics reduced their numbers and broke their political organization, with the result that most of the survivors were assimilated into white society, accepting inferior status but adopting Western culture. Imported slaves also took on much of the culture of their masters, and racial mixture between the whites, the

Khoikhoi, and the slaves produced the racial group that was to be known later in South African history as the "Cape colored." By the early nineteenth century, Cape society was multi-racial, but all races shared a similar Western culture, spoke a kind of Dutch ancestral to modern Afrikaans, and mostly practiced the same brand of Calvinist Christianity.

This settler community expanded geographically during the course of the eighteenth century, as frontiersmen moved eastward along the relatively well watered coastal strip or took up semi-nomadic pastoralism as trekboers in the more arid interior. About 1775 they met Bantu-speaking Africans, who had been settled for several centuries as far south as the Fish River. With that encounter, the Afrikaners faced the Xhosa across a frontier line, and the Xhosa were too numerous to be easily moved aside. They traded across that frontier for guns and horses, which made it possible for them to meet the Europeans on nearly equal terms in a long series of wars beginning about 1780 and lasting into the 1850s. Though the Europeans pushed forward the frontier of European control in short stages, a relatively dense African population remained on the land. The easy advance of the trekboers came to an end—at least in that direction.

The pastoral trekboers of the frontier districts were already in chronic conflict with Cape authorities. They resented political domination by the city, but they also needed metropolitan help to push the frontier line forward against African resistance. These tensions became still more serious when control of the Cape passed from Holland to Britain during the Napoleonic Wars. The British, like their Dutch predecessors, wanted to restrict frontier expansion. They also established tighter control of the frontier districts under British officials, who were resented on national grounds and because they occasionally acted to protect the rights of Khoikhoi servants.

By the mid-1830s, frontier resentment was nearing the crisis stage. When Britain emancipated the slaves in all parts of the empire in 1834, it seemed to the Afrikaners that Britain was determined to overthrow the social patterns of Cape society—based as it was on white supremacy. Then came the Mfecane. The Xhosa on the frontier were not directly affected, but word came through from the north that the high veld and central Natal were abandoned by their inhabitants and open to white settlement. With that, trekboers from the eastern Cape formed organized parties of migrants and began crossing the colonial boundaries toward the north. This movement, centering on the decade after 1835, is known as the Great Trek. It was partly an act of rebellion or flight from British rule, partly a search for new land to settle, and partly an effort to reestablish the kind of society the trekboers had come to value—a society where Europeans ruled and other races were kept in "proper" subordination.

The Voortrekkers who left Cape Colony were relatively few in number, but they gained a distinct military advantage from by-passing the Xhosa on the old eastern frontier. The Africans on the high veld were disorganized and scattered by the Mfecane. Large areas had been depopulated as smaller groups fled the ferocity of Shaka's army. The domino effect of war, flight, and famine caused the death of large numbers of Africans and left others in a vulnerable position. Guns were rare both there and in Natal, and the trekkers were skilled in the tactics of mounted infantry that could concentrate, strike a blow, and then retire. It was therefore comparatively easy to defeat the Zulu and lay claim to the temporarily depopulated lands of central Natal. On the high veld, the trekkers also defeated the Ndebele and drove them off toward the Limpopo. Since the British declined to push their authority north of the Orange River, the trekkers were free to set up two republics on the high veld, though the British did move forward and annex Natal to protect the strategic control of the sea lanes.

The Great Trek not only led to secondary empire, it also changed the nature of Afro-European relations in southern Africa. Where the old Cape Colony had been culturally Western, both Natal and the Boer republics remained African in culture. The Europeans were strong enough to assert their over-all dominance and to seize part of the land, but they were only a small minority within the territory they claimed. Most African communities remained intact and self-governing in local affairs for many decades. In the longer run, some Africans took on aspects of the Western way of life, but whole communities were not shattered and assimilated as the Khoikhoi had been in the eighteenth century. South Africa therefore became a plural society with African and Western culture existing side by side.

Secondary Empire from the North

In these decades of the Mfecane and the Great Trek in southern Africa, another secondary empire was rising in the Nilotic sudan. Its origins lay in the Ottoman Empire, which had fallen behind the technological progress of western Europe. After one sultan had tried unsuccessfully to modernize the army, Muhammad 'Ali, a military leader in the Ottoman province of Egypt, led a successful revolt, seized control of the province, proclaimed himself pasha (or provincial governor), and brought in mercenaries to train a new army in the latest techniques of European warfare. Though he recognized formal Ottoman sovereignty, Muhammad 'Ali's military modernization made him virtually independent as ruler of Egypt, and at one point he almost gained control of the whole empire.

As a side line to the Egyptian drive for power in the eastern Mediterranean, Muhammad 'Ali also turned south toward the Nilotic sudan. The most important state on the Nile beyond the Sahara was the sultanate of Funj, founded in the fifteenth century; to its west lay Kordofan, a province of the larger state of Darfur. Neither Darfur nor Funj was a match for the modernized Egyptian army. Both were easily conquered in 1821. Funj and Kordofan were annexed to become the nucleus of a sub-Saharan secondary empire. Over the next half century, Egyptian forces using Western methods, often under the command of Western mercenaries, gradually extended the size of Egypt's empire. They established a measure of control over the Arab and Beja nomads of the desert, pushed down the Red Sea as far as Massawa in present-day Ethiopia, up the Nile into northern Uganda and a corner of Zaire, and westward into Darfur. They tried and failed in the 1870s to conquer Abyssinia as well, but the Egyptian secondary empire was nevertheless the largest territory under one rule up to this point in African history.

Perhaps because of this vast extent of territory, the administrative structure was always fragile. The Egyptians could profit from borrowed technology to conquer almost anywhere they chose, but they lacked the means to establish effective day-by-day administrative control in the outlying areas. This was especially true in the far south and southwest, where the principal Egyptian interest was the slave trade. Egypt used slaves as domestic servants, occasionally as agricultural workers, but especially as soldiers. Recruitment by purchase was an ancient Turkish military practice which Muhammad 'Ali retained, even though he turned to Western tactics and weapons. On the fringes of the sudanic empire, therefore, the Egyptian presence was little more than a series of fortified slave-trading posts, and these were often controlled by private merchants who maintained their own armies—in effect, a secondary empire within a secondary empire.

The regime thus suffered from one of the fundamental weaknesses of secondary empires in general—modern weapons gave power, but they gave power indiscriminately. An individual on the fringes, in command of a private army, could easily detach himself from Egyptian power and set out on his own course of empire building. The most spectacular example is that of Rabih

Zubayr, who began as a slave trader in the Bahr al-Ghazal region in the 1880s. He then set out with a force armed with modern rifles and marched to the west, fighting and raiding a variety of African states as he moved. By the 1890s he had reached the vicinity of Lake Chad, more than twelve hundred miles from his point of departure. There he destroyed the ancient empire of Borno and set himself up as ruler of an extensive kingdom until he was finally hunted down and killed by the French in 1900.

By that time the Egyptian empire in the sudan had disappeared. Secondary empires were marked by a number of peculiarities and weaknesses. Since the ultimate source of their power was in Europe, not in their own technological capacity, the secondary empires were fundamentally unstable—at the mercy of any European state that chose to bring even greater power to bear. In the middle decades of the nineteenth century, however, European states preferred to avoid direct annexation and administration of weaker states overseas. They preferred the kind of indirect control sometimes called "informal empire." The weaker state was allowed to retain its formal sovereignty, but only on condition that it follow certain policies dictated from Europe. Part of the price Egypt paid for its military modernization was a growing debt owed to European bankers. When, in the 1870s, Egypt was unable to repay or meet interest payments, an international commission dominated by France and Britain took control of Egyptian finances, treating the country as though it were a private firm put in receivership. This kind of informal empire was almost as unstable as secondary empire, since the threat of force could easily turn into active intervention. This happened to Egypt in the 1880s when Britain took over effective control of the Egyptian government, even though Egypt continued in theory as an autonomous province of the Ottoman Empire.

When Britain acquired effective control over Egypt in 1882, it also acquired responsibility for Egypt's secondary empire in the sudan, which was just then at the point of collapse. In 1881, only a few months before the British intervention, a religious leader, Sheikh Muhammad 'Ahmad ibn 'Abdallah, declared himself to be the expected Islamic savior, or Mahdi. He rose in revolt against the Egyptian authorities in Khartoum, capitalizing on the unpopular policies of Western officials in Egyptian service and on a variety of other grievances, both secular and religious. By 1885, the revolt succeeded in capturing Khartoum and the whole core area of the Egyptian sudan. Muhammad 'Ahmad then set up a new Islamic state. For the British in Cairo, this posed a serious problem. It would have been possible to call on enough military power to destroy the new state, but the British had come to Egypt to collect old debts, not incur new ones. The caliphate in the sudan was therefore allowed to stand for the time being, and it lasted until 1898, when the British were finally impelled by new considerations to go ahead with the conquest. Meanwhile, the fringe areas of the Egyptian secondary empire fell to local control.

The Net of Secondary Empire in East Africa

Secondary-empire building took a somewhat different form in East Africa. During the eighteenth century, new currents of trade began to move in the East African interior. Direct trade from the coast began to reach inland as far as Lake Victoria in return for ivory and, for the first time, a significant export trade in slaves. The pioneers of these long-distance trade routes were people from the interior, especially the Nyamwezi of central Tanzania, but they were soon joined by Swahili and Afro-Arabs from the coast, who pushed their caravans inland after about 1800. The seaborne portion of this growing trade fell more and more under the control of Oman, in Arabia, which had already developed important interests on the East African coast during the eighteenth century. In the early nineteenth century, the Omani were able to take advantage of a British concern to have a strong and friendly maritime power help police the waters of the Persian Gulf and Arabian Sea. Britain was willing to supply financial and technical assistance and to sell modern warships that made Oman the strongest Asian naval power short of Japan. In the 1830s Sultan Seyyid Said moved his capital from Arabia to Zanzibar, and from Zanzibar it was possible to dominate the range of coastal ports from north of Mombasa down to Kilwa.

Zanzibari power was based on exploitation of a commercial system, not merely on British support in becoming a secondary maritime power. The islands of Zanzibar and Pemba were ideally suited for clove plantations, which could be developed with supplies of slave labor drawn from southeastern Africa. Other caravans could also bring ivory, which found its way into world trade along with the clove crop. To meet increasing demand for ivory and slaves, Zanzibari and Swahili traders from the coast reached farther and farther into the interior. By 1830 Tabora in west-central Tanzania had become the key Zanzibari trading post in a network that reached on to Ujiji on Lake Tanganyika by 1840, northward into present-day Uganda by the 1850s, and then still farther west across Lake Tanganyika into the whole eastern third of Zaire.

The Zanzibari trade network in the interior of East Africa was a secondary empire, based on Zanzibar's access to the latest European firearms, but it was a special form of secondary empire. Guns were used to protect the trade routes, on occasion to encourage warfare in the interior so as to increase the supply of slaves for sale, but not to establish Zanzibari rule over territory or people. Political control was limited to trading-post enclaves. The Zanzibari "empire" was thus a trading-post empire—an economic operation equivalent to the North American or Siberian fur-trade empires of the seventeenth or eighteenth centuries—and it succeeded admirably, from a Zanzibari point of view, until the 1860s.

It was then that Zanzibar began to encounter difficulties with its patron, Great Britain. Having suppressed the slave trade in the Atlantic, the British were anxious to suppress the East African slave trade as well. If Zanzibar acquiesced, it would lose control over the thousands of Zanzibari traders scattered through the interior, since these men lived by the slave trade and were hardly likely to abandon it until they were forced to do so. But acceptance of British dictates would protect the clove plantations and increase Zanzibari control over the coastal cities. In 1873 Sultan Bargash seized one horn of this dilemma and agreed to an anti-slave-trade treaty. In return, he received British assistance in training a modern army, hence tightening his control over the coastal region.

One result of this decision was the detachment of the trading-post empire of the interior. The up-country Zanzibari, and any African states that had managed to arm themselves with modern rifles, began to form their own secondary empires over any neighboring territory they could seize. Dozens of new states sprang up in the 1870s and 1880s. To the north of the principal trade route, Buganda and Bunyoro in present-day Uganda began to build secondary empires of their own. (Since Bunyoro had a common frontier with the Egyptian sphere to the north, a nearly continuous band of secondary empires stretched by this time from the Sahara to the Orange River.) In central and western Tanzania two Nyamwezi warlords, Mirambo-ya-Banhu and Myungu-ya-Mawe, each united a large number of previously independent chiefdoms to create two substantial states. Across the mountains, in the upper Congo basin, a Zanzibari trader called Tippu Tib founded a new state in the region west of Lake Tanganyika, while a Nyamwezi trader, Msiri, created still another in Shaba in southern Zaire.

All of these states were short-lived, but they are important examples of the impact of Western technology as it penetrated into Africa well in advance of Western missionaries or Western colonial

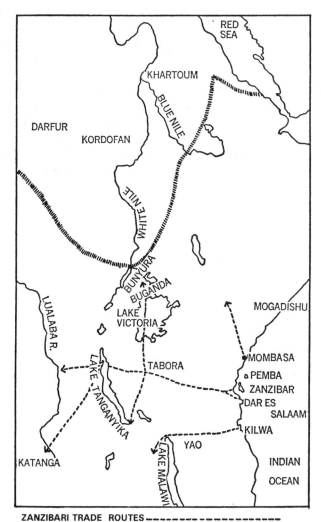

ZANZIBARI TRADE ROUTES ------------------

APPROXIMATE MAXIMUM EXTENT ⁄⁄⁄⁄⁄⁄⁄⁄⁄⁄⁄⁄⁄⁄⁄⁄⁄⁄⁄⁄⁄⁄⁄⁄⁄⁄
OF EGYPTIAN PENETRATION

Figure 11. Secondary empires in eastern Africa.

rulers. It is futile, but intriguing nonetheless, to speculate on the African states' possible development if they had been left to their own devices for a century or so. Some, like Buganda, had modern governments as early as the 1890s and began to adopt elements of Western and Islamic culture and technology. Others might have done the same, and large parts of Africa might possibly have taken a course toward modernization without colonial rule—as did Thailand or Japan. As it was, they had no such choice. Within two or, at most, three decades after many of these states had been founded, the Europeans invaded and annexed east-central Africa to their colonial empires. Even Zanzibar, which chose the road toward modernization under British aegis in 1873, was caught up in the rivalries of the European powers and accepted a British protectorate in 1890.

16

COMMERCE AND ISLAM
THE DUAL REVOLUTION IN WEST AFRICA

During the century from about 1780 to 1880, West Africa passed through its own period of dramatic change, with a pattern and style that contrast sharply with those of secondary empires to the east. Part of the explanation may be the slave trade itself. The sale of slaves had introduced firearms on a wide scale—a form of inoculation against secondary-empire building. Since the military technology was widely distributed, West Africa, rather than being convulsed by a sequence of wars like the Mfecane, passed through a process of adjustment to the end of the slave trade. The savanna belt also passed through a simultaneous process of readjustment to the eralier and still incomplete introduction of Islam. As so often in African history, part of the impetus for these important changes came from the intercommunicating zone outside Africa and part came from the internal change in the special conditions of quasi-isolation.

Islamic Reform

The introduction of Islam into West Africa was a slow process—one that had already been under way for a thousand years before the revolutionary upheavals of the nineteenth century. The barrier of the Sahara had not prevented the spread of Islam, but it had a profound influence on the nature and form that Islam took, once it was accepted in West Africa.

In other places where Islam became dominant, it was often introduced by conquest and spread through state influence. In West Africa (as in Southeast Asia) it came through the individual efforts of merchants who happened to be Muslim and chose to act as unpaid missionaries. For the most part, these North African merchants were not members of the learned class, the 'ulama of the North African cities. Their version was seldom the Sunni orthodoxy of the urban elite but rather less orthodox doctrines preserved on the northern fringes of the Sahara.

Over the centuries, these doctrines were modified by new influences. Where the institutions of an Islamic state were rarely present to articulate religious life, the religious brotherhoods took on much of the role that would have belonged in North Africa to the urban 'ulama. The brotherhoods (turuq, sing. tarīqa) first became important to Islam in the eleventh century, with the growing influence of mysticism. Hundreds of different orders sprang up, each grouping together followers of a particular religious leader—followers who accepted his way of achieving a sense of personal communion with God. Only a few turuq crossed the Sahara, but of those that did, the most important was the Qadirīyya, an order founded in eleventh-century Baghdad. It grew in time to become one most orthodox and broadly tolerant, as well as the largest, in the Islamic world.

The Qadirīyya was especially well suited to the religious condition of West Africa. The mystical element of the Islamic religion helped to make an effective tool for enforcing the Muslim law where the state was either unable or unwilling to do so. In this connection, it is important to remember that Islam is far more secular than Christianity. While both look forward to a life after death, Islam also aims at using the law to improve the moral quality of life on earth. All Muslims have a religious obligation to obey the law and to see that it is properly enforced on others. While some West African states embraced Islam as the official court religion, few if any tried to enforce Islamic law or to insist on the conversion of the whole population. Although the mass of the people continued to follow one of the traditional religions. Islamic elements could easily creep into traditional religions and commonly did. At the same time, in the absence of a clerical class closely associated with the power of the state, it was equally easy for those who considered themselves good Muslims to incorporate many pre-Islamic practices and beliefs.

This is not to say that well-educated clerics, like the leaders of the Qadirīyya, were always tolerant of unorthodoxy. On the contrary, many were profoundly disturbed by the condition of Islam, but they were rarely able to make their political influence felt. As a minority, even where nominal Muslims might be a majority, they tended to seek safety for themselves within their own community, and orthodoxy through the brotherhoods. At times, it was possible to secure the right of internal self-government for the Muslim community, and Muslim groups with special privileges were found up and down the trade routes. Creating Muslim enclaves for self-protection, however, made it harder to convert others to Islam. But Allah's command to wage holy war, in both a physical and spiritual sense, was not altogether forgotten. It was recalled with ever greater frequency from the seventeenth century onward—not only against genuine pagans, but also against rulers who were only lukewarm in the faith or who tolerated pagan practices.

The Fulbe

These recurrent calls for holy war were more often internal than external. That is, they sought to overthrow rulers who were too secular and to substitute theocratic government. Only after a theocratic state had been created was the call turned outward toward the conquest and forcible conversion of non-Muslim peoples. It may seem surprising, then, that a very high proportion of these jihads, or holy wars, also contained an ethnic or national element. All of the most prominent leaders of the large revolts were Fulbe (sing. Pulo), a nationality that speaks the Fula language and originated in Fuuta Tooro on the middle Senegal River, though they are found today (as they were in the eighteenth and nineteenth centuries) scattered throughout the savanna belt of West Africa from Senegal to northern Cameroon.

It is not surprising that the Fulbe were often associated with Islam. Their homeland is in the far north of the savanna country, where the Senegal River makes a swing to the north near the edge of the desert. The banks of the river have long been capable of supporting an unusually dense population, based on irrigation agriculture. The early Fulbe were therefore among the most northerly of dense populations in West Africa, and they were among the first to accept Islam. Indeed, one Arabic word for a black muslim is Takruri, derived from Takrur, the Arabic word for Fuuta Tooro.

Several theories have been advanced to explain the Fulbe diaspora which produced their present spread from one end of West Africa to the other. Today, the descendants of the emigrant Fulbe far outnumber those of Fuuta Tooro itself. The most reasonable hypothesis at the present state of knowledge is based on the ecological peculiarities of the Senegal Valley. The people along the river are sedentary farmers, but the land to the north and south of the river is well suited to grazing during the rainy season which lasts from June through September. In the distant past, some of the Berber pastoralists of the Sahara fringe apparently detached themselves from the patterns of nomadic life and began to return each dry season to the perennial supply of water along the Senegal. In time, they intermarried with the sedentary Fulbe, producing an element in the general Fulbe population that has a partly European appearance; this physical type is somewhat more common among the pastoral than among the sedentary Fulbe. All Fulbe nevertheless speak the same language and share most cultural features.

Once the pattern of transhumant pastoralism was established alongside sedentary farming on the riverbanks, the problem of periodic dry periods remained. If the rains failed, pastoralists were driven far off to the south in search of wet-season pastures. At times, they must have found themselves unable to return for the customary dry season near the Senegal. As a result, they were forced to seek a new dry-season base somewhere else, while continuing the transhumant northward move each wet season. Given the annual north-south migration, it was easy to drift eastward as well, over a period of years. Since the Fulbe were expert cattle keepers, they were usually welcome among sedentary populations, though their semi-nomadic life tended to preserve much of the original Fulbe language and culture.

A second occupational group among the Fulbe also tended to travel widely. These were the Islamic clerics who were literate and skilled as merchants and makers of charms; these skills made them readily employable elsewhere. They, too, often settled down away from home to become a permanent community of Muslim teachers living in an alien society. Still other Fulbe of the noble or warrior class also emigrated, perhaps because the pastoralists and clerics had already set the pattern and established emigrant Fulbe communities that might welcome them. By the seventeenth century, political conflict in Fuuta Tooro normally ended in the *fergo*, or emigration, of the losing faction and its supporters. They often tried to settle somewhere in the vicinity to wait for a change of fortune, but many kept moving and permanently joined other Fulbe communities.

The result was a network of Fulbe scholars in West Africa towns, who were in touch with one another and shared a common nationality, language, and religion. They were not the only group of wandering scholars, but, unlike the others, they shared the nationality, language, and often the religion of the pastoral Fulbe, who might be a large minority of the rural population almost anywhere in West Africa. Thus, in the event of conflict between the Muslim community and a secular ruler, the Fulbe scholars had the possibility of rallying the Muslim community on religious grounds and their pastoral kinsmen on national grounds to create an alliance that stood some chance of success in battle.

The great religious revolutions of the nineteenth century were based on this tradition of an Islamic jihad under Fulbe leadership that went back at least as far as the seventeenth century. The first recorded jihad among the Fulbe came in Fuuta Tooro itself in the 1670s, though the leadership in this case was partly Fulbe and partly *zwaya*, clerical nomadic tribes of Berber extraction in southern Mauritania. In this instance, the clerical party managed to hold Fuuta Tooro for only a few years before it was defeated and the secular dynasty returned to office. A second and more successful attempt was made in the 1690s, when a Pulo cleric named Malik Sy founded the *almamate* of Bundu just beyond Fuuta's eastern frontier. This was the first of a series of dynasties that proclaimed their theocratic intentions by taking the title of "Almami" in Fula from the Arabic *al-Imam* and denoting religious rather than simply political leadership. The second almamate followed a generation later, when in the 1720s Fulbe in the Fuuta Jaalo highlands started a successful revolution under clerics who were also kinsmen of Malik Sy. In the 1770s the example was followed by a third almamate, this time in Fuuta Tooro.

The Nineteenth-Century Jihads

While the first three almamates set a precedent, they were small kingdoms that were (or soon became) mainly Fulbe. The nineteenth-century jihads, however, led to political structures that rivaled the scale of earlier empires like Mali or Songhai. The earliest in time began in Hausaland of present-day Nigeria, an area that had never before been united as a single state. Between the old centers of political power in Borno near Lake Chad and Songhai in the Niger Valley lay a region dominated by the Hausa city-states. In each of these, a walled town served as a commercial and political center and ruled over the surrounding countryside. At various times in the past, either Borno or Songhai had been able to incorporate some of the Hausa cities and establish its general hegemony, but neither Borno nor Songhai was especially powerful at the beginning of the nineteenth century. The main centers of power were the Hausa states themselves, especially Zamfara, Katsina, and Gobir.

Islamic reform was already an issue in several of the Hausa cities in the last decades of the eighteenth century, and the spark that set off a general jihad came from Usuman dan Fodio, a Pulo cleric whose activities centered on Gobir. Many of the clerical class, both Fulbe and non-Fulbe, shared his distress at the laxity of Hausa rulers, who claimed to be Muslim but made no effort to enforce Muslim law, and the clerics were in communication through the network of Qadirīyya. In 1804 Usuman dan Fodio called for a holy war against Gobir. Some Hausa Muslims joined him, but the greater part of his military strength came from the pastoral Fulbe and the Tuareg nomads of the desert to the north. By 1808 Usuman dan Fodio was in command of Gobir.

Even before this success, religious revolt broke out in other Hausa city-states. In each case, the leadership tended to be drawn from the clerical Fulbe, though the rebel alliance differed considerably in different regions. Usuman dan Fodio was not the direct leader of these additional jihads, but the leaders recognized his spiritual authority and over-all leadership—largely because of his immense religious prestige. By the 1830s the rebels had succeeded in conquering most of what later became northern Nigeria and northern Cameroon, and the movement spilled over into non-Hausa states like Nupe and parts of the old Yoruba empire of Oyo. The resultant empire was organized as a series of emirates, each of them ruled by descendants of the original leaders of the jihad. Each recognized the caliphate of Usuman dan Fodio's heirs, with its capital at the new city of Sokoto. Thus the Fulbe clerics became a new ruling class in Hausaland, and they were able to extend their power under British rule and to keep much of it into the post-colonial period.

A second but separate jihad with similar inspiration and a similar following was led by Sheikh Ahmadu Lobbo of Maasina, beginning about 1818. But the region of Maasina (in the Niger basin upstream from Timbuktu) was very different from Hausaland. Here the Fulbe herdsmen were a majority of the population. The holy war was therefore an assertion of clerical control over the Fulbe themselves, rather than a Fulbe and clerical conquest of non-Fulbe states that were incompletely Muslim. The result was nevertheless the establishment of a second new caliphate, this one centered on the newly founded city of Hamdullahi, which dominated the Niger Valley from Timbuktu on the north to Jenné in the south. Sheikh Ahmadu had less prestige than Usuman dan Fodio in the field of Islamic scholarship, but he achieved more of the declared aims of religious reform, perhaps because he led a single revolt, rather than assuming leadership over a series of quasi-independent revolutions.

A generation later, the third of the major Islamic empires was founded still farther to the west. While it rested in part on the inspiration and example of the predecessors, its organizational base was no longer the Qadirīyya, but a new order, the Tijanyya, recently founded in North Africa. The founder of this Tijani Empire was Sheikh Umar Tal, a Pulo cleric whose original home was Fuuta Tooro. After making the pilgrimage to Mecca, he established himself in 1839 on the frontier of the old Fulbe and Islamic state of Fuuta Jaalo. From this base he began to recruit followers and import European arms from the coast. By 1848 he was ready to launch his holy war, first pushing northward toward his own homeland in Fuuta Tooro. Though he failed in his effort to seize Fuuta, he attracted many thousands of followers from among the Fuutanke, who departed in a great fergo toward the east, thus providing Sheikh Umar with his principal support in the conquest of the pagan states

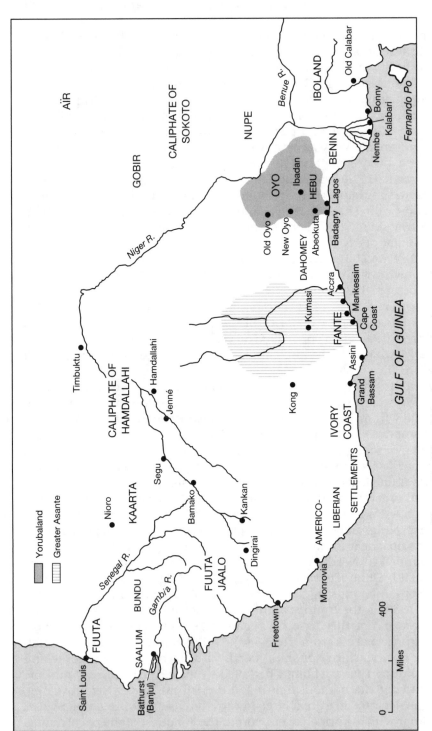

Figure 12. West Africa in the early nineteenth century.

of Kaatta and Segu and the caliphate of Hamdullahi. By the time of Sheikh Umar's death in 1864, he had established the largest of all the new Islamic empires in West Africa.

Like the secondary empires elsewhere on the continent, the Islamic empires were submerged by European conquest at the end of the century. They nevertheless had a profound influence on the history of West Africa. Not only did they remake the political map; they also established Islam more firmly than ever before, setting the stage for its spectacular growth in the twentieth century. In spite of the hiatus of colonial rule, many members of the religious and political elite in West Africa today belong to families which trace their power and position to the role of an ancestor in one of the jihads.

Commercial Revolution on the Coast

In a narrow sense, the commercial revolution was simply the substitution of other products for slaves as Africa's principal export. In the broader context of Atlantic history, however, it was the African manifestation of a much larger and more diverse set of political, economic, and social changes. The American and French revolutions, with an ideology drawn from the rights-of-man philosophy of the Enlightenment, marked the first steps toward the end of slavery in the Americas. The Christian revival in the early nineteenth century brought a new humanitarian concern and a new burst of missionary zeal. The Industrial Revolution produced a stream of new products in search of markets, and at prices that declined steadily. It also brought a new demand for tropical products, especially fats and oils for food, lighting, lubrication, and soap. In military affairs, Europe became more powerful in comparison with non-industrial societies like those of Africa. By 1850, medical discoveries made it safer than ever before for Europeans to visit the African coast; the death rate of Europeans in Africa dropped by 75 percent between the first and second half of the century, even before the true cause of malaria or yellow fever was known. All of these factors were, of course, part of the background of the conquest of Africa after 1880, but Europe had not yet decided to conquer Africa. The dominant European aims in the pre-colonial century were to end the slave trade, to increase "legitimate trade," and to establish European influence through informal empire and conversion to Christianity.

To achieve any or all of these goals required the physical presence of many more Europeans in Africa than was necessitated by the slave trade. In the French sphere, the old slave-trade posts in Senegal became more substantial bases for the trade in gum from the Sahara and peanuts from the immediate hinterland. In the 1820s, the French reestablished an up-river fort on the Senegal at Bakel, reached by the newly invented steamboat. In the 1840s they built new fortified trading posts in Gabon and on the Ivory Coast. The British meanwhile returned to the Gambia, which they had abandoned, and built the new town of Bathurst (now Banjul) as a British commercial enclave at the mouth of the river. Sierra Leone was established in the 1790s as a settlement colony, though the settlers were mainly African-American loyalists displaced by the American Revolution. The Gold Coast trading forts gradually became a center for influence in the hinterland. By mid-century British steamboats were operating on the lower Niger, and British merchants were especially active in the palm-oil trade along the coast of present-day Nigeria. Given the disparity of power, a larger European presence meant more frequent European intervention in African affairs, even though actual annexation was limited, and the web of informal influence surrounding the Western enclaves grew broader and tighter as the 1880s approached.

Within Africa, the commercial revolution brought dramatic changes, at least to some regions. The long-distance routes of the slave trade were diverted to internal markets, as the export trade dropped and then disappeared. Since the new "legitimate" exports were harder to transport, their production was concentrated near the coast or the riverside. In these restricted areas, the peanuts of the Senegambia, timber in Sierra Leone, and palm products from the Gold Coast to Cameroon brought a new level of affluence to the peasantry and to new groups of traders, who had not been in a position to profit from the slave trade. Income from the new commerce also increased progressively through the first two-thirds of the century, as the prices paid for European manufactures declined while those of the African exports remained steady or rose slightly. In effect, some of the benefits of European industrialization were passed to African economies through this favorable shift in the terms of trade—even though that shift was to be reversed in the final third of the century.

Fringe Westernization

The new intensity of contact on the West African coast brought a conscious effort to change African cultures as well—from the Europeans in the form of Christian missions, and from some

Africans who wanted to modernize their societies by borrowing Western technology. Africans near the slave-trade posts had already begun to shift toward some aspects of Western culture, and the pace of change accelerated in the nineteenth century. The "French" traders in the Senegal Valley and southward along the coast of present-day Guinea were actually Africans from Saint-Louis and Gorée, some with one or more European ancestors. The citizens of these Senegalese towns were recognized as French citizens in 1848, and they later sent elected representatives to the National Assembly in Paris. An equivalent group of Anglo-African merchants grew up in Gambia, the Gold Coast ports, Lagos, and Calabar in Nigeria.

Sierra Leone, however, was the principal center of culture change in the British sphere. The colony of black Americans began to receive new settlers after the legal abolition of the slave trade, as British cruisers of the anti-slavery patrol began to unload cargoes of recaptured slaves. Missionaries paid special attention, because the liberated Africans were associated with their humanitarian campaign against the slave trade. As a result of their proselytizing and educational work, combined with the normal pattern of rapid culture change among those who are uprooted and set down in a strange community, the liberated Africans of many origins rapidly formed a new group known as Creoles, partly African and partly Western in culture.

Since the mountainous peninsula of the original colony was not well suited to agriculture, many Creoles turned to trade with the hinterland and then to coastal trade by sea as well. During the 1840s, Creole merchants from Sierra Leone, especially those of Yoruba origin, began to settle permanently in Lagos and Badagry in Western Nigeria. Others moved into the Yoruba hinterland, and sent for missionaries to join them. By mid-century a Creole Christian clergy had come into existence, and many of the missionaries to Nigeria and elsewhere along the coast were Sierra Leonean. After the British annexation of Lagos in 1861, Creoles served as officials of the British colony.

Other returned slaves from the Americas also brought back Western cultural influences, as they too found it possible to resettle in Africa. Ex-slaves from the United States began to settle in Liberia in 1822. In the 1840s, ex-slaves from Brazil began to arrive in present-day western Nigeria, Dahomey, and Togo. They were generally less well educated than the Creoles from Sierra Leone, but they became important in commerce and in the skilled trades. By the 1880s they dominated the trade inland from the French post in Dahomey (now the People's Republic of Benin), just as the Creoles dominated that of Lagos. Even today, the older houses in Western

Nigeria show the influence of Brazilian architecture, brought back by the returned ex-slaves. Nor was Western influence limited to the European enclaves. Both the Fante states of the Gold Coast and Abeokuta in Nigeria experimented with modernized constitutions under the influence of Western-educated Africans, and other African authorities sometimes sought Western technical assistance.

It is hard to know where this process might have led, if there had been no European conquest. However, the European *did* conquer Africa, and many tendencies of the pre-colonial century were reversed. With the colonial period, Europeans reasserted their authority over the missionary movement. Europeans replaced most of the Africans who had held high posts in government administration, medical services, and the like. The African middle class of traders in Senegal, Sierra Leone, Liberia, and elsewhere found it increasingly hard to compete with large European firms in the export trade to Europe, though Africans continued to fill the role of middlemen between African producers and European firms. In the colonial setting, the Western impact increased immensely, but with Africans playing a diminished role as responsible participants in the process.

17

FORMS AND CONDITIONS
OF CONQUEST

n retrospect, the European conquest of Africa looked inevitable. It was part of a worldwide pattern of annexation reaching a highwater mark in about 1920. By that time almost the whole world was under the formal or informal control of the European powers, or ruled by overseas Europeans. The non-Western countries that escaped formal annexation did so only by a process of defensive modernization like that of Siam, Turkey, or Japan—or else by the fortuitous circumstance of falling between rival European empires as a buffer zone that was prudently left neutral, though it might be honeycombed by several varieties of informal empire. Circumstances of this kind preserved the independence of Afghanistan, Iran, China, and Ethiopia. In the perspective of world history, it is hard to imagine a combination of circumstances that would have prevented or delayed the European annexation of Africa.

From an African perspective, however, the final conquest was both sudden and unexpected. The European powers had been satisfied with slow encroachment here and there during the pre-colonial century. African isolation was coming to an end more rapidly than ever before. In West Africa, moderation within the coastal trading enclaves, and beyond, suggested a satisfactory course and direction of change. Most of the secondary empires in eastern Africa looked substantial enough in the 1870s—substantial enough, that is, to serve Europe's interest in stability and expanding trade, without calling for the expensive commitments to imperial administration. For that matter, Zanzibar, the Boer republics, and the Egyptian sudan were already within the sphere of "informal empire." But then, after 1880, the whole structure came apart, and the Europeans fell into a frenzy of competitive annexation.

The Background

Some causes of the sudden change lay in Europe, others in Africa. Underlying both was the continued progress of European technology. The military hardware that had made possible the earlier secondary empires was replaced by still newer and more effective weapons. By the 1880s machine guns and light artillery capable of firing explosive shells gave the Europeans an incomparable advantage over any African opponent. Medical progress meant that European soldiers and administrators could be sent to tropical Africa without the old constraint of astronomical death rates from disease. Naturally, none of these changes could *cause* the conquest of Africa, but they slashed the price of any military action a European government might choose to consider, European economic growth made the cost smaller still in terms of resources available.

Other changes in Europe made empire building seem desirable— at least to some. England, with the lion's share of informal empire and African trade, was content with the established pattern of influence. But France, having lost the Franco-Prussian War in 1870–71, had reason enough in wounded national pride and the web of international rivalries to seek spectacular victories overseas. Still other nations, seeing Britain as the economic leader of Europe and also in possession of the largest overseas empire, could easily assume that empire brought wealth—a point that historians now believe to have been true in exceptional cases only.

In Africa, the low cost of informal European control over secondary empire was advantageous. However, secondary empires failed to maintain relatively peaceful control over their territory. Political instability, in European eyes, was bad for business. Some of the secondary empires began to break up in the 1870s, when Zanzibar lost control over the East African interior. At the beginning of the 1880s, Egypt became hard to manage, with the result that Britain took firm control of Cairo. Cairo in turn lost its control of Khartoum and the sub-Saharan secondary empire. In these two instances, the Europeans found that the wreck of a secondary empire lay beyond the remedy of informal control. Only reconquest and direct administration would serve. Both the Nilotic sudan and East Africa fell to European conquest as the pressures of competitive annexation and international rivalry mounted during the 1880s and 1890s.

In the Boer republics, the situation was somewhat different. After an attempted British annexation of Transvaal in the 1870s, British informal control became very weak, but the British were not concerned until after 1884, when the gold of the Witwatersrand became known. These deposits were the largest ever discovered, but to mine ore of this quality in this location required heavy capital expenditure. The mining companies that put up the capital were mainly British, and the companies wanted a more docile government than Transvaal could supply. Tensions between the mining community and the Transvaal secondary empire were a major cause of the Anglo-Boer War of 1899–1902, after which the British finally annexed both Transvaal and the Orange Free State, as they had already annexed the Egyptian sudan and parts of the Zanzibari sphere in East Africa. Thus, the major secondary empires fell to full European control, either because they were too fragile or because they were unwilling to bow to informal pressure.

Similar temptation to change informal to formal empire existed in West Africa as well. Central governments in Europe were often reluctant to annex African territory, but the Europeans in the trade enclaves were tempted to use force whenever they came into conflict with weak or recalcitrant African states. Whenever diplomacy became difficult, as it often did across lines of cultural difference, it was all too easy to shoot first and consult the home government afterward. From the African side, European power presented a dilemma. A strong African state was likely to use its strength to protect its control of trade in the face of European pressure. If it did so, its resistance to European demands could be an invitation to conquest. If, on the other hand, it was weak, unable to maintain peace and order or to keep open the flow of trade, that too could be an excuse for a European take-over. The line between these two dangers was very thin indeed. A halting encroachment had been spreading outward from the British and French trade enclaves for some decades before 1880, but in the next two decades encroachment turned to conscious conquest sanctioned by the home government.

Competitive Annexation

The first round of competitive annexations in western Africa was touched off by a series of French moves in 1879–82—a projected railroad inland from the upper Senegal into the empire founded by Sheikh Umar, seizure of new trading posts along the Gulf of Guinea, and some territorial annexations north of the lower Congo. Diplomatic historians still dispute among themselves as to which of these moves was most important in alarming other powers; the crucial fact is that they were alarmed. Germany and Portugal joined France in annexing African territory for fear of being left out, and Britain shifted from informal to formal control for the same reason.

From that point on, the European annexation took place on two separate spheres—one in Europe, and one in Africa. In Europe, competitive annexation led to a series of diplomatic crises. After each new crisis, the powers bargained and agreed among themselves, drew lines on maps indicating what territory each should be allowed to conquer, and then settled down to prepare their bargaining position for the next crisis a few years later. Looking back, this whole process has a ring of unreality, as diplomats met and assigned one another sovereignty over peoples they had barely heard of, most of whom had never seen a European. It was nonetheless important for the future of Africa. The lines drawn on maps in the European capitals became the boundaries of the European colonies, and these boundaries in turn became the frontiers of modern African states.

This map work was mainly completed between 1882 and 1902, while the actual conquest took place in Africa itself. During the first phase, the Europeans marched small armies here and there to establish their claims. They also fought wars against major African states, and in some cases the conquest was drawn out over a period of years. But military victory was only the first step toward creating a colony. Administrations capable of governing followed later, and their main framework was barely completed on the eve of the First World War. Several of the more isolated African states were not conquered until the 1920s, and a few fringe areas were left until the 1930s.

A New Generation of Secondary Empires

While most of the first generation of secondary empires collapsed faster than did African states with a long-standing tradition of loyalty and support, a new group of secondary empires came into existence during the conquest period. One of these was the Congo Independent State, a private creation by King Leopold of Belgium. He began by organizing an "association" which was actually a regular business firm in the European tradition of corporate enterprise. In Africa, the association began by assuming the powers ordinarily held by a sovereign state. It conquered a part of the Congo basin and succeeded in getting the European powers to recognize its sovereignty. This late-blooming secondary empire lasted from 1884 to 1908, when the Belgian government took it over as an ordinary European colony.

Liberia also acquired most of its present territory during the period of the European conquests. The Americo-Liberian settlers had already gained recognition of their independent status in the middle of the nineteenth century. As Europeans advanced into Africa's interior, the Americo-Liberians also advanced into their own hinterland, conquering the indigenous peoples. The result was a secondary empire, dominated by settlers from America and their descendants, though often under a measure of informal control by the government of the United States. From the point of view of local Africans, the result was hardly different from conquest by Europeans, but Liberia continued to be marked on the maps as "independent" rather than "colonial."

The only traditional African state to survive the general conquest was Ethiopia. The Christian kingdom of Abyssinia had the good fortune to be located at a strategic intersection of imperial rivalries between Britain, France, and Italy—with the natural protection of mountain barriers as well. It also had an especially able leader in Menelik, who ruled from 1889 to 1913 and was able to manipulate international rivalries in the lower Red Sea and Nile Valley in order to acquire modern arms from France. With these, he defeated an Italian invasion in 1896 and went on to conquer the neighboring peoples in the Ethiopian highlands to create the present-day empire of Ethiopia. Like Liberia, this was not merely an African state that kept itself free of European control; it was also a secondary empire built by conquest and maintained by the dominance of the Christian Amhara from the old core area. Though Ethiopia passed through a phase of Italian occupation from 1935 to 1941, that period was too short to be truly comparable to the colonial experience elsewhere.

A final exception to the usual pattern of conquest and colonization is found in southern Africa. The British victory in the Anglo-Boer War was a clear case of a secondary empire defeated by a European power, but the aftermath of the war was different. Within a few years, the British granted the right of self-government to the white minority in the Union of South Africa, which included former Boer republics. This move was partly an effort to conciliate the defeated Boers; the exclusion of non-whites was a concession to the prevalent racism of the times. After the First World War, a similar grant of control over Rhodesian affairs was made to the overseas Europeans in that colony.

Forms and Conditions of Conquest

Given the disparity of military power, the Europeans had no great difficulty conquering the areas they had assigned to one another. But conquest was rarely on the basis of unconditional surrender, giving the victors a free hand to do as they liked. Instead, the pattern of conquest and pacification was enormously complex and variable from one local situation to the next. The form taken by the conquest itself, the implicit or explicit terms of surrender, and fear of rebellion all set limits on the policies the Europeans might follow.

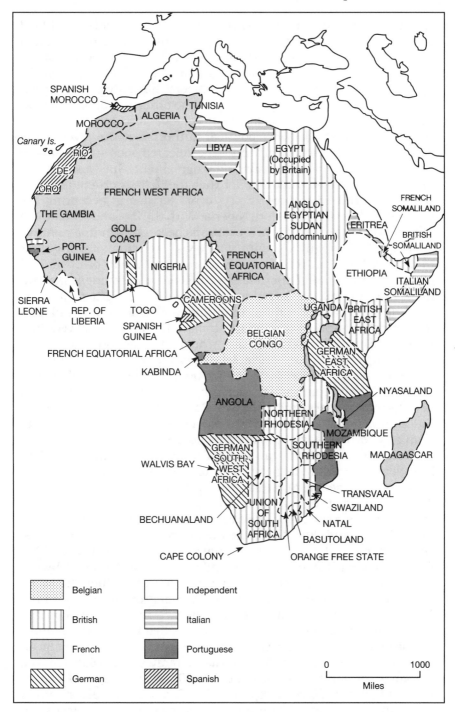

Figure 13. Africa in 1914.

One major determinant was the nature of pre-colonial political structures. Some were as large and powerful as the empire created by Sheikh Umar in the mid-1800s, and ruled at the period of the European conquest by his son, Ahmadu. It was finally conquered by an African army under French officers, but only after a dozen years of intermittent campaigning. At the other end of the political spectrum were stateless societies; these, too, often posed a military problem. With the highest political authority at the level of the village, there was no central army to be defeated once and for all—no central authority to make a surrender agreement. One aspect of this problem is illustrated by the fact that the British ordered no less than five hundred printed treaty forms for use in accepting the surrender of the Ibo in eastern Nigeria. With the Ibo, and with others like the Tiv farther north, the Europeans began by sending punitive expeditions through the country as a way of demonstrating their military power, but this was only a first step. Real "pacification" could come only after they had established a permanent government administration, and this could only be a gradual process. Typically, it was a matter of military patrols and gradually increasing pressure for peaceful submission. In the end, it required some measure of consent on the African side, as individuals and then groups within African society began to see the possibility of using the alien presence for whatever advantage it might offer. The process therefore stretched over a considerable time—at least a decade in most cases, and often two. Chinua Achebe's novel, *Things Fall Apart*, explains the varied Ibo reactions in a single village better than any formal work of history could do.

Other African societies accepted European influence, and then European rule, without the need for military action. In some cases, European rule seemed preferable to other dangers that threatened. The Fante and other peoples on the Gold Coast, for example, were caught between the European forts on the shore and Asante power in the hinterland. For them, the first step, as early as the 1820s, was to bring in the British as military allies against Asante. This led to informal British influence and a partial protectorate by the 1840s—accepted voluntarily by the African leaders, though always with the threat of Asante power in the background. When, in the 1870s, Britain converted the partial protectorate into full control, hardly more than a threat of force was needed to gain acceptance.

Elsewhere, Europeans were sometimes invited in to help an African regime against its internal enemies. In 1858, in the almamate of Bundu (founded in the 1690s by Malik Sy and located in what is now eastern Senegal), Bokar Saada Sy, a descendant of the founder, was one of a number of contestants in a succession crisis. He entered into a military alliance with the French, on terms that left him as an independent monarch. As a result he won control of Bundu until his death in 1885, and the French made him a *Chevalier de la Légion d'Honneur* out of gratitude for his cooperative attitude toward their expansion farther to the east. During his long reign, however, he made enemies—some in Bundu itself and even more in the surrounding countries. In 1886–87 a revolt broke out, aimed partly at the almamate and partly at the French on the upper Senegal. The French suppressed it, using African troops, but Bundu had now become so dependent on foreign support, it was impossible to avoid a French protectorate on French terms. This meant incorporation in the colony of Senegal, but it was not the end of political power for the descendants of Malik Sy. They continued to rule Bundu as the appointed local government right through the colonial period and for some years after Senegal had emerged as an independent republic.

Similar cooperation between the Europeans and an African political faction was an underlying condition of conquest in other African societies as well. One of the best-known examples is Buganda, the African kingdom on the north shore of Lake Victoria, which had turned to secondary-empire building well before the European arrival. In the 1880s and 1890s Buganda was in religious ferment, with competing factions supporting Islam, Protestantism, Catholicism, and the traditional Ganda religion. With British help, the two Christian factions joined together, deposed the king, and seized power for themselves as an oligarchy. In 1900 they made a written agreement with the British, which guaranteed their position within the British colony in return for their support of British rule. Among other things, this agreement turned over more than half of the land in Buganda to less than four thousand of their own followers, and Apolo Kagwa, the principal leader of the Protestant faction, received a British knighthood. Buganda was preserved as a semi-autonomous administrative unit within the larger British protectorate of Uganda, and the descendants of the religious revolutionaries of the 1890s became an aristocracy with effective power over local affairs until the end of the colonial period.

Still another African response was the attempt to amalgamate small African states into a unit large enough and powerful enough to stand off the European invaders. Perhaps the most spectacular effort of this kind was that of Samori Touré, a Malinké from what was to become French Guinea. In about 1870, he first emerged as a local military and political leader. For the first decade or so, he extended his power base by conquest. Then, in 1880, he took the title of Almami and proclaimed himself the head of a new religious revolution in the tradition of Sheikh Umar. Some authorities doubt the seriousness of his concern for Islamic reform, but all agree that he was a military genius. His wars against the French invasion began in 1882 and continued with only a few periods of truce until his final defeat and capture in 1898. As he stood off the French to the north and west, gradually giving way as necessary, his armies continued to conquer African territory to the east until, at the end of his career, his empire stretched across the northern part of the present-day Côte d'Ivoire and Ghana.

Unlike most of the earlier West African jihad leaders, Samori Touré mobilized the economic resources of the country in order to buy European weapons from the coast. In this respect, his conquests were in the pattern of secondary empire, and he also set up his own arms industry on a small scale, gathering together several hundred African smiths for the manufacture of breach-loading rifles and cartridges. Since the guns were all handmade, the total output was low, but the effort itself shows that the European challenge could lead to technological innovation. In this case, however, innovation was not enough to stave off defeat.

An initial defeat and surrender was not necessarily the end to resistance. Many African societies were caught unprepared for the initial European impact; they had emerged too recently from their previous isolation to put up more than a brief fight. The reality of the colonial situation was slow to emerge. The initial stage was often no more than the march of a European-led force through the country—hardly enough for ordinary people to comprehend the coming trauma of alien rule. Only when the Europeans began to take control was the reality of their occupation brought home. At that point the Africans began to regroup and prepare for a serious fight, which the Europeans often labeled a "rebellion," though it was actually the first serious opposition to conquest.

Organized rebellion in the early stages of colonial rule often came along with an attempt at state-building, assembling a larger political unit than any of the pre-colonial states in the region. In Rhodesia, for example, the British government assigned the conquest to the British South Africa Company, under a charter that gave it some of the sovereign powers of the British Crown. In 1890–91, the company first conquered the Shona of eastern Rhodesia, then turned to the west and defeated the Ndebele of Matabeleland in 1893–94. The Ndebele themselves were an offshoot of the Mfecane, and they had been chronic enemies of the Shona up to this time. Nevertheless, in 1896–97, the Ndebele and Shona rose simultaneously against the company forces in a movement that was remarkably successful in its early stages, and the new unity was based on religion—just as Samori had used Islam as a unifying force in West Africa. The Europeans soon brought in overwhelming force and broke the rebellion, but the legacy of combined action was passed on to become part of the present-day Zimbabwean identity.

In considering the conditions of conquest in Africa generally, the most obvious point is that Europeans wanted to gain control as easily and cheaply as possible. It was therefore in their interest to form alliances with some African states and with some social classes or other groupings within states. When this happened, there had to be a pay-off to those who favored the European occupation. The Africans most often coopted into the European structure were the local aristocracy, and that aristocracy sometimes remained in power to the end of the colonial period—as it did in Zanzibar, Rwanda, Burundi, Buganda, or northern Nigeria. Even without a clear and lasting alliance between the Europeans and a local group, the form and conditions of conquest became a key factor in the political and social patterns of the colonial period and beyond. The legacy of the Rhodesian revolts is a case in point. So too is the carry-over from resistance which served as the foundation of nationalism in West Africa. For example, Sékou Touré of Guinea made political capital out of his claim to be Samori's grandson.

Conquest was experienced in ways that were still more subtle and complex—too subtle and too complex to be traced here in detail. Even the indecisive and time-consuming penetration of stateless societies like those of the Tiv or Ibo in Nigeria were reflected in Tiv and Ibo responses during the heyday of colonial rule. Similar legacies of the conquest period are still important in the social and political patterns of post-colonial Africa.

18

THE COLONIAL ERA

In the Europeans' rush to annex as much territory as possible before some other power beat them to it, they had little opportunity to learn much about Africa—and the cultural arrogance prevalent in the early twentieth century provided little incentive to do so until after they found themselves with the responsibility of running an African empire. Aside from the desire to exploit known mineral deposits, they began with no fixed ideas of what they wanted to do with the colonies, once they had them. This made for an early uncertainty about ultimate objectives, but as the colonial era moved along, a variety of different goals appeared.

Certain aims were universal. First of all, any colonial government had to set up an administration—"to keep the peace," in the phrase of the times. This implied at least minimal control over the African population—enough to stop local warfare and slave raiding and to allow free access for missionaries, administrators, and traders. This much was an essential first step, no matter what other policies followed. But administration was expensive, and the first step led automatically to the second—the colonies had to pay their own way. The taxpayers at home were hardly inclined to view empire acquisition as a philanthropic enterprise, but making the colonies pay was not an easy matter. The European administration was usually an additional layer of government, above and beyond the existing African authorities, and there was seldom a system of regular taxation that could simply be diverted to the alien government. As a result, some form of economic development had to be fostered, especially a kind that would create taxable income.

Theories of Empire

Beyond this general agreement that they should keep the peace and make the colonies pay their way, Europeans had a wide choice of possible policies. However, the choice was limited in practice by the fact that Europe already had a body of theory about the government of non-Western empires. Europeans also had a body of received opinion about the nature of Africa and Africans, largely built up in the nineteenth century and based on pseudo-scientific racism and cultural arrogance. (See chapter 12.) This heritage of ideas helped to confine European attitudes to a limited number of general ways of looking at "the colonial problem."

One tradition carried down from the early nineteenth century can be called "conversionism." It held that the best possible future for Africa, or any other society, was to adopt as much as possible of the European way of life. This implied conversion to Christianity, Western education, Western manners, and in time, a Western political system. Some conversionists had a long-run expectation that a colony sufficiently "advanced" toward "civilization" would become an independent state. Others hoped that it would join the European mother country as a part of "overseas France" or "overseas Portugal." The conversionist tradition was weakening in the early decades of the twentieth century, but it still had many followers.

One reason for the decline of conversionism was the rise of a competing group of ideas that can be labeled "permanent trusteeship" or paternalism. The point of departure was pseudo-scientific racism, with its view that Africans were permanently inferior to Europeans and could never successfully adopt the "civilization" of Europe. Believers in trusteeship nevertheless regarded Africans as human beings deserving the protection of their "superiors." The best policy for a European empire was therefore to treat Africans as minors, incapable of running their own affairs, but entitled to the guidance and discipline of those who were wiser than they. The crucial difference between conversionism and this new doctrine was its expectation for the future. Conversionists might advocate guidance and discipline as a step toward full maturity and Westernization, but the new school of trusteeship saw Africans as minors who could never grow up. In this view, it served no purpose to hold out the goal of conversion to "civilization." Racial inferiority placed that goal beyond their reach. Better to let them develop "in their own way," even though one recognized that that way was inferior to the European way.

Conversionism and trusteeship had a certain moral tone in common, and both were used to justify the existence of empires as well as directing the course they should follow. A third general category of imperial theory was less concerned with moral principle, even more rigorous in its insistence on racial inferiority, and infested with cultural arrogance. This school of thought can be called "racial subordination," though the Afrikaans word, *baasskap* (domination), may be even better in catching the essence. In this view, the best possible future for Africans was neither Westernization nor autonomous development but subordination as servants in a Western society—and permanently so. It began with the underlying belief that anything Africans could develop on their own was not worth having. At least as servants of Europeans, they would enjoy some of the material benefits of industrialization. They would be protected in their weakness, and they would be given the kind of discipline they needed. This view was not very common in government circles. Its greatest following came from the overseas Europeans in South Africa and Rhodesia—to a lesser extent in the Belgian Congo and to a still lesser extent in Kenya. However, it was common enough in Europe, though it tended to be muted in public discussion because it was open to the charge of self-serving immorality. Even in South Africa, the official defense of racial subordination came to be set in terms of *apartheid*, or separate development, which is actually a variant form of permanent trusteeship.

In practice, the clusters of ideas or attitudes identified here as conversionism, trusteeship, and subordination rarely occurred in isolation. An official government policy might be guided by a mixture pulling together separate and even contradictory elements from all three. The administrators who translated policy into practice had their own attitudes, which could easily warp the original intentions beyond recognition. Nevertheless, in tropical Africa the ideas of permanent trusteeship dominated the early colonial period, and they were gradually modified by an increasing element of conversionism, especially in the 1940s and 1950s. In much the same way, racial subordination was dominant at first in southern Africa, changing only gradually to the slightly softer doctrine of permanent trusteeship.

No colonial system was ever built on intentions alone; reality was bound to be different from European intentions. Administrators went to Africa as adults, already set in the forms of Western culture and prepared to see Africa only in the light of attitudes they brought from home. Africans saw the colonial situation against a background of African society, culture, and the modes of thought they had learned in childhood. A common humanity and common experiences in the setting of colonial Africa assured that, for some matters, the two evaluations would be complementary. Just as surely, historical and cultural differences made other matters diametrically opposite. Once the first period of conquest and "rebellion" had passed, the great majority of Africans tried to make the best of the situation. But the nature of the colonial experience made it unlikely that they and their rulers could ever see eye to eye on all issues—or even come to a mutual understanding of what the issues were. Communication is likely to be faulty across cultural barriers in any case, and between rulers and ruled, faulty communication is even more common. Major changes took place with a large element of European and African cooperation, but the process was accompanied by a constant suspicion of tyranny, stupidity, and lack of good faith on both sides as things rarely turned out as either group expected. The result was a pattern of "working misunderstanding."

Keeping the Peace

One important part of this working misunderstanding was the nature of administration itself. All colonial governments had to use some African administrators; there were simply too few Europeans to do the job by themselves. Whenever possible, they turned to Africans who were already in authority. Traditional rulers had prestige, could work through existing habits of compliance, and had a base in local support. The British in particular made a virtue of necessity and developed the theory that indirect rule through the chiefs was the best possible form of colonial government. The ideal of trusteeship suggested that it was better to "develop" African institutions than to import new ones. All the colonial powers therefore made an effort to promote the study of African societies, so as to understand their point of departure. They then tried to modify and reform them whenever possible. In some cases, when the existing political system appeared not to be suitable, they went so far as to invent new "African" institutions for local government. Even the French, who preferred a more direct administration, with authority from the top and obedience from the bottom, were forced to depend on African authorities at the village level, As they did in Bundu, the French often kept the old rulers in office.

Indirect rule could hardly work as planned. A traditional chief at any level ruled through an intricate balance of political and constitutional forces. The very fact of his being coopted into the colonial administration upset that balance. If he stuck by the traditional ways, he might keep his local power base, but he could hardly be an effective agent for the Europeans. If, on the other hand, he took the European side, as often happened, he lost his local following and continued in power only because the Europeans were willing to keep him there.

More important still, the European attitude toward African institutions was highly ambivalent. Few administrators really believed that the African way was best—only that it was best for Africans. They therefore sought to preserve and alter at the same time. While they might keep African forms of government at the local level, the colonial governments added new ranges of government services at the top—veterinary departments, health services, railway departments, labor recruiting bureaus, agricultural services—and these expanded in time to work at the local level as well. These services had to be staffed by Africans, at least in part. They needed trained personnel to serve as clerks, typists, medical assistants, and mimeograph machine operators. The European commercial firms and mining firms needed similar personnel. As a result, the foreign rulers were forced to introduce at least some elements of Western education. Missionary societies were ready to supply it, often with financial support from the colonial government. Most administrators claimed to admire "the unspoiled African from the bush" and despised the Western-educated class that began to appear in the coastal cities. But the "unspoiled African" was unable to drive a truck or pound a typewriter—and could therefore find no place in the modernized sector where the economic and political rewards were greatest.

Africans were also ambivalent in their assessment of African and Western cultures. They soon learned that Western education was the gateway to success in colonial society. One common reaction at the earliest stages of Western penetration was to reject African culture as much as possible and to imitate the Europeans in everything. But Africans were rational people who could see that the West had not created a perfect society, no matter how useful their technological advances. Western-educated Africans therefore began to mix their own combinations of traditional culture and Western learning, varying the combination according to opportunity and personal preference. One important variable was the amount of education; a person with only a primary education had access to only part of the Western tradition, and thus a limited range of choice. But Africans who took advanced degrees in European universities ended most often with the hope of making Africa modern, yet at the same time preserving the basic traditional values and African identity.

This African ambivalence toward the West was quite different from the Western ambivalence toward Africa. The point of departure was different, and the long-range goals were different, but the "working misunderstanding" contained enough common ground for Africans in the modern and traditional sectors alike to cooperate with the European goal of keeping the peace. In the realm of politics, many of the traditional elite survived the colonial period and emerged with continued power in the era of independence. Alongside them arose a new elite whose status came from Western education and whose power increased as they took over the administrative positions vacated by departing Europeans.

Making the Colonies Pay

When colonial rulers thought of economic development, they thought first of government revenue. In the early days of minimal government, revenue came from import duties. Imports in turn depended on having exports that could be sold on the world market. It was only natural for administrators to look for a few commodities that could be sold overseas, rather than considering the general health of the local economy. From their point of view, a general increase in local production and the consumption of locally produced goods was hard to translate into government revenue, while an increase in external trade could be easily taxed. For that matter, external trade might be increased, even if there were no appreciable change in total productivity. Colonial economic thought therefore began with a special emphasis on exports—and all too often it ended there as well.

Economic development rarely went according to plan. The most successful export crops were those the Africans discovered for themselves. That is, African farmers responded on their own initiative to produce what Europeans were willing to buy at an attractive price. This had happened in the pre-colonial growth of peanut exports from Senegambia or palm products from the Niger delta. It happened again in the colonial period with the spectacular growth of cocoa farming in the southern Gold Coast. Agriculture departments might push a particular crop for some region of Africa, but African farmers would not respond voluntarily if the economic advantage seemed marginal or uncertain. This fact occasionally led colonial governments to resort to force, laying down quotas for each farmer in cotton or some other crop—quotas with penal sanctions for those who failed to produce. While this system no doubt induced the desired production, the cost of enforcement was often so high that the net return to government was negligible.

Resource endowment was far more important than planning in dictating that some regions would be centers of relative prosperity, while others became economic backwaters. Africa is not a rich continent for agriculture; rainfall is often low and irregular. Production for the market might well be profitable near easy transportation routes, but a long haul to the coast cut deeply into the price that could be paid to the peasant producer. Export crops therefore tended to be concentrated in the more favored regions.

Mineral deposits were even more concentrated, although they were sometimes valuable enough to justify special transportation facilities like the net of railroads that reached to the Witwatersrand at an early date and later to the Zambian copper belt and Katanga.

Another uncontrollable factor was the shifting nature of European demand for particular commodities. The great depression of the 1930s was a special kind of disaster for Africa, since the prices of primary products dropped further and faster than those of manufactured goods. This meant not only a steep drop in production, but also an unfavorable shift in the net barter terms of trade as African producers received less per unit for what they sold and paid more per unit for the imported goods they bought. Other shifts in demand grew out of technological change in Europe. Beginning in the 1890s, the coming of the automobile in the developed world brought a sharp increase in the demand for wild rubber, but high prices also encouraged the development of plantation rubber in Malaya and elsewhere. By the 1920s the price of wild rubber had dropped so low that it was hardly worth gathering except in the most favorable circumstances.

Technological factors were also important in encouraging the economic development of some regions and not others. Africa had a long history as one of the world's main sources of gold, but some forms of gold deposit can be exploited by the new industrial technology, while others cannot. The old gold fields of Bambuk, for example, were widely scattered placer deposits, easily mined by hand. They are still in production and still mined by hand, because modern technology has little or nothing to offer in exploiting deposits of this kind. The South African gold fields, on the other hand, are the largest ever found anywhere, but the ore is poor in terms of gold per ton of rock mined. The mining boom that began in the 1890s and set South Africa on the road to industrialization was therefore made possible by the fortunate coincidence of newly discovered resources at the exact time when techniques for dealing with them became available.

One field in which government policy was crucial in encouraging or discouraging economic growth was railroads and later the construction of motor roads. Private capital was available to build railroads to transport mineral resources, but not for other railroad uses. Most of the railroads were built either with government funds or under government guarantees to the investors. The private investors were right in their reluctance—outside the mining regions, most privately financed railroads failed, and the others ran at a loss. In some cases the planners simply miscalculated. Other lines were built as a form of subsidy to economic development—investment in infrastructure, it would be called today. Still others were built for a variety of political reasons. The Uganda railway from Mombasa to Lake Victoria required a special vote of funds from the British Parliament, justified as a subsidy to "legitimate trade" and also because the cost of holding and administering Uganda without it would have been even greater. The French Congo-Océan line was even more clearly a political rather than an economic venture. It connected Brazzaville on Stanley Pool with Pointe-Noire on the Atlantic. Since the Belgians had already built a parallel railroad south of the Congo, its only justification was the desire to keep a vital transportation link entirely within French territory.

Railroad investment, so often political in motivation, also had political consequences. A railroad bound the hinterland to the coast, and it set up internal lines of circulation for people as well as goods. The Nigerian railroad system, for example, attached the Hausa and Muslim north to the coast by two lines—one through eastern Nigeria and one through the west. These lines helped to bind the country together—in contrast to French West Africa, where each port had a rail line to its own hinterland, but no links to a general rail network. Partly as a result, the internal lines of circulation ran inward from the port towns to the local hinterland, and, in time, each rail terminus became the capital of an independent republic. Even the efforts to join together some of these states, such as in the brief Mali Federation linking Senegal and Mali, were based on the economic and political realities that grew up around the rail line—in this case, the railroad from Dakar east to Bamako on the Niger.

Railroads also multiplied the tendency of other factors (such as resource endowment) to "pile up" economic development in a series of regional centers. These, in turn, drew population from the comparatively undeveloped regions. With the railroad finished from Mombasa to Lake Victoria, Uganda farmers became prosperous growing cotton for export, drawing in thousands of migratory workers from Rwanda, which was both over-populated and hard to reach with cheap transport.

Economic development was not only irregular in spatial distribution, it was also irregular in timing. In spite of the high price some parts of Africa paid in the pain of colonial conquest, the early colonial years, up to the mid-1920s, were a period of economic growth. Growth brought some regions like the cocoa-growing areas of Nigeria and Ghana not only increased gross territorial product, but rising real wages as well. Then, with the beginning of the Great Depression of the 1930s, most of tropical Africa passed into a period of comparative economic stagnation. The colonial powers had all they could do to handle the economic problems at home, and small African entrepreneurs had insufficient resources to do much on their own. Once the depression, the war, and the post-war crisis had passed, however, sharp recovery set in during the early 1950s and continued well into the 1960s. It was this economic spurt that helped to pave the way for independence and for the great optimism that both Africans and foreign observers felt during those years. It was followed, unfortunately, by the post-independence slump from the mid-1960s through the 1970s, then by the economic disasters of the 1980s.

Only South Africa seemed to keep the momentum of the early post-war decades—another example of lopsided development in sub-Saharan Africa. Development was geographically lopsided, concentrated in the south and other favored areas. It was racially lopsided in territories where settlers were present, with incomes very unevenly distributed. It was lopsided in its concentration on production for export, rather than production for local sale. It was technologically lopsided, with some regions and some industries using the most up-to-date processes Western technology could provide, alongside other means of production that were backward and inefficient.

Africa was altered beyond recognition during the course of the colonial period. Some Africans were better off materially, but the important change was not so much in the size of income; it was the new ways incomes were earned. Migratory labor, or permanent migration into mining towns, river ports, rail junctions, and market centers, brought Africans together who had little contact across ethnic lines in pre-colonial Africa. It also brought them into contact with the fruits of Western technology, Western culture, and Western education. Many were converted to one of the outside religions—Christianity or Islam. They formed new kinds of associations in the towns—new associations linking the new townsmen with their kin who remained in the villages. There was, in short, a new intensity of intercommunication both within Africa and between Africans and the West. One inevitable result was to increase the problems of personal adjustment to an unfamiliar and rapidly changing world. Another was an increase in social friction between ethnic groups caught in new and highly competitive situations. Still another result was to channel intercommunication within the boundaries of a colonial territory. As colonial frontiers created new barriers, colonial transportation and communication networks erased some of the old ones. In time, this opened the possibility of colony-wide political organization which could give effective voice to a new demand for independence.

19

TOWARD INDEPENDENCE

J ust as the conquest of Africa was part of a worldwide movement of imperial expansion, the coming of independence was part of a worldwide liquidation of European empires. It can be fully understood only in the perspective of world history, which would take account of events as diverse and distant as the modernization of Japan, the success of the Communist revolution in China, and the physical and emotional state of Europe in the aftermath of the Second World War. Whatever the causes, near and remote, most of the non-Western world achieved its independence in the very short period of only two decades, from 1945 to 1965. For Africa, the process reached its climax in 1960, and the process of achieving independence in tropical Africa was more peaceful and orderly than in any other major region of the world.

However, the success story of the independence movement should not obscure the other side of the picture. Southern Africa was not included. Angola and Mozambique continued as Portuguese colonies until 1976 and then gained independence only in a setting of continued civil war into the mid-1990s. The white-dominated government of Rhodesia refused "decolonization" and remained under white domination until 1980. Even then, independence came only after a prolonged insurrection and international pressure.

The final act, the removal of racial domination in South Africa came three full decades after African independence elsewhere, and the final achievement or peace and stability in South Africa is still somewhat uncertain at the time of this writing.

Nationalism

Most accounts of the African independence movement deal with the force of "nationalism," while far too many accounts of post-independent Africa emphasize the importance of "tribalism" as a disruptive force. Nationalism is ambiguous in itself. Tribalism is not only ambiguous but loaded with pejorative overtones drawn from the myth of a savage Africa. (See chapter 1.)

The term nationalism applied to African affairs has a similar history. Ever since the late 1940s, political commentators have written about the rise of nationalism—meaning resistance and

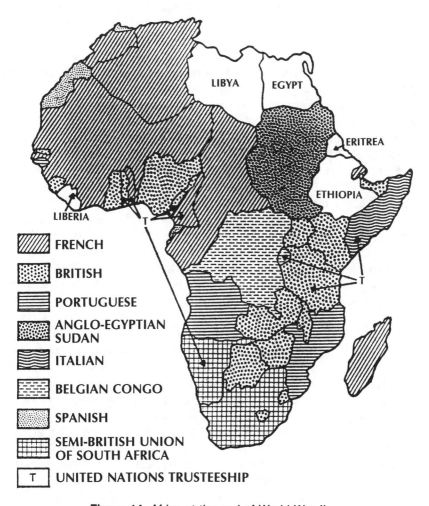

Figure 14. Africa at the end of World War II.

protest movements against colonial rule, and political parties demanding independence for each colony. The term was borrowed from European history, and especially from the nineteenth-century political movements in which people with a common culture, common territory, language, and historical tradition claimed to be a nation—and claimed for that nation the right of self-determination, the right to join together under an independent state. At times, as with Germany and Italy, the aim was to bring together a group of small states to form a larger unit with borders approximating those of the "nation." With Yugoslavia and Poland, it was a matter of separating out and joining together bits and pieces from larger multi-national states. By the 1990s, it was clear from the contested nationhood in Northern Ireland, the former Soviet Union, and the former Yugoslavia, among other places, that ethnic identities are far from stable. The ideal of forming ethnically homogeneous political units is a practical impossibility.

African nationalism had no such emphasis on ethnicity. Most precolonial African states had long since been swallowed up in the political structures of the European colonies, and there was remarkably little disposition to rejuvenate them. Only a few—such as Swaziland, Lesotho, Rwanda, and Burundi—kept their territorial identity during the colonial period and reemerged as independent states. Elsewhere, the African leaders in the independence movement claimed independence, but not a right based on common ethnicity. Theirs was the reverse of European nationalism; Europeans began with the nation, which they wanted to become an independent state. The Africans had states—the existing colonial units through which the Europeans ruled—and they wanted independence for these units, so that they could become nations.

The goal of nation building was not really central to the purposes of African leaders. First and foremost, they were against foreign rule, against European arrogance, and against European racism that branded them as inferior. Insofar as nationhood was a mark of equal status with other nations in the world, they were for it. Insofar as a feeling of patriotism or nationality could help persuade individuals to make sacrifices for a common cause, this too was useful. But these were merely means to other ends—to recognized equality of status, to independence, to modernization and economic development. Of these, the keys were equality and modernity, not nationality. The term nationalism has nevertheless been used to describe the African independence movement far too long to make it worthwhile trying to invent a better one. But it remains important to recognize that nationalism in Africa means something quite different from nationalism in Europe.

Given the colonial experience, it is remarkable how little anti-European sentiment there was in African nationalism. The nationalists wanted to get rid of European rulers, of course, but the ambivalence toward European culture that first emerged in the "working misunderstanding" of the colonial period still continued. In some aspects, Europe still served as a model for the aspirations of independent states. Africans who had been educated abroad wanted better health services, better education, and higher incomes for their own people. They preferred most aspects of African culture, and they wanted a technologically modern society that would still be African.

This is not to say that the sense of loyalty to an ancient national identity was absent in Africa. Many African kingdoms had the same kind of loyalties that go with the European type of nationalism— loyalties based on common historical traditions, language, and way of life. Asante was certainly a nation in this sense; so was the kingdom of Kongo; so too was Buganda. Yet these nations were incorporated in the new independent states without a serious struggle, and this fact itself seems to call for explanation.

It is clear that a sense of loyalty to pre-colonial nations did not disappear, or even weaken markedly, when faced by new claims of loyalty to the post-colonial African states. The older of these loyalties, often and wrongly called tribalism, still plays an important role in African politics. When states weaken, they can emerge as crucial centers of violent conflict, even as they did in Bosnia and elsewhere in Europe. The role of ethnicity after or along with the collapse of the state in Ethiopia, Somalia, Angola, and Liberia is all too clear. But the recent violence in those countries should not obscure the fact that most of the former colonies received independence as a unit, and almost all survived as a unit through the first three decades of independence. Attempted secessions, of Katanga from the ex-Belgian Congo and of Biafra from Nigeria, were defeated by force of arms.

Part of the explanation lies in the fact that it is easy psychologically for an individual to have two simultaneous national loyalties, as long as they are not in direct conflict. Americans of Irish descent have no trouble taking pride in their Irishness, while remaining patriotic Americans. It is just as easy to combine a dual loyalty to Asante and to Ghana, and the desire for modernization favors the new state against the old nationality. The strength of the African National Congress in South Africa is a remarkable victory over ethnic splintering, in spite of the actions of the Nkatha Freedom Party representing Zulu ethnic loyalty.

Resistance and Protest

The movement for African independence began far back in the colonial period. In a sense, it began with primary resistance to European conquest on the part of African states—or even more clearly in the several attempts to pull together larger political units in order to oppose the Europeans. But primary resistance failed, the early revolts were defeated, and the traditional framework of government either disappeared from the scene or was coopted into the lower reaches of the European administration.

Ordinary people then found themselves face to face with incomprehensible changes. Once physical resistance had failed, it was only natural to seek supernatural help to cope with the circumstances. Some found solace through a traditional African religion, some through Islam which made enormous gains in partly Muslim areas during the early colonial period, and some turned to Christianity, the religion of the conquerors themselves. The search for comprehension and consolation through religion was usually an alternative to protest, not a form of protest; but resistance to the Europeans could also be expressed through religious organizations. Part of the popularity of Islam lay in the fact that it offered itself as a modern religion, and thus a useful vehicle for religious change, but was not closely associated with the colonial governments. Many of those who adopted Christianity protested against missionary control over the churches by breaking away and setting up their own African churches. Thousands of new churches were formed in this way, more than two thousand in South Africa alone.

Some of these religious movements hoped for supernatural aid in handling earthly problems, while others placed their main hope in a better life after death. All three religious alternatives—traditional African, Muslim, and Christian—might also turn millenarian. The idea of a millennium, a last judgment after a thousand years, is specifically Christian, but present usage classifies any system of religious belief as millennial if it predicts drastic measures of divine intervention in the world in the relatively near future. A predicted millennium is usually not a sign of Christian influence, but rather of widespread loss of hope and understanding in the face of cataclysmic change. A classic example was the reaction of the Xhosa in 1856, after repeated defeats in their frontier wars against the advancing whites from the Cape Colony. It followed the typical pattern of millennial movements. They usually require two people to get them started—some sort of visionary or prophet and an impresario or organizer. In this case, the vision was seen by a young girl, interpreted by an important religious leader as a command from the gods to kill all the cattle, destroy all grain, and sow none for the coming season. The prophecy held that, if this were done, new cattle and grain would appear, ancient heroes would rise from the dead, and the Europeans would be swept into the sea. Many of the Xhosa killed their cattle, burned their grain, and waited for "the day"; but the millennium failed to come. Tens of thousands of people died of starvation. Though the Xhosa cattle killing was the most spectacular event of its kind, it was to be repeated again and again on a smaller scale with the same elements—the prophecy, the call for sacrifice in expectation of the millennium, and then disappointment.

Quite different reactions to conquest appeared among the more sophisticated Africans, especially those of the former trade enclaves along the west coast. From Saint-Louis-du-Sénégal to Calabar in eastern Nigeria, many of the old port towns were allowed representative government at the municipal level. Africans also held a few seats on legislative councils in many of the colonies. The port towns of Senegal began sending a representative to the National Assembly in Paris from 1870 onward, and Blaise Diagne was elected in 1914 as the first African representative. These channels of legal representation were also supplemented by organized pressure groups. The Western-educated elite of the Gold Coast joined with some of the traditional chiefs to form the Aborigines Rights Protection Society, and the ARPS could sometimes influence the colonial government. On occasion it bypassed the colonial governor and took its case directly to the Colonial Office in London.

Other protest took the form of spontaneous or nearly spontaneous riots against specific grievances, and these could sometimes spread into open rebellion over a wide region. In 1927–30, protest against forced labor and forced cotton planting among the Gbaya of the present-day Central Africa Republic became a general insurrection. The French lost control of the rebel territory for months or years and were finally forced to repeat the conquest at great expense. During the same period in eastern Nigeria, rebellion came as a result of a cross-cultural misunderstanding. The British had recently introduced direct taxation in the form of a head tax payable by every adult male. The rumor began to circulate that women were to be taxed as well. The head tax was a serious threat to the Ibo, since many believed that counting people could cause their death. They also took the tax to be a form of tribute, symbolic of servile status. As the rumor spread, bands of women began attacking colonial courts and administrative offices and sacking European-owned shops. The movement spread over a considerable area and was only suppressed by force after several months, with some fifty-five women killed by the military.

Appeals to the supernatural, polite protests of the educated elite, and sporadic rioting or local rebellion were not, strictly speaking, nationalist movements in either the African or European sense of the term. They could be effective in forcing the Europeans to modify their policies; but the true nationalist movement that emerged after the Second World War was not aimed at influencing policy—it wanted to capture colonial administration itself. Its most effective weapon was the Western-style political party, organized on a colony-wide basis by members of the Western-educated elite, with mass participation at the local level. No movement of this kind existed in tropical Africa before 1945, in spite of certain forerunners like the West African National Congress of the 1920s, which was still limited to elite groups.

The first example of a political party with a mass following came instead from South Africa. There, young men, some of whom had been abroad for education, had founded the forerunner of the African National Congress in 1912. Though the ANC did not aim immediately for a mass following, it was soon paralleled by the Industrial and Commercial Workers Union of Africa, founded in 1919 by Clements Kadalie as a dock workers' union. In a short time, it spread to other trades and became a mass party, even though Africans had no effective means of representation through an electoral process. By 1928 Kadalie had enrolled about 250,000 members, but the authorities simply disregarded peaceful protest. The white trade unions refused to cooperate with ICWU in strike action. The alternatives were violent revolution or a general strike by all African workers, but Kadalie held back from these stronger measures. The membership gradually became disillusioned and drifted away during the early years of the Great Depression. The lesson then and since in the South African setting is that mass organization and peaceful protest are not enough where the government has a strong military position and the intention to maintain white domination at any cost.

The Coming of Independence

The independence movement in tropical Africa developed in a broader world setting. Demands for independence were especially strong from Asia. The United States had promised independence for the Philippines before the Second World War, and it made good on the promise in 1945. A British plan for Indian independence had been built into the structure of Indian government since 1935. In 1947, Britain came through with independence for India (which soon split into India and Pakistan).

In Southeast Asia, the struggle was tougher. The Dutch set out in 1945 to reconquer Java, where the nationalists had seized control on the surrender of Japan. The Dutch won the war in its early stages, but the pressure of world opinion led them to grant independence to Indonesia in 1949. The French had also been dispossessed by a Japanese occupation of Indochina, but they reconquered southern Vietnam. When the Vietnamese forced the surrender of a large French army at Dien Bien Phu in 1954, France gave up and recognized the independence of a puppet ruler in the south and the de facto independence of the north.

The lesson was clear for African nationalists and colonial powers alike—colonies could only be held by force in the face of a resolute local opposition. An insurrection broke out in Algeria in 1945, modelled on the French resistance to the Nazis in Europe. It failed, but the French counter-measures left a bitter legacy for the future. Another insurrection followed in Madagascar in 1947, and again the French retaliation was so severe that Malagasy resentment of French rule redoubled.

The independence movement elsewhere in tropical Africa speeded up immediately after the Second World War. Wartime dislocation and shortages increased people's dissatisfaction. A new generation of Africans had gone overseas for education in the 1930s and now began to return, more militant than the older leadership and determined to gain independence—not the small increases in self-government the Europeans were willing to grant. France liberalized the forms of colonial government in 1946, and the British began to introduce new constitutions that gave a larger voice to elected African representatives in each colony. Between 1944 and 1948, the first parties with mass support began to emerge—the National Council of Nigeria and the Cameroons, the Convention People's Party (CPP) in the Gold Coast, the Rassemblement Démocratique Africaine (RDA) in French West Africa.

As African politicians began to increase their pressure for greater self-government, the colonial powers began to retreat, first in West Africa, then elsewhere. For the British, the crucial decision was reached before 1951. In that year, Kwame Nkrumah and the CPP won an election in Ghana, though he was in jail for sedition at the time. The governor freed him and allowed him to take office as premier under a new constitution that gave broad powers of self-government to an elected legislature. The very act of introducing a constitution of this kind implied British willingness to move more rapidly toward self-government and then to independence. The acceptance of Nkrumah's election in 1951 meant that independence would come sooner rather than later. After that, it was only a matter of time and arrangements, as far as the West African colonies were concerned.

In British eastern and central Africa, the situation was different, partly because British settlers were more numerous there. At first, through the 1950s, the British experimented with a constitutional expedient called "multi-racialism," the practice of giving a certain number of seats in the legislature to each separate racial group rather than following the rule of one-man-one-vote. African pressure for one-man-one-vote increased through the 1950s, however, and Britain finally agreed in 1958 to grant independence to most of eastern and central tropical Africa on that basis. The one exception was Rhodesia, where the legislature was controlled by whites and already had powers of self-government. In the face of British reluctance to grant independence without effective African representation, the Rhodesian whites declared their own independence in 1965 and set out down the road toward racial domination of the South African type.

The French decision to decolonize had a different timing and intent, but it produced the same result. The colonial reforms of 1946 increased the number of African representatives in the National Assembly of France itself. By 1956, it looked as though the French African colonies might be willing to accept self-government without independence. A new constitutional reform, called the *loi-cadre*, or framework act, was piloted through the French Assembly by Felix Houphouet-Boigny, one of the founders of the RDA who would later be the long-term president of Côte d'Ivoire. One of DeGaulle's first acts as president was to give African colonies a choice between independence—and an end to all French aid—or continuing as part of France under the loi-cadre. Although only Guinea voted for independence at that time, the pace of movement toward independence elsewhere in Africa was too strong for the French plan to succeed. Refusal to grant independence, once self-government had already been granted, would only deprive France of influence in their ex-colonies. By 1960, the major French colonies in sub-Saharan Africa were all on their way to independence, and Algeria followed in 1962.

In the first decade after the Second World War, Belgium followed a somewhat different policy toward the Congo, hoping to isolate the colony from the nationalist virus by rigid controls. By the mid-1950s, however, the policy was clearly not working, and the government began to prepare for eventual independence a few decades in the future. By 1960, it was clear that the only alternative to immediate independence would be an expensive and futile war of liberation. At that point, the Belgians hoped that a rapid move to independence would preserve the substantial Belgian economic and political interests in the former colony. That too failed in large part. The Congolese army mutinied immediately after independence. After several years of disorder, the country settled down under the corrupt and autocratic government of Mobutu Sese Seko.

By the early 1960s, the wave of independence had advanced east and south across Africa, until it ended at the frontiers of Angola, Rhodesia, and Mozambique. There it stopped for a decade or more, as the Portuguese and the dominant whites in Rhodesia and South Africa were determined to stand firm and fight if necessary. Guerrilla movements began early—from 1961 in Angola and 1964 in Mozambique. They were not strong enough to win immediately, but they were strong enough to demonstrate the high cost of empire. In 1974, the army in Portugal revolted and overthrew the long-standing Portuguese dictatorship. In 1975, Portugal granted independence to its mainland African colonies, Angola, Mozambique, and Guinea-Bissau.

This shift was crucial for Rhodesia as well. It had long frontiers, hard to protect, on three sides. In 1976, two important guerrilla movements began operations against the white government. Britain took a hand in trying to work out a settlement that would provide independence along with security for the whites—who had themselves been in rebellion against Britain since 1965. In 1979, the contenders reached an agreement, held an election, and in 1980, the former Rhodesia became the independent Zimbabwe.

Once again, the limits of African independence seemed to have been reached. South Africa was technically independent, but it was ruled under a political system where only whites could vote. In 1989, however, the government of the National Party—the creators of the apartheid system of racial domination—began a slow reversal of its previous stand under the leadership of F. W. De Klerk in cooperation with the efforts of Nelson Mandela of the African National Congress. In April 1994, after a long period of negotiation between various political factions, the ANC won the first non-racial South African election. With that Africa had finally reached independence under African governments. Many problems remained, but the colonial era, at least, had ended.

Part IV

EPILOGUE

20

AFRICA SINCE INDEPENDENCE

T he underlying patterns of African culture and the African past are a necessary guide to understanding the African present and future; to provide that background has been the primary premise of this book. We have made no effort to analyze the contemporary scene—many other books make that their specific task. In this final chapter, however, we hope to highlight longer-running trends that are not obvious in the daily press.

One of the most obvious changes over these thirty to forty years has been the shift in attitudes about Africa's possible future. In the late 1950s and early 1960s, Africans were immensely optimistic about what they could accomplish once the incubus of colonial rule had been removed. One of us recalls meeting an automobile dealer in a provincial Nigerian city in 1955. After hearing our favorable reactions to Nigeria's recent achievements, he said, "But you came too soon. If you'd only waited five years, you'd really see something!"

Africans were not alone in this optimism. Western observers, and especially the professional Africanists, had first-hand evidence of the important economic and political advances over the past decade or so. By the early 1960s, to be sure, cracks had already began to appear in the democratic beginnings of independent rule, but some slips had to be expected.

By the mid-1990s, the universal optimism of the early 1960s had been replaced by a general pessimism. The recent past provided grounds enough for that belief. As of the mid-1990s, however, some hopes for a brighter future were visible through the gloom—liquidation of apartheid in South Africa, an occasional move toward more democratic governments, and some economic up-turns here and there. Contrasted with those hopeful signs were the inexorable continued population growth, the AIDS epidemic, the near-total collapse of the post-colonial state in Somalia, Liberia, and Zaire, and chronic warfare in societies that had experienced a thirty-year arms build-up.

Modernization and Nation-Building

One of Africa's fundamental problems has to do with its reaction to "modernization"—a term used here simply to mean getting the benefits of industrialization for African use. African leaders have sought these benefits, even though the extent of economic development over recent decades is no true measure of the effort. They use air-conditioned cars, have their offices in skyscrapers—and all too often, keep their spare cash in numbered Swiss bank accounts. From the mosque tower, the call for prayer comes from a public address system, even where the leaders may preach Islamic fundamentalism. The tools of industrial technology can thus mask the cultural reality, and few African leaders want a carbon copy of what the West has to offer.

Even the most modernizing people appeal to values of an African past. For example, Léopold Senghor of Senegal wrote about *négritude* as an abstract quality that permeates African thought, art, and achievement. But he wrote in superb French, not in Serer, his home language. Kwame Nkrumah of Ghana also had a lot to say—in English—about African philosophy and the "African personality." Julius Nyerere gave himself the Swahili title of *mwalimu*, or teacher, and tried to reorganize Tanzania's rural life along lines dictated by *ujamaa*, an African sense of community. Joseph Mobutu changed his name to Mobutu Sese Seko, changed his country's name from the Congo to Zaire, and insisted that his fellow countrymen also change their names to "authentic" African forms and wear a cut of suit that was broadly Western, but not the current fashion of the Western world. Some of this window-dressing no doubt represents a genuine effort to get back to values, real or imagined, of Africa as it was before the conquest, but the myth of the noble African lurks there as well.

In fact, the living traditions of African culture do not have to be recovered. They were never lost—modified to make innovation possible, but not lost. In the villages, a whole body of custom lives on. It controls relations between families, land tenure, and worship of the gods (including the Christian/Muslim God). Even in adapting practices suitable to modern life, some possibilities feel "right" and others feel "wrong" and are likely to be rejected.

This sense of "rightness" attaches less easily to the new life of rural migrants in the slums that surround all African cities. It never attached very easily to the colonial state. The post-colonial state inherited that weakness and added new weakness on its own. The state is rarely perceived as an institution to which every person should owe ultimate loyalty. It demands taxes, and it gives back benefits like schools, roads, medical care (sometimes), and jobs. It is the focus of political life, but it is not often the focus of a sentiment that could be called patriotism. This is not to argue that patriotism is a "good thing" in all circumstances, but African loyalties, since independence as before, have gone in other directions.

Institutions other than the state are the first source of group loyalty. Even urban Africans tend to keep foci of loyalty similar to those of the villages—based first on age and kinship, secondly on common language and common standards of behavior. These feelings are not unlike the sources of ethnic loyalty found elsewhere in the world—in the former Soviet Union or Yugoslavia, where the collapse of a state removed an important way to resolve conflict peacefully. In Africa, too, similar ethnic loyalties have had a major role in the civil wars that have ravaged Rwanda, Angola, Somalia, Ethiopia, or Liberia.

Post-Colonial Economics

One way to see present-day Africa in the world is to picture the African economy as part of the world economy. At the time of independence, the world was divided into the developed economies of western Europe, North America, and Japan and less developed countries (LDCs) that were much poorer. All of tropical Africa was in that group, and it was not very much poorer than the poor on other continents—in 1960, the gross national products per capita in South Korea and Ghana were about the same. By the early 1990s, several countries in south and east Asia had risen to become newly industrialized countries (NICs), especially Singapore, Korea, Hong Kong, and Taiwan—with Thailand, Malaysia, Indonesia and China beginning to catch up. Latin American countries like Mexico, Brazil, and Chile also showed marked economic growth. Even south Asia, the world region closest to the African poverty level, had begun to move ahead in terms of gross domestic product per person. In tropical Africa as a whole, GDP per capita rose by about 2 percent per annum over the period 1961–73, then fell slightly each year over the period 1973–1980, and finally dropped with an average loss of more than 1 percent per annum in the period 1980–91. Over that last dozen years, the GDP per capita in the East Asia/Pacific rose at about 6 per cent per year. For Africa, however, the worst had passed with the 1980s, and several African countries have shown positive rates of growth from the late 1980s onward.

Part of the greater economic success of Asia came from the "green revolution"—the new seeds and fertilizers that increased the productive capacity of much of the tropical world. India went from being a grain-deficit area to become a net exporter. Other rice-producing areas also profited. Africa, unfortunately, lacked the climate and soil resources to make good use of these new techniques.

Gross domestic product *per capita* measures both production and population. Governments elsewhere in the less developed world sought lower birth rates. China has been a leader. By the 1980s, in much of Latin America and Southeast Asia the rate of population increase began to slow down. In sub-Saharan Africa, on the other hand, the rate of net population growth has remained steady at around 3 per cent per year and is projected to continue at that rate to the end of the century. With that rate, the population doubles every twenty-three years. Sub-Saharan African population had more than doubled between 1960 and 1990. As of the mid-1990s, Africa had the highest population growth rate in any region of equivalent size in the world. The AIDS epidemic may change the pattern, but data on infection rates are not accurate enough to make serious prediction possible.

To generalize about a sub-Saharan African economy is somewhat deceptive. Growth, or lack of it, was uneven within tropical Africa, and it was uneven over time in particular places. Oil resources in the era of OPEC could bring enormous wealth. As a result Gabon, which has both oil and a small population, is off the scale of African productivity per capita. Elsewhere, oil wealth could be used to promote other kinds of productivity—or it could be squandered on government extravagance and private corruption.

Nigerian oil wealth turned out to be a windfall of dubious value. It was an important cause of the attempted secession of Biafra and a bloody civil war between 1967 and 1970. In the next decade, it grew to become nearly the only source of foreign exchange. In the process, it distorted other possibilities for economic growth. By 1980, oil brought in $20 billion a year and a binge of public and private spending. By 1988, oil revenues had fallen to less than $2 billion a year, and the rest of the Nigerian economy was a shambles from which it showed no signs of recovery by the mid-1990s.

What mineral resource endowment could give to one region, the fragile climate could take away from another. Many of the countries with the most serious negative growth rates were also those along the desert edge from Senegal in the West to the Sudan Republic, Ethiopia, and Somalia in the east. That was the zone that experienced the devastating drought of 1968–74, followed by the return of drought in 1977–78, and a third episode in 1983–85, most serious for Sudan and the Horn of Africa. These periods of drought were not just a temporary aberration, like the American dust-bowl of the 1930s; they represented a movement of increasing aridity stretching over several decades and dating back to the beginning of this century.

Farther west along the desert edge rainfall over the period from 1960 to 1990 was 25 per cent lower than it had been between 1930 and 1960. As a result, the Sahara advanced to the south by about 100 kilometers, adding about a half-million square kilometers to the desert—an area roughly equal to the whole of Ohio, Indiana, Illinois, and Iowa. Lake Chad, which has no surface outlet, lost 90 per cent of its area between 1960 and 1983.

Directions in Economic Policy

All African countries exert substantial government control over, or government participation in, the economy. This can take the form of indirect measures like currency manipulation, but it almost always includes substantial government ownership and management of major industrial and commercial enterprises. Even in "capitalist" South Africa, the government owned and operated the important iron and steel industry.

As the post-colonial economic disaster became clearer, Western economists began to place more importance on errors of policy than they did on natural disasters. In certain instances, it seems clear that good intentions lead to bad policies and unnecessary poverty. Tanzania is a case in point. Under Julius Nyerere, the leader at independence, Tanzania set out to escape both the capitalism of the colonial economy and the Marxian model as it existed in the Soviet Union. Nyerere called for "African socialism," based on African communal traditions of mutual self-help. Among other things, he nationalized the banks and some other foreign firms, and he tried to reduce the country's dependence on international trade. "Dependency theory," popular in the 1960s and 1970s, suggested that, for poor countries, foreign trade meant "unequal exchange" and the diversion of wealth to rich countries.

The center-piece of Nyerere's economic plan was the idea of *ujamaa* (community). Since most Tanzanians had lived in small and scattered hamlets, the institution of this communal village program had both a long- and a short-term aim. In the short run, it was designed to bring people together so they could better enjoy educational, medical, and social services—and so their farming could be regulated by government agents. In the longer run, it aimed at voluntary collectivization of agriculture with genuine communal farming.

The peasants, however, did not respond to the government

appeal. By 1974, the movement of the peasantry into villages had to be forced, not voluntary. The government created some 7,000 new villages, populated by 13,500,000 people by the end of the 1970s. Many observers at the end of the 1970s thought the program might well succeed, but by the mid-1980s, few thought so. The peasants' interests were ignored in favor of government interests which led to very low agricultural productivity until the scheme was finally abandoned.

Just as Tanzania is used too often as an example of the failures of socialism, Côte d'Ivoire is used as an example of success for a "free market" system. The success was undoubted for a time. The Ivory Coast maintained a growth rate of 7.2 percent per year over the whole period from 1960 to 1981. The United States did not do as well. But the Ivoirian system was not quite "economic liberalism" in our sense. The government siphoned off income from exports. In 1977, a boom year, small producers received only about a quarter of the world price for their export crops. The government diverted the surplus to pay for as much as two-thirds of the public-sector investment at that time.

The government encouraged cocoa and coffee production, even though the producers were taxed for the sake of the rest of the economy. It allowed prices to rise with inflation, made it easy to hire cheap foreign labor, and it guaranteed security of tenure to farmers producing for the market. The main beneficiaries, however, were not the peasants but government officials and the urban middle class.

The Ivoirian system worked very well through the 1970s. Then, in the early 1980s, the growth rate dropped and by 1983 had turned negative, as it did in so many other African countries in that decade. Part of the problem was slackening demand in Europe and America, but another part was the diversion of income to non-productive uses. President Houphouet Boigny built a new capital at his home village, with the largest Catholic basilica in the world (for a country where only a minority of the population were Catholic). Much of this non-productive investment was paid for by foreign borrowing, and the debt service was a further drag on the economy.

General economic stagnation was bad enough, but food production was worse still. No country in sub-Saharan Africa produced as much food per capita in 1990 as it had done in 1960. Drought was a major cause of this short-fall, but common forms of government policy also played a role. Even before the end of the colonial period, African governments experimented with several forms of price manipulation designed to isolate the local economy from the world market.

Marketing boards had been a common device in the British colonies and continued in use after independence. The boards were ordinarily given a monopoly over the purchase of an important export commodity. The boards collected the world price at the port, paid the farmers somewhat less, and held the balance—in theory against some future time when the world price might drop. In fact, no marketing board ever paid out a significant part of its funds to compensate for a low world prices. Governments soon discovered that such funds were a convenient source of revenue for all kinds of economic development. All too often, this meant that the farmers were systematically underpaid for the sake of development projects, which were rarely for the benefit of rural areas.

Price control on food for local consumption was another way to drain wealth from the agricultural sector for the sake of cheap food in the cities. Rigging the value of the currency could accomplish the same thing more indirectly. An African government could overvalue the currency, thus lowering the domestic price of exports. This favored the urban consumers at the expense of the farmers. When oil also entered the picture, as it did in Nigeria from 1974 onward, oil revenue could be used to pay for imported processed food, and the local farmers found it hard to compete. This policy very nearly ruined Nigerian agriculture.

In the formerly French states, the post-colonial currency was kept tied to the French franc, with the result that the value of that currency reflected the French place in world markets—not that of the African economy attached to it. This system, however, was kept in place until 1994.

By the mid-1980s, it was clear that African economies were in serious trouble. The fall in productivity, the distortion of the value of African currencies, and excessive government spending often produced a fiscal crisis—either serious problems with balance of payments or untenable deficits for the public treasury. In many cases, the only way out of the problem was a thorough reform of the economy, aimed at restoring the currency to its actual exchange value and encouraging economic growth by exposing the economy to the play of market forces.

Many African countries began seeking a return to a market value for their currency, government financial stringency, encouraging farm production and exports, and discouraging imports. These remedies were called structural adjustment programs. The World Bank and the International Monetary Fund recommended them; foreign-aid donors and the international banking community also brought pressure to bear. It was not a way many African politicians would choose to go, but the Bank insisted on these reforms as a condition of further assistance. The price was a painful period of economic adjustment, but in some cases the result was a striking success, as in Ghana. In other cases, an African country rejected the program and continued in the economic doldrums. Or, as in Nigeria, it began structural adjustment but then abandoned it before it could produce much change.

Political Order and Disorder

Many of Africa's economic shortcomings after independence can be traced directly or indirectly to political conditions. These conditions, in turn, depend in large measure on underlying culture and on the history of the colonial period. That the colonial powers failed to prepare Africa for independence is all too obvious, but it is important to remember that the colonial powers did not expect Africa to become independent in the 1960s. Independence caught them by surprise, even when it came peacefully.

The lack of preparation shows in a number of important ways. On the British side, the long-term colonial policy for tropical Africa was based on indirect rule through the chiefs. In the quest for independence, the organized groups that demanded an end to European rule demanded an end to chiefly rule as well. Some of the bloodiest struggles during and after decolonization were fought on precisely this issue. The Zanzibar revolt against the Afro-Arab elite in 1972 and the peasant risings against the Tutsi elite in Rwanda and Burundi in 1972–73 were directed against deeply resented class and caste power that had been sustained by the colonial rulers.

Neither France, Belgium, nor Britain, made a serious effort to prepare Africa for electoral democracy. Portugal *had* no electoral democracy, even at home, until 1974. In the French sphere, the Senegalese communes had a long electoral experience with representation in France, but the Framework Law was passed in time to allow only one local election before independence was declared. For the Belgian Congo, the only national election was the one that led directly to independence. In the British sphere, the electoral politics that existed were limited to the old port towns and to a very limited electorate. In tropical Africa generally, some politicians had the experience of being elected; but few indeed had the experience of leaving office voluntarily after a defeat at the polls. Politicians were therefore loath to leave office, suspecting—correctly as it turned out—that their successors were unlikely to give them another chance.

A third source of non-preparation for independence was the colonial treatment of the military. The conquest of Africa had been carried out largely by African troops under European officers. Africans had fought in two world wars, but almost no public attention was paid to the place of the military under the newly independent governments. It was as though the colonial administrators and the rising African politicians shared a belief that the armies would behave under their new officers just as they had under the old.

The colonial powers made the military problem more serious by the way they recruited their armies. The British in particular had a theory that certain peoples, whom the British called "martial races," were better soldiers than other colonial people. The so-called martial races tended to come from the fringe areas of any colony, often from its poorest sections where soldiers could be recruited for little pay. Sometimes, as with Gurkhas from Nepal, the British even recruited their armies from outside the empire. In East Africa, some of the earliest British forces were from the Sudan, recruited there by purchase well before the British had conquered the Sudan. Later on, in Ghana, Nigeria, and Uganda, the recruits (though not necessarily the local officers) were drawn from the comparatively impoverished northern territories. This meant, in the longer run, that such soldiers had ties to their home districts, to their fellow soldiers, and to their officers at times, but rarely to people in the core area of the colonial state.

The colonial powers transferred power to democratically elected African governments, but democracy was short lived. In British territories, independence usually began with the "Westminster model"—that of the British Parliament with a prime minister responsible to the majority of a parliamentary body. A common next step was to move to a presidential system, with a powerful president. Ghana became independent in 1957. By 1960, President Kwame Nkrumah secured a new constitution which gave the president the right to veto any legislation, to pass laws without calling on parliament for approval, and to control the budget. In 1964, Nkrumah made his Convention People's Party the sole legal party. In theory, important decisions would be reached by democratic means, but within the single party. In 1966, Ghana reached a fourth stage: the military seized control of the country while Nkrumah was overseas. Supreme power then passed to a group of officers that called itself the National Liberation Council.

These stages—from the Westminster model, to a powerful presidency, to a one-party state, to a military dictatorship—were not universal, but they were common enough to represent a process. Some stopped short at the stage of one-party state. Several one-party states were remarkably stable, and some of their leaders remained in office for a very long time, as with Kenneth Kaunda in Zambia until 1991, Sékou Touré in Guinea-Conakry to 1984, Félix Houphouet Boigny in Côte d'Ivoire to 1993. The party often continued in power even after the first leader died or resigned, as the ruling party did after the death of Jomo Kenyatta of Kenya in 1978, the resignation of Léopold Senghor of Senegal in 1981, or that of Julius Nyerere of Tanzania in 1985.

The more usual course, which became dominant in tropical Africa, was to move on to military dictatorship. Military governments changed, but most often they did so only when one military group overthrew its military predecessors. Others who began as military dictators sometimes moved toward the forms a one-party state, like Mobutu Sese Seko's Zaire. Others claimed to be interim regimes, ready to pass control over to a new civilian government when circumstances warranted—like Nigeria, where the promise was rarely kept for long.

One final category of government went well beyond the usual rules of military take-over. In the late 1960s and into the 1970s, Africa had a few governments whose record for tyranny was among the worst in the post-war world. These were Equatorial Guinea under Macias Nguema from 1968; Jean Bedel Bokassa of the Central Africa Republic from 1965, which he renamed the Central African Empire; and Idi Amin in Uganda from 1971. This phase of military-based tyranny may well have passed for tropical Africa. These three worst tyrants were all deposed in 1978.

The most tragic of the three was Uganda, if only because the country had a record of rapid modernization and great expectations at the time of independence. Part of the background was a conflict between the previously dominant Ganda people near the capital, and their neighbors. Milton Obote became the first president, mainly with non-Ganda support. He was not generally popular, and he quickly suspended the constitution and created a one-party state. His lack of support made it all the easier for the army to revolt under Idi Amin, whose followers were mainly badly educated soldiers from the poverty-stricken north. Most were Muslim, though the majority of Uganda was Christian. The soldiers set out to rule Uganda like a conquered country; they are credited with killing more than one hundred thousand people before they were driven from power by a Tanzanian invasion in 1979. But the fall of the tyrant was only the beginning of a long process of rebuilding a once stable and prosperous country.

Frontiers and Secessions

At the time of independence, some people expected old, "tribal" loyalties to re-emerge and to dominate African international affairs as one tribe after another tried to bring all its members within a single state. The early predictions focused on such possibilities as the secession of Muslim northern Nigeria, of the Asante from Ghana or the project for a united Ewe state carved out of Togo and Ghana. Nothing came of those projects, and the crucial leadership in the early decades of independence was united in accepting colonial borders, despite the fact that they had been determined somewhat arbitrarily by European conquest.

Attempted secession movements in the early independence period failed. Some Belgians tried to organize the secession of Katanga province (now Shaba) from the ex-Belgian Congo in 1960–63. It ended with UN intervention on the side of the Republic of Congo-Kinshasa (later Zaire).

The Nigeria civil war of 1967–1970 came closer to the European pattern of a war for "national" independence. It began in southeastern Nigeria, where the Igbo-speaking people had a poor and overpopulated homeland. Igbo-speakers had been unusually quick, however, to take advantage of missionary education, which made it possible for them to migrate to cities all over Nigeria looking for work or business opportunities. By the 1960s, more than a million Igbo-speakers were scattered through other parts of Nigeria, where they were known as Ibo. Other Nigerians disliked Ibo pushiness and envied Ibo success.

In Northern Nigeria in 1966, anti-Ibo sentiment turned to violence following a military coup led by Ibo army officers. Riotous crowds roamed the strangers' quarters of northern cities, beating or killing any Ibos they could find. Estimates of the dead run from five to thirty thousand. As a result, many Ibo from other parts of Nigeria fled back to Iboland.

In 1967, the Igbo-speaking region declared its independence as Biafra. The new state was also the center of the oil boom; the secession set off a civil war that lasted until 1970. The federal government won, but the victors went out of their way to welcome the defeated Biafrans back into the Nigerian federation. Ibos gradually worked their way back into government posts and into businesses, and they enjoyed more security after the war than they had before the riots.

The secession of Eritrea from Ethiopia did succeed, but only after a long struggle. After the Second World War, the United Nations gave the former Italian colony of Eritrea to the Ethiopian empire.

Culturally, Eritrea had more in common with the dominant Amhara of Ethiopia than most other parts of the Ethiopian empire did, but the Eritreans resented Amharic rule and claimed self-determination for the political unit created by Italian conquest less than a century earlier. Guerrilla resistance began in the 1970s, and it finally achieved an independent Eritrea in 1993—an outcome that was only one part of a massive upheaval in the Horn of Africa from the mid-1970s onward into the mid-1990s.

The civil war in the southern Sudan is still another long-standing struggle. When the British took over the old Egyptian secondary empire, it included the Muslim northern Sudan, just to the south of the desert, and a non-Islamic region in the far south. Out of deference to Muslim feelings, the British allowed missionary work only in the south, which led to education in English, not Arabic, and extensive conversion to Christianity. The result was a linguistic and religious split, superimposed on animosities going back to the northerners' pre-colonial slave raids into the south. After independence, the south was comparatively poor and backward and regarded itself as oppressed by the mainly-Muslim government in Khartoum. The first guerrilla war broke out in 1962. Although interrupted by a brief truce in the mid-1970s, fighting continued into the mid-1990s.

The Rise of Political Violence

The massive upheaval in the Horn of Africa and the prolonged struggle in the southern Sudan began a new phase of political violence in sub-Saharan Africa—a phase where the post-colonial state itself threatened to disappear in the face of dispersed military power in the hands of many and diverse groups. Sometimes the military represented the professional interests of the officer corps, sometimes ethnic interests, sometimes class or caste interests, at other times simple banditry by teen-age gangs.

The new phase began about the late 1970s with fall of the Ethiopian empire in 1974 and the reopening of war in the southern Sudan. The coup in Portugal (also in 1974) was nearly simultaneous with the beginning of the upheaval in the Horn. Angola and Mozambique became independent and embarked on a generally Marxist economic policy—provoking internal opposition and foreign intervention which turned to civil war.

Liberia entered the picture in 1980, with a military revolt against the Americo-Liberians who had formally controlled that country. Master-Sergeant Samuel Doe led a revolt, killed the principal members of the former government, and set up a military regime with a political base among his own ethnic group. It lasted as a stable but repressive government until 1990 when it was overthrown and the Liberian state collapsed into anarchy.

The new phase had several ingredients. One of these was the continued militarization of Africa. It was not merely that military men often seized governments. Whatever the dangers to the state—either internal or external—few civilian or military regimes were willing to risk their future by making substantial cuts in their military budgets, which gradually took a larger and larger part of government revenue.

The increasing intervention by the Soviet Union and the United States was even more serious. Independent Africa had been a minor theater in the cold war from early 1960s. The Soviets intervened with some aid to the exiled opposition to South African apartheid and racial dominance in Rhodesia. The United States intervened through the CIA and international diplomacy to keep Patrice Lumumba from taking office as president of Congo-Kinshasa. The United States supported Mobutu's repressive and corrupt government because it was anti-Soviet.

A few military regimes—for example, Madagascar, Benin, and the ex-French Congo—called themselves socialist with more or less Marxist-Leninist trappings. However, they received comparatively little Soviet aid and they moved very little in the direction of a directed economy based on the Soviet model.

After 1976, Angola and Mozambique began their independent careers based on Marxist models, though not an out-and-out copy of the Soviet pattern. Neither was an outstanding success, but the "Communist" threat seemed serious to the United States and South Africa, both of which intervened with more or less covert supplies of weapons to any opposition they could find. The full extent of American involvement is not yet public knowledge. The South African involvement was more overt; it involved direct military intervention as well as a flow of military supplies for Jonas Savimbi, a leader who mainly rallied the Ovimbundu people of southeastern Angola. South Africa's chosen instrument in Mozambique was RENAMO, a guerrilla faction operating in Mozambique from bases in Rhodesia and South Africa itself.

In the Horn of Africa, the United States supported the Ethiopian empire with military and other aid until the overthrow of Haile Selassie in 1974. The Soviet Union had supported Somalia in their territorial claim to the large Ogaden region in southeastern Ethiopia. After the revolution, the Soviets switched support to the new pseudo-Marxist military regime in Addis Ababa, and Somalia changed sides to accept military aid from the United States. Over the decades that followed, the two super-powers armed their surrogates. However, the most serious problem was not open Ethiopian-Somalian warfare, it was the fact that neither Ethiopia nor Somalia was able to keep the weapons in the hands of people under government command. The victory of the Tigrinya and Eritrean forces that overthrew the Marxist Ethiopian government was mainly won with weapons captured from the Ethiopian army. The collapse of the Somalian state and the spread of anarchy and civil war in Somalia were equally products of weapons originally supplied by one or the other of the two superpowers.

The End of the Cold War

Just as the mid-1970s seemed to mark a turning point in African affairs, the years from 1989 onward marked another. The main lines are apparent at the time of writing, but the outcome is far from certain. The crucial events were two: One was the economic crisis of the 1980s which, almost everywhere in tropical Africa, began the shift in economic policies from a more directed and inward-looking stance toward an effort to reintroduce free market forces. The second was the beginning of reform in the Soviet Union, followed by the break-up of the Soviet Union itself and the end of the cold war. In international affairs, this meant that Soviet client-states like Ethiopia could no longer count on Soviet aid. It suggested to the pseudo-Marxist-Leninist states that they might also change direction, which Madagascar, Congo-Brazzaville, and Benin all did in the early 1990s, followed by the governments of Angola and Mozambique.

The end of the cold war also meant that American clients like those in Somalia, or Savimbi in Angola, would receive little or no more American aid. Once cut free of American aid, they were also free of American guidance or influence. They had the guns the Americans had given them, and they could use these to fight their way into power. This change lay behind the collapse of the Somalian state and the rise of the "warlords" in its place; it also lay behind Savimbi's refusal to accept defeat at the polls and his intensification of the Angolan civil war.

By 1994, violence in many parts of the continent led to enormous increases in the number of refugees forced to leave their homes by fighting or by other threats to their safety. As of 1960, the number of refugees in sub-Saharan Africa was negligible. By 1981, estimates suggested that as many as 3,500,000 people had become refugees.

By 1994, the total was at least twice that. In the southern Sudan, three million people, half the total population, had been forced to leave their homes. About 2,000,000 Liberians were refugees in neighboring countries or in Liberia itself. The fighting, still continuing in Angola and just ending in Mozambique, would add at least 2,000,000 more, without counting the continuing refugee problems in Somalia and Ethiopia or the massive flights in Rwanda and Burundi. Worldwide, more than half of all refugees are Africans.

On the positive side, the removal of the Soviet Union as a perceived threat to white South Africa raised the question of what people of good will should now do about the failed apartheid policies of the past forty years. When Frederick Willem De Klerk became leader of the National Party in 1989, no one expected the National Party to change direction, but De Klerk nevertheless released Nelson Mandela, the leader of the African National Congress from prison, and set about repealing the main legal foundations of apartheid. He opened negotiations with Mandela and other African leaders with the goal of giving South Africa a new constitution based on racial equality. The first non-racial election was held in 1994, with an electoral victory for the ANC.

Epilogue

From the perspective of 1995, it seems clear that Africa since independence has passed through three distinct stages. The first lasted from about 1960 to the mid-1970s, The second ran from the mid-1970s to about 1990. The beginning of the third is clear, though its future course is still very clouded. It began in the late 1980s with the swing away from earlier errors in economic policy. The end of the superpower rivalries followed. Then came the end of apartheid and the beginning of true independence for the African population of South Africa. In tropical Africa, the end of the political and economic drift of the 1980s is equally clear, but the rise of political violence, in some cases including anarchic conditions, is also marked in many countries. It is, of course, a tendency that began well back in time, but it is too soon to guess whether it will get worse before it gets better.

To return to the alternation of optimism and pessimism about Africa outlined at the beginning of this chapter, we must admit that our unguarded optimism of the 1960s was mistaken—no matter how much it seemed to be supported by events at that time. Most trends of the post-colonial decades, however, might leave little room for optimism today. Although superpower rivalry endorsing African violence has ended, plenty of violence continues without outside help. Civil wars, tribal and other conflicts, corrupt and dictatorial governments, military rulers who schedule elections and then void the results, poverty, disease, drought, famine—all hinder or prevent long-term development. However, not all of Africa is unstable and devastated; there is scattered economic progress, and a half-dozen countries have had free elections. A variety of specialized projects— yielding everything from clean drinking water, to inoculations for children, to greater literacy—have been instituted.

Indeed, a few bright spots exist. Zimbabwe and Botswana are generally regarded as success stories. For example, when Botswana gained independence in 1966, it was surrounded by hostile white minority regimes, had a per capita income of $35, and exported nothing. It did have a centuries-old tradition of consultation and consensus between its Tswana leaders and the people. Using that tradition as a foundation, Botswana has carved a successful democracy which has steadily improved in economics, health care, education, and protection of resources. In addition, Namibia, formerly South West Africa, is making it, as are Ghana, Zambia, and the Ivory Coast. Uganda, after the atrocities of Idi Amin, is progressing. Malawi recently held a peaceful election, naming a successor to H. K. Banda who headed the government there for the last thirty years. Finally, the coming of true independence for South Africa, Africa's most developed nation, could make an enormous difference far beyond South Africa's borders. Perhaps the near-universal pessimism about Africa among present-day commentators will be as mistaken as the optimism of the early 1960s. We hope so.

PHOTOGRAPH CAPTIONS AND CREDITS

Part I opener (pages 2–3) Agricultural agent testing yield at pond stocked with fish in Nigeria. (© Beryl Goldberg) **Chapter 1** (page 5) Young girl. Kano, Nigeria. (Philip Curtin) **Chapter 2** (page 17) Preparing grain beside a baobob tree. Bolgatanga, Ghana. (© Beryl Goldberg) **Chapter 3** (page 33) Map of Africa in 1626. Facsimile by North Wind Picture Archives.

Part II opener (pages 46–47) Village near Bobo-Dioulasso (Upper Volta), Burkina Faso. (© Beryl Goldberg) **Chapter 4** (page 49) Brass worker in Bida, Nigeria. (Philip Curtin) **Chapter 5** (page 63) Extended family. Ouahigouya, Burkina Faso. (© Beryl Goldberg) **Chapter 6** (page 77) Member of coffee and cocoa growers' cooperative harvesting coffee. Toumanguie, Ivory Coast. (© Beryl Goldberg) **Chapter 7** (page 87) Political rally. Kano, Nigeria. (© Beryl Goldberg) **Chapter 8** (page 101) Makola market. Accra, Ghana. (© Beryl Goldberg) **Chapter 9** (page 115) Praying. Ouahigouya, Burkina Faso. (© Beryl Goldberg)

Part III opener (pages 126–127) Fishing village. Dixcove, Ghana. (© Beryl Goldberg) **Chapter 10** (page 129) Father and son. Ouagadougou, Burkina Faso. (© Beryl Goldberg) **Chapter 11** (page 139) Cultivation in Burkina Faso. (Philip Curtin) **Chapter 12** (page 151) Mosque. Mopti, Mali. (© Beryl Goldberg) **Chapter 13** (page 165) Scene near the Cape Coast in Ghana. Elmina castle can be seen in the distance. (United Nations) **Chapter 14** (page 179) Immigrants from Africa transported to America in chains in crowded quarters below ship decks. (Culver Pictures) **Chapter 15** (page 191) Menelik II, Emperor of Ethiopia 1889–1913. (Culver Pictures) **Chapter 16** (page 205) Praying. Ouagadougou, Burkina Faso. (© Beryl Goldberg) **Chapter 17** (page 217) The Zulu War: Attack on an escort of the 80th Regiment at the Intombi River. (Culver Pictures) **Chapter 18** (page 229) Two colonial officers sitting in a Tiv gathering in Nigeria in 1950. (Paul Bohannan) **Chapter 19** (page 239) A. L. Adu, an African administrator, toward the end of British rule in the Gold Coast. (Philip Curtin)

Part IV opener (pages 250–251) Commerce near train station in Ouagadougou, Burkina Faso. (© Beryl Goldberg) **Chapter 20** (page 253) School children. Abidjan, Ivory Coast. (© Beryl Goldberg)

Cover photographs by Kent Eimers.

FURTHER READING

A flood of new writing about Africa has appeared in the past forty years. The vast majority of the best work on Africa has, indeed, appeared since the first edition of this work came out in 1964. The books and articles listed below are little more than a sample of where to begin on particular topics.

Bibliographies

Hector Blackhurst (ed.), *Africa Bibliography 1984* (Manchester: Manchester University Press, 1985) is the first volume of a recent annual series which adds to the already established series published by the International African Institute in London. More up-to-date references can be found in the principal periodicals listed below, and in the bibliographies of recent books on several of these topics.

Bibliographical Guidance

In the 1980s and early 1990s, the Social Science Research Council/American Council of Learned Societies, Joint-Committee on African Studies supported a series of reviews of the literature in various fields of African Studies. These were presented at the African Studies Association meetings and later published in *African Studies Review*. The articles not only listed recent work in their particular fields, they also discussed the development of knowledge in these fields in recent decades. They are listed below under the appropriate subject headings. Each is marked JCAS to indicate its sponsorship.

Periodicals

Africa Report (bi-monthly) is a quality journal that reports on current African Affairs. *West Africa* (weekly) and *Southern Africa* (monthly) have similar coverage for those regions. *The Economist* (London) also prints an American edition, and it has good coverage of African news. The *Journal of Modern African Studies* is somewhat more technical and covers the special fields of international relations, political science, and economics. *Cahiers d'études africaines* (Paris) is also multidisciplinary, dealing with literature, politics, anthropology, and history. It publishes some articles in English, though French is its principal language. *Africa*, published by the International Africa Institute in London is more concerned with social anthropology, including linguistics. *African Studies* (London) is somewhat broader and publishes a good deal on history. The principal historical journals, however, are *Journal of African History* and *International Journal of African Historical Studies*. For archaeological developments, the relevant journal is *African Archaeological Review*. *African Arts* is also valuable for that field.

General Books

The best of the recent general books on all aspects of African studies is Phyllis M. Martin and Patrick O'Meara, *Africa*, 2nd ed. (Bloomington: Indiana University Press, 1986). In addition, two atlases are far more than collections of maps. These are Jocelyn Murray, *Cultural Atlas of Africa* (New York: Facts on File, 1982) and J. F. Ade Ajayi and Michael Crowder (eds.), *Historical Atlas of Africa* (Cambridge: Cambridge University Press, 1985).

Specialized Sources

Geography

William A. Hance, *The Geography of Modern Africa*, 2nd ed. (New York: Columbia Press, 1975) is a useful summary for the entire continent. A regional geography of prime quality is R. J. Harrison Church, *West Africa*, 7th ed. (London: Longman, 1974). A. T. Grove, *The Changing Geography of Africa* (London: Oxford University Press, 1989).) provides a convenient up-date.

Catherine Coquery-Vidrvitch surveys the early history of urbanization in "The Process of Urbanization in Africa (From the Origin to the Beginning of Independence)," *African Studies Review*, 34:1–98 (1991) JCAS, while Alin Mabogiunje takes up the post-colonial period in "Urban Planning and the Post-Colonial State in

Africa: A Research Review," *African Studies Review*, 33:121–203 (1990) JCAS.

Prehistory

For the earliest evidence of man in Africa see Roger Lewin, *The Origin of Modern Humans* (New York: Scientific American Library, 1993). Graham Connah, *African Civilizations. Precolonial Cities and States in Tropical Africa: An Archaeological Perspective* (Cambridge: Cambridge University Press, 1987) is a useful introduction through a number of case studies. Peter Robertshaw (ed.), *A History of African Archaeology* (London: James Currey, 1990) is a convenient survey of what archaeologists can tell people in other specialities. John Sutton, *A Thousand Years of East Africa* (Nairobi: British Institute in Eastern Africa, 1990) is a convenient regional survey. David Phillipson, *African Archaeology*, 2nd ed. (Cambridge: Cambridge Press, 1993) is the most recent general survey of the later archaeology of Africa. J. Desmond Clark, and Sven A. Brandt (eds.), *From Hunters to Farmers* (Berkeley: University of California Press, 1984), is an important collection of papers on the transition to agriculture, while Christopher Ehret and Merrick Posnansky (eds.), *The Archaeological and Linguistic Reconstruction of African History* (Berkeley: University of California Press, 1982) correlates linguistic with archaeological evidence.

General History

Two recent landmarks in the historiography of Africa are the eight-volume sets dealing with African history from the beginning to the post-colonial world. These are *The Cambridge History of Africa*, 8 vols. (Cambridge: Cambridge Press, completed in 1986) and *UNESCO, General History of Africa*, 8 vols. (Paris: UNESCO, completed in 1993). The Cambridge volumes are principally the work of British historians of Africa, while each of the UNESCO volumes is edited by an African scholar, though the contributors are drawn from the international community of Africanists.

In briefer form, Philip D. Curtin, Steven Feierman, Leonard Thompson, and Jan Vansina, *African History: From the Earliest Times to the end of the Colonial Period*, 2nd ed. (London: Longman, 1994) deals with the history of the whole continent in a single volume. Roland Oliver, *The African Experience: Major Themes in African History from the Earliest Times to the Present* (New York: Icon, 1992) has more of the quality of a protracted essay than a reference volume. For the colonial period, Adu Boahen, *African*

Perspectives on Colonialism (Baltimore: Johns Hopkins University Press, 1987) contains the reflections of one African historian on the events of the colonial period.

At the regional level of synthesis, each major region has had a multivolume work. In some respects, these have been superseded by the UNESCO and Cambridge histories, but David Birmingham and Phyllis M. Martin, *History of Central Africa*, 2 vols. (London: Longman, 1983) is recent and of unusually high quality. Central Africa in this case means the whole region from Chad on the north, southward through Zaïre and Angola and east to Mozambique on the Indian Ocean. J. F. Ade Ajayi and Michael Crowder, *History of West Africa*, 2 vols, (London: Longman, 1971–76, third edition of volume 1, 1985). This edition does much the same kind of job for West Africa and the first volume has been recently revised.

For South Africa, the recent crisis has encouraged a stream of books, many of high quality. Two recent surveys of South African History are J. D. Omer-Cooper, *History of Southern Africa*, 2nd ed (London: James Currey, 1993) and Leonard Thompson, *A History of South Africa* (New Haven: Yale University Press, 1990). For more detailed studies, see Shula Marks and Anthony Atmore (eds.), *Economy and Society in Pre-Industrial South Africa* (London: Longman, 1980) and Shula Marks and Richard Rathbone (eds.), *Industrialization and Social Change in South Africa: African Class Formation, Culture, and Consciousness 1870–1930* (London: Longman, 1982).

On particular themes, Paul H. Lovejoy, *Transformations in Slavery: A History of Slavery in Africa* (Cambridge: Cambridge University Press, 1983) and Patrick Manning, *Slavery and African Life: Occidental, Oriental, and African Slave Trades* (Cambridge: Cambridge University Press, 1990) are useful surveys of slavery and the slave trade from different points of view.

Polity

Two classic accounts of "traditional" African polity are Meyer Fortes and E. E. Evans-Pritchard, *African Political Systems* (London: Oxford Press, 1940) and John Middleton and David Tait, *Tribes Without Rulers* (London: Routledge and Kegan Paul, 1958). For more recent studies of the interaction of culture and politics, see Crawford Young, *The Politics of Cultural Pluralism* (Madison: University of Wisconsin Press, 1976) and Igor Kopytoff (ed.), *The African Frontier: The Reproduction of Traditional African Societies* (Bloomington: Indiana University Press, 1985).

For a survey of contemporary politics see Gwendolen Carter and Patrick O'Meara (eds.), *African Independence: The First Twenty-Five Years* (Bloomington: Indiana University Press, 1985). Bruce Berman and John Lonsdale, *Unhappy Valley: Conflict in Kenya and Africa* (London: James Currey, 1992) is a thoughtful study of late colonial and post-colonial political life.

For political instability and military regimes, John W. Harbson (ed.), *The Military in African Politics* (New York: Praeger, 1987) presents a series of articles surveying the military/political scene in several different countries.

Economy

For the pre-colonial economy, some of the older works are again useful. See, in particular, S. F. Nadel, *A Black Byzantium* (London: Oxford Press, 1942) and Paul and Laura Bohannan, *Tiv Economy* (Evanston: Northwestern University Press, 1968). Among more recent theoretical works see Claude Meillassoux, *Maidens, Meal, and Money: Capitalism and the Domestic Community* (Cambridge: Cambridge University Press, 1981) and Sara S. Berry, *Fathers Work for their Sons: Accumulation, Mobility, and Class Formation in an Extended Yoruba Community* (Berkeley: University of California Press, 1985), an exemplary study of the ways in which present material life responds to the on-going traditions of an African society. See also Sara S. Berry's "The Food Crisis and Agrarian Charge in Africa: A Review Essay," *African Studies Review*, 27:59–112 (1984), JCAS, along with Frederick Cooper, "Africa in the World Economy," *African Studies Review*, 24:1–86 (1981), JCAS. Allen Isaacman surveys the role of the peasantry in social movements in "Peasants and Rural Social Protest in Africa," *African Studies Review*, 33:1–120 (1990) JCAS. For recent problems, Paul Richards, "Ecological Change and Politics in African Land Use," *African Studies Review*, 26:10–72 (1983) JCAS is useful survey of the field, as is Bill Freund, "Labor and Labor History in Africa," *African Studies Review*, 27:1–58 (1984) JCAS.

Disease

For the role of disease in Africa, Gerald W. Hartwig and K. Davis Patterson, *Disease in African History* (Durham: Duke University Press, 1978) is a good introduction. John M. Janzen and Steven Feierman (eds.), *The Social Basis of Health and Healing in Africa* (Berkeley: University of California Press, 1992) is a useful collection of recent articles on African disease problems.

Women in Africa

Gender studies about Africa have blossomed in recent decades, as they have for the social sciences at large. Jane I. Guyer, "Household and Community in African Studies," *African Studies Review*, 24:87–138 (1981) JCAS, surveys a slightly broader field that includes women's studies. Among individual studies, Iris Berger, *Threads of Solidarity: Women in South African Industry 1900–1980* (Bloomington: Indiana University Press, 1992) and Belinda Bozzoli and Mmantho Kkotsoe, *Women of Phokeng: Consciousness, Life Strategy, and Migrancy in South Africa, 1900–1983* (London: James Currey, 1991) are especially recommended.

Art

Many attractive books deal with African art. Frank Willett, *African Art* (London: Thames and Huston, 1960) is especially valuable because Willett is both art historian and anthropologist; his book contains a well-chosen selection of plates, good descriptions of techniques, and a thorough and interesting review of the literature from the 1860s through the 1960s. Among the older picture books, the classic work is William Fagg and Eliot Elisofon, *The Sculpture of Africa* (New York: Praeger, 1958) is a beautiful match between the art historian and the photographer.

Jan Vansina, *Art History in Africa: An Introduction to Method* (London: Longman, 1984) is concerned not simply with styles, style changes, and aesthetic factors, but even more with the way art interacts with society, history, and other aspects of culture.

Language

The accepted language classification for Africa is Joseph H. Greenberg, *The Languages of Africa*, 3rd ed. (Bloomington: Indiana University Research Center, 1970). For social aspects of language use and literacy see also John R. Goody (ed.), *Literacy in Traditional Societies* (Cambridge: Cambridge Press, 1968,) and Joseph A. Greenberg, *On Language: Selected Writings of Joseph H. Greenberg* (Stanford: Stanford University Press, 1990) contains many important articles on African linguistics.

African literature in English is now represented by a wide variety of works by different authors from the plays of Wole Soyinka to the novels of Amos Tutuola and Nadine Gordimer. Harold Scheub, "A

Review of African Oral Traditions and Literature," *African Studies Review*, 28:1:1–72 (1985) is the relevant JCAS-sponsored survey of oral literature.

Religion and Philosophy

E. Bolaji Idowu, *African Traditional Religions: A Definition* (Maryknoll, NY: Orbis Books, 1973) and John S. Mbiti, *African Religions and Philosophy* (New York: Praeger, 1970) provide an introduction to African traditional religion. Terrence O. Ranger and Isaria Kimambo (eds.), *The Historical Study of African Religion* (Berkeley: University of California Press, 1972) deals with some of the historical problems. Among individual studies, Wyatt MacGaffey, *Religion and Society in Central Africa: The Bakongo of Lower Zaïre* (Chicago: University of Chicago Press, 1986) is especially valuable, and Valentin Mudimbe, *The Invention of Africa: Gnosis, Philosophy, and the Order of Knowledge* (Bloomington: Indiana University Press, 1988) is a recent consideration of Africa by an African philosopher.

The JCAS sponsored three separate studies in this increasingly important field of knowledge. They are: Wyatt MacGaffey, "African Ideology and Belief," *African Studies Review*, 24:227–274 (1981); V. Y. Mudimbe, "African Gnosis: Philosophy and Orders of Knowledge," *African Studies Review*, 28:149–223 (1985); and Terrence O. Ranger, "Religious Movements and Politics in Sub-Saharan Africa," *African Studies Review*, 29:1–69 (1986).

INDEX

Abbasid Caliphate, 161
Abeokuta, Westernization and, 216
Aborigines Rights Protection Society (ARPS), 245
Abyssinia, fighting over, 176. *See also* Ethiopia
Achebe, Chinua, 39, 53
  Things Fall Apart of, 224
Acheulian culture, 135
  disappearance of, 136
Addis Ababa, Soviet Union and, 266
Aesthetic judgments, 152–153
Aesthetics, of African art, 58–60
Affonso I, 175
African Americans. *See* Afro-Americans
African history, teaching of, 6–7.
African legal systems. *See* Courts; Government; Law(s)
African National Congress (ANC), 243, 268
  forerunner of, 246
  Mandela and, 249
Africans
  in colonial governments, 233–234
  survival as slaves, 181–182
African Studies programs, 6–7
Afrikaans language, 197

Afrikaners, 197. *See also* Boer secondary empire
Afro-Americans
  African heritage of, 7
  cultural and racial mixes of, 13
  in Sierra Leone, 214, 215
  U.S. population of, 185–186
Afro-Asiatic languages, 39, 141–142
Age grade, 193, 194
Age-set, and labor, 83–64
Aging, grandparenthood and, 74–75
Agriculture, 140–144. *See also* Bantu languages, expansion of; Droughts; Subsistence areas
  communal village program and, 258–259
  crops from Americas, 143
  domestication of animals and, 147–148
  and economic development in colonial Africa, 235–236
  Iron Age and, 144–145
  revolution in, 140–144
  rices and, 143
  soils and, 23–26
  subsistence areas and, 43–45
Ahmadu, 224
AIDS, 31

Aksum, kingdom of, 155
Akwamu, slave trade and, 183
Algeria
  insurrection in, 247
  Ottoman Turks in, 175
Almamates, 210
  of Bundu, 210
Almami
  leadership and, 210
  Touré as, 225–226
'Alwa, kingdom of, 163
Americas, slavery and, 181–182,
    185. See also Brazil; Cuba;
    United States
Amharic language, 36, 40
Amin, Idi, 7, 263, 268
Anglo-African merchants, 215
Anglo-Boer War (1899–1902), 220
Angola. See also Kongo
  fighting in, 268
  independence of, 240, 249, 265,
    266
  Portugal and, 175
Angoni kingdoms, 196
Animal husbandry, 140. See also
    Agriculture
Animals
  domestication of, 147–149
  jungle myths and, 8
  as religious sacrifices, 121
  trypanosomiasis and, 30
Annexations, competition among
    European powers, 220–221.
    See also Colonialism and
    colonization
Anthropoid forms, 130
Anthropology. See also Human
    origins
  culture areas and, 34
  human origins and, 130–137
Apartheid, 7, 232. See also South
    Africa
Apes, and hominids in ancient
    Africa, 133–135
Apolo Kagwa, 225
Arabia, Islam and, 158
Arabian Desert, religion and, 159
Arabian peninsula, 18
Arabic numbers, 161
Arabs, historical records of, 166.

See also Islam
Archaeology, human origins and,
    135–137. See also Human
    origins
Armies. See also Wars and
    warfare; Weapons
  military innovation and, 193
  recruiting of, 262
Aro people, slave trade and, 184,
    185
Art(s)
  aesthetic judgments and,
    152–153
  aesthetics of African, 58–60
  communication through, 51
  dance as, 52
  forms and techniques of, 51–54
  history of, 54–56
  Ife bronzes and, 27
  impact on Western world, 60–61
  of Kingdom of Benin, 55–56
  literature as, 52–53
  masked drama as, 57
  masks as, 57
  music as, 52
  Nigerian sculpture, 54–55
  painting, 53
  and religion, 57
  role of, 51, 56–57
  sculpture, 53–54
  theater and, 52–53
  in Western museums, 60–61
Artillery, 174
Asante people, 167, 224
  development of, 190
  gold fields of, 174
  as nation, 243
Asia
  green revolution in, 256–257
  independence in, 246–247
  industrialization in, 256
Atlantic region, slavery in, 181,
    185
Australopithecus, 133
Automobile, rubber prices and,
    236
Azande people (Sudan), ordeals
    and, 98
AZT, 31

Baasskap (domination), 231
Bachwezi empire, 172
Badagry, Creole merchants in, 215
Bahr al-Ghazal region, 200
Bakel, fort at, 214
Balance of power, kinship and, 93
Bambuk, 167
Band, 92
Banda, H.K., 268
Banjul, as British town, 214
Bantu languages, 37, 39
    expansion of, 146–147
    Khoikhoi and, 196
    spread of, 146–147
Bantu states, 91
    courts in, 95–96
Bathurst. See Banjul
Bedoin Arabs (Cyrenaica), 80
Belgian Congo. See also Zaire
    elections in, 261
    Katanga province and, 264
    stabilized labor in, 85
Belgium
    Congo Independent State and,
        221
    independence movements and,
        248
    preparation for electoral
        democracy by, 261
Benin. See also Dahomey;
        People's Republic of Benin
    Kingdom of, 55–56
    military regime in, 266
    Portugal and, 175
Benue-Congo language family, 39
Berbers, 156
Biafra, 257
    independence of, 264
Bicentric organizations, stateless
    societies as, 94–95
Bight of Biafra, slave trade and,
    185
Bini, sculptures of, 55–56
Birth rates, of North American
    slave population, 187
Blixen, Karen, 8
Bneue River, 19
Boer republic
    African culture of, 198
    as secondary empire, 196–198

Bokar Saada Sy, 224–225
Bokassa, Jean Bedel, 7, 263
Bolia states, 171
Bonny, slave trade and, 184
Borno
    Hausa cities and, 210
    Ottoman Turks in, 175–176
Botswana, successes in, 268
Bouré, 167
Brass sculpture, Nigerian, 55
Brazil
    African settlements by ex-slaves
        from, 215, 216
    anti-slave trade laws in, 188
    slave trade to, 185
Bridewealth, 65, 69–71
British South Africa Company,
    226
Bronze Age, 145
Bronzes, 54. See also Art(s); Ife
        bronzes; Sculpture
    as ancient art form, 55
    Benin plaques, 56
Brotherhoods, West African
        religious, 206–207
Buganda
    European-African cooperation in,
        225
    government in, 204
    as nation, 243
    secondary empire of, 202
Bundu, 224–225
    France and, 225
    rulers of, 224–225
Bunyoro, secondary empire of,
    202
Burundi, 242
    peasant risings in, 261
    refugee problems in, 268
Burundi Pygmies, Bantu
        languages and, 146
Bushmen. See San people
Bush telegraph, 107

Caliph
    Abbasid, 161
    Islam and, 159–160
Camels, 148
    herders of, 42

Canary Islands, plantations and slavery in, 181

Cape. *See* Boer republic, as secondary empire; Cape Colony; South Africa

Cape Colony, 196–198
European culture of, 198
Xhosa resistance in, 244

Cape of Good Hope, 196

Cape Town, trade and, 173

Cape Verde islands, languages in, 40

Caravans. *See also* Nomads; Trade
camels, oases, and, 148–149
East African trade and, 102, 106, 201

Caravels, Portuguese, 173

Carbon-14 dating, of human origins, 132

Caribbean islands, slave trade to, 185

Carving. *See* Sculpture

Cattle
domestication of, 147–148
Fulbe and, 209
use among Bantu-speaking peoples, 170
Xhosa killing of, as protest, 244–245

Cattle belt, 42

Caucasian peoples, 35, 36

Central Africa Republic
Bokassa in, 263
Gbaya protest in, 245

Chad, Lake, 18
Kanem and, 169
languages spoken around, 39

Changamire dynasty, 172
Portugal and, 177

Chiefs. *See* States

Childbearing, 66

Children. *See also* Family life; Women
polygyny and, 67
Tiv (Nigeria), 73–74

China
nomadic-sedentary conflict in, 157
trade with, 172–173

Chinese, in South Africa and Mascarene Islands, 36–37

Christianity. *See also* Religion
in Arabian Desert, 159

Creole clergy and, 215
impact on African religion, 123–125
independent churches and, 244
Monophysite, 155, 158–159
myth of savage Africa and, 9–10
Portuguese conversion and, 174–175
struggles with Muslims, 176–177

Churches, independent African, 244. *See also* Christianity; Religion

Civilization(s)
early, 153–154
and myth of savage Africa, 8–10

Civil war
in Biafra, 264
in Nigeria, 264
in southern Sudan, 265

Clan, 72

Clerics, Fulbe and, 210

Climate
change after Pleistocene period, 136
civilizations and, 167–168
and vegetation, 19–23

Coffee crops, 143

Coinage, 111

Cold War
end of, 267–268
and political alignments in Africa, 13–15

Colonial Africa, 6, 88, 89–90, 216

Colonialism and colonization. *See also* Technology
amalgamation of small states into larger unit and, 225–226
economic development and, 235–238
European-African cooperation in, 225
forms of European conquest, 222–227
governing and, 230–238
government during, 94
lack of preparing for electoral democracy and, 261–263
languages of 39–40
legacies of, 227
market places and, 107
market principle and, 110–111

by Portugal, 175
  resistance to, 243–244
  society under, 82
  Tiv moots during, 97–98
  traditional viewpoints and,
    230–231
Columbus, Christopher, Gold
    Coast voyage of, 173–174
Commerce, along West African
    coast, 213–214. See Trade
Common law, 97
Communal Land Rights (Vesting
    in Trustees Law (1958), 82
Communal ownership, 81, 83
Communication. See also
    Migration; Trade;
    Transportation
  art as, 51, 57
  colonialism and, 232–233
  markets and, 107
  rise of Islam and, 161–162
  technological progress and, 154
Communism, 240, 266
  and Africa, 13–14
Communities, space, territory,
    and, 78
Congo. See also Belgian Congo;
    Zaire
  independence and, 248
  military regime in, 266
  as Zaire, 255
Congo Basin, marketing system
    of, 109
Congo Independent State, 221
Congo-Kinshasa, 264
  United States intervention and,
    266
Congo River, 18
Conquests. See Colonialism and
    colonization; Independence
    movements; Warfare
Convention People's Party (CPP),
    247, 262
Conversion. See also Christianity;
    Islam; Religion
  decline of, 231
  Islam and, 159–160, 207
Convicts, as enforced labor, 181
Copper, 26–27
Coptic Church, 123–124

Côte d'Ivoire (Ivory Coast), 259
  French trading posts in, 214
  leadership in, 263
  successes in, 268
Courts. See also Law(s)
  law and, 95–96
  state organization and, 97
Co-wife. See Polygyny
Creole languages, 40
Creoles (people), 215
Cro-Magnon immigrations, 136
Crops, 43–45. See also Food
    production
  agricultural migration and, 143
  from Americas, 143
  in Bantu-speaking areas, 147
  diffusion of, 143–144
Cuba, slave trade and, 188
Cultivation, 141. See also
    Agriculture
  shifting, 23–24
Cultural institutions, 50–61
Culture(s). See also Human
    origins; Race(s); Religion;
    Society
  aesthetic judgments and,
    152–153
  African assessments of African
    and Western, 234
  appeals to past and, 255
  arts and, 51
  bicultural style of, 51
  colonialism and, 232–233
  comparative technological
    progress of, 153–156
  languages as, 146
  Nok sculpture and, 54–55
  of North American Afro-
    Americans, 13
  political order, disorder, and,
    261–263
  Portguese impact on, 177–178
  race and, 11–13
  of Sub-Saharan Africa, 152–164
  value judgments and, 152–153
  Westernization and, 214–216
Culture areas, 34–35
  of art, 56
Currencies
  in formerly French states, 260

problems with, 260
Cyrenaica, Bedoin Arabs and, 80

Dahomey, 215. *See also* People's
    Republic of Benin
  arts and culture of, 61
  ex-slaves in, 215
  gun-slave cycle and, 189
  priesthood in, 116
  religion of, 118
Dakar, trade and, 106
Dance, 51
Darfur, 199
"Dark Continent", Africa as, 6
Dart, Raymond, 130
Date palm, spread of, 148
DeGaulle, Charles, independence
    movements and, 248
De Klerk, F. W., 249, 268
Demand, economic development
    and, 236
Democracy, 262–263
Demographics, of slave trade, 187
Denmark, abolition of slave trade
    and, 187
Dependency theory, 258
Descent groups, 72–73
Desert regions, 20
  camels in, 148
  oases, agriculture, and, 148–149
  states on edge of, 167
Developed countries, 256
Developing world, 25
Development. *See* Economic
    development; Urban
    development
Diagne, Blaise, 245
Diamonds, 27
Dictatorships
  in Equatorial Guinea, Central
    Africa Republic, and
    Uganda, 263
  military, 262–263
Diet, and agriculture, 43, 44
Diffusion
  of crops, 143–144
  spread of iron technology,
    145–146
Dingiswayo (Mtethwa chief),
    military innovation of, 193

Dioula. *See* Juula
Diseases, 28–32
  isolation caused by, 32
  plantations, slavery, and, 181
Dispute settlement, 97–98. *See*
    also Courts; Law(s)
  self-help tradition and, 98–99
Divination, 120–121
Divorce, 67
  inheritance and, 71–72
Doe, Samuel, revolt by, 265–266
Dogma, in African religions,
    119–121
Domestication, of animals,
    147–149
Drama, masked, 57
Droughts, 257
  food production and, 259
  news coverage of, 7
  in 16th and 17th centuries, 175
Dry farming, shifting cultivation
    as, 23–24
Dry lands, 22–23
Dutch East India Company, 196
Dynasties, religious orientations
    of, 210. *See* Empire(s); groups
    by name

East Africa
  European conquest of, 219
  prosperity in, 164
  secondary empire in, 201–204
  time of troubles in, 176
  trade and, 173
Ebi people, of Yoruba, 82–83
Ecology, of Senegal Valley, 208.
    See also Geography; Land
Economic change, money and,
    111–112
Economic development
  in colonial Africa, 235–238
  shifting demand and, 236
  technology and, 236
  timing of, 237–238
  transportation and, 236–237
Economy. *See also* Slaves and
    slavery
  African difficulties with,
    260–261
  labor and, 83–86

marketing boards and, 260
monetary systems in, 112–113
policy directions in, 258–261
polity and, 78–86
post-colonial, 256–258
reciprocity and, 112
redistribution and, 112–113
regional specialization in, 170
slavery and, 187
subsistence, 43–45
trade and, 102–114
Egypt
African and Asian culture of,
    142
British annexation of Egyptian
    sudan, 220
British control of, 200–201
empire in sudan, 199
Muhammad 'Ali in, 198–199
Ottoman Turks in, 176
Elections
lack of preparedness for
    independence and, 262
preparation for, 261
Electoral democracy, lack of
    preparation for, 261–263
Elmina, Portuguese castle at, 174
Empire(s). See also Colonialism
    and colonization; Europe;
    Ghana; Jihads; Kanem; Mali;
    Roman Empire; Secondary
    empires; Takrur
Bachwezi, 172
Egypt, 199
Ghana, 166–167
Lunda, 177
Monomotapa, 172
Oyo, 188
in precolonial century, 192
theories of, 230–233
Tijani, 211–213
of western sudan, 166–169
Zanzibari trade network as, 202
England. See Great Britain
English language, 39, 40
Epstein, Jacob, 58
Equatorial Guinea, Nguema in,
    263
Eritrea, 267
secession of, 264–265

Erythriote peoples. See
    Ethiopian/Somali peoples
Ethiopia
Eritrea secession from, 264–265
fall of empire, 265
government overthrow in, 266
independence of, 222
Portuguese-Turkish conflict
    over, 176
refugee problems in, 268
Ethiopian/Somali (Hamite,
    Erythriote) peoples, 35, 36
Ethnic groups, trade specialization
    by, 106
Ethnicity, African nationalism
    and, 242
Europe. See also Belgium;
    Colonialism and colonization;
    France; Great Britain;
    Portugal; West
African conquest by, 218–227
African culture compared with,
    11
conquests by, 192–204
early civilization in, 153
military innovation from, 193
secondary empire weaknesses
    and, 200
slavery in, 180–181
Europeans. See also Belgium;
    France; Great Britain;
    Portugal
African labor and, 84–85
African sentiment toward,
    242–243
Boer secondary empire and,
    196–198
impact on African art, 59
myth of savage Africa and, 8–11
West African commerce and
    settlement of, 213–214
Evil, in African religions, 118, 119
Evolution, 132
Exports, in colonial Africa,
    235–236

Fairs, market places and, 109
Family law, Western, 96–97
Family life, 64–75

and labor organization, 83
non-familial kinship groups and,
72–75
polygyny and, 65–69
widow inheritance and, 71–72
Famine
in savanna belt, 169
slavery and, 188
Fante people, 224
Fante states, Westernization and,
216
Farmers, nomads and, 157
Farming, 145. *See also*
Agriculture; Food production
animals and, 24–25
land relationships and, 79–80
methods of, 43–44
shifting cultivation as, 23–24
Fergo (emigration), 209
Fertile Crescent, 159
Firm, as social organization, 84
First World War. *See* World War I
Fishing, agricultural revolution
and, 143
Folk tales, 53
Food, price controls and, 260
Food production. *See also*
Agriculture; Diet; Farming
drought and, 259
early humans and, 137
in sub-Saharan Africa, 25
Foraging, 41
Forced labor. *See* Slavery
Forests, 20
cultures of, 136
Fossils, human origins and,
132–133
Framework Law, 248, 261
France
African control by, 225
African empire and, 219
African-French traders and, 215
annexations by, 220
decolonization by, 248
in Egypt, 200
Indochina and, 246
insurrections against, 247
preparation for electoral
democracy by, 261
slave trade and, 185

West African forts of, 214
Freemarket system, 259
French Guinea, Touré in, 225–226
French language, 39, 40
Frobenius, bronze sculptures and,
55
Frontiers, and secessions,
264–265
Fulani people, 80
Fulbe people, 208–210˙
diaspora of, 208
and Hamdullahi, 211
as Hausaland ruling class, 211
Islam and, 208
as network of West African
scholars, 209
as teachers, 209
Funj sultanate, 199
as Muslim state, 163
Fuuta Jaalo (state), Tijani Empire
and, 211
Fuuta Jaalo highlands, Fulbe
revolution in, 210
Fuutanke, 211
Fuuta Tooro, 155, 208
political conflict in, 209
slave trade and, 183

Gabon
French trading posts in, 214
oil and, 257
Gambia, British town in, 214
Gambia Valley, expansion into,
167
Gaza empire, 196
Gbaya, protest by, 245
Gender, in farming, 44. *See also*
Women
Genealogical map, of Tiv people,
80–81
Genetics
human origins and, 131
migration and changes in,
142–143
Geographers, historical records of,
166
Geography
of Africa, 18–19
in Muslim world, 164
space, territoriality, and, 78–83

Geology
  of Africa, 18
  human origins and, 132–133
Ghana, 155
  government of independent, 262
  historical records of, 166–167
  Nkrumah in, 247
  religion in, 162
  sack of capital, 167
  slave trade and, 183
  successes in, 268
Gifts, trade and, 112
Gobir, 210
God, in African religions,
  117–119. See also Religion
Gods Must Be Crazy, The (movie),
  10–11
Gold, 26. See also Minerals;
  Mining
  economic development and, 236
  in Transvaal, 219
Gold Coast
  Columbus and, 173–174
  Convention People's Party (CPP)
    in, 247
  exports of, 102
  peoples of, 224
  Portugal and, 174
  slave trade and, 185
  trading forts of, 214
Gold trade, 176
Goods, trade in market places,
  110. See also Demand; Trade
Government. See also Law(s);
  Political institutions
  under colonialism, 230–238
  conversionism and, 231
  economic policy and, 258–261
  and labor, 83
  law in African societies and,
    95–99
  local, 233–234
  as peacekeeping function,
    233–235
  political order, disorder, and,
    261–263
  representative, 245
  stateless societies and, 92–95
  states and, 90–91
  trusteeship and, 231

Grain crops, 43–45, 143
Grandparenthood, 74–75
Great Britain
  abolition of slave trade, 187
  African annexations by, 220
  African control by, 224
  African empire and, 219–220
  African independence and,
    247–248
  Boer empire and, 197
  Buganda and, 225
  efforts to halt slave trade, 188
  in Egypt, 200–201
  Indian independence and, 246
  maritime interests in East
    Africa, 201
  preparation for electoral
    democracy by, 261
  slave trade and, 185
  and Zanzibari trade network,
    202
Great Depression (1930s)
  economic development and,
    237–238
  labor movement during, 246
Great Trek, in southern Africa,
  197–198
Great Wall of China, nomads and,
  157
Great Zimbabwe, 171–172
Greenberg, Joseph, 38
Green revolution, 25
  in Asia, 256
Gross domestic product (GDC),
  257
Gross national products,
  comparative, 256
Guerrilla faction, RENAMO as, 266
Guinea, independence in, 248
Guinea-Bissau
  independence and, 249
  languages in, 40
Guinea-Conakry, Touré in, 263
Gunpowder, 174
Gun-slave cycle, 189

Haley, Alex, myths about Africa
  and, 10
Hamdullahi, 213

Hamite peoples. *See*
Ethiopian/Somali peoples
Hausa
jihads and, 210
trade of, 106
Health
AIDS and, 31
diseases and, 28–32
Heidelberg man, 134
Herding, 24, 41
Holy war
idea of, in West Africa, 207
Muslim, 210
Hominids, in ancient Africa,
133–135
Homo erectus, 133–134
Homo habilis, 133, 135
Homo sapiens, 134, 135
rhodesiensis, 135, 136
sapiens, 136
Horn of Africa
peoples in, 36
political violence and, 265, 266
Hottentots. *See* Khoikhoi peoples
Houphouet-Boigny, Felix, 248,
259, 263
Human origins, 130–137
Human sacrifice, 122
Hunters-gatherers, 140–141. *See
also* Agriculture; Food
production
in Sahara, 142
Husband. *See* Bridewealth; Family
life; Women

Ibn Khaldun, 157
Ibo peoples
Igbo-speaking people known as,
264
slave trade and, 184
surrender of, 224
Ife bronzes, 27, 55
Igbo-speaking people, 264
Igbo Ukwu style, of bronze
sculpture, 55
Ijo peoples, slave trade and, 184,
185
Illness. *See also* Diseases
Imbangala people
attacks by, 175

slave trade and, 184
Immigrants, African, 13
Immigrations, human origins and,
136Independence
economic development and, 238
frontiers and secessions after,
264–265
lack of preparedness for,
261–263
Independence movements,
240–249
regional nature of, 240
resistance and protest as,
243–246
worldwide, 246–249
India, independence of, 246
Indian Ocean, trade on, 172–173
Indian peoples, 35, 36
Indirect Rule, 89–90
Industrial and Commercial
Workers Union of Africa, 246
Industrialization
post-colonial economics and,
256–258
and Westernization, 14–15
Industrial Revolution
technology and, 192
and West Africa, 213–214
Inheritance, by widows, 71–72
Institutions, 50–61. *See also*
Culture(s); Family life;
Political institutions; Society
political and economic, 78–86,
88–99
Intercontinental trade, 170
International Monetary Fund, 260
Iron Age, 144–145
Iron ore, 27
Islam
in Africa, 161–164
carried by traders, 169
conversions to, 162–163
culture and, 178
effect of writing on historical
records, 166
and Egypt, 200
Fulbe people, and 208–209
impact on African religion,
123–125
literacy and, 190

new empires and, 192
  rise of, 158–161
  in West Africa, 206–207
Islamic jihads. *See* Jihads
Isolation, disease as cause of, 32
Italian language, 40
Ivoirian system. *See* Côte d'Ivoire
Ivory Coast. *See* Côte d'Ivoire
Ivory trade, 184

Jaga, invasion of Kongo, 177. *See*
  Imbangala people
Jahaanke, 106
Japan, Indochina and, 246–247
Java, independence for, 246
Java Man, 134
Jihads
  of Ahmadu Lobbo (Sheikh of
    Maasina), 211
  of Fulbe, 210–211
  holy war against Gobir and, 210
  in 19th century, 210–213
  Tijani Empire and, 211–213
  Touré as leader of, 226
Joker, as source of evil, 118
Jolof, Portugal and, 175
Judaism, in Arabian Desert, 159
Jungles, myths of, 7–8
Juula (Dioula), 106

Kaatta, 213
Kadalie, Clements, 246
Kalahari Desert, 19, 20
  slave trade and, 184
Kanem, 169
  conversion to Islam, 162
  historical records of, 166
Karanga people, 171–172
Katanga province, secession
  efforts of, 264
Katsina, 210
Kaunda, Kenneth, 263
Kenya
  Kenyatta in, 263
  language of, 40
  population in, 25
  Portuguese impact on region,
    177
Kenyatta, Jomo, 263
Khartoum, Islamic rising in, 200
Khoikhoi peoples, 36, 196

Khoisan peoles, 35, 36, 136. *See*
  also San peoples
Kikuyu, religious sacrifices in, 116
Kilwa, 201
  coast trade and, 177
  sack of, 177
  trade and, 163
Kingdom of Benin, arts of, 55–56
Kingdoms, 90–91. *See also*
  individual kingdoms and
  peoples by name
  almamates, 210
  Angoni, 196
  growth of, 155–156
  Kongo, 170–171, 177
  loyalty to, and nationalism, 243
Kinship, 64–75. *See also* Lineage
  systems
  non-familial kinship groups,
    72–75
  and stateless societies, 92
Kongo. *See also* Angola
  Jaga invasion of, 177
  kingdom of, 170–171, 172, 243
  kings of, 175
  Portugal and, 175
Kordofan, 199
Krio language, 40
Kush, kingdom of, 155

Labor, 83–86
  in Belgian Congo, 85
  and markets, 104
  migratory, 85
  in modern Africa and West, 84
  slavery and, 181
  whites and, 85–86
Labor union, in South Africa, 246
Lagos
  British annexation of, 215
  Creole merchants in, 215
Lake Chad, 18
  Kanem and, 169
  languages spoken around, 39
Lake Mai Ndombe, 171
Lake Nyasa, 18
Lake Rudolf, 18
Lakes, 18–19
Lake Tanganyika, trade and, 201
Lake Victoria, 18

empires near, 201
Land. *See also* Geography; Geology;
  Maps and mapping; Social
  relationships; geographical
  features by name
allocation and market price, 104
climate, vegetation, and, 19–23
and labor, 83–86
and markets, 104
nomadic-sedentary conflict in, 157
and property system, 81–83
space, territoriality, and, 78–83
Yoruba ownership of, 81–82
Language(s), 37–41
  Afro-Asiatic, 141
  Amharic, 40
  classification of, 38–39
  Creole, 40
  English, 40
  impact of colonial, 39–40
  as issue in Africa, 40–41
  Krio, 40
  as migration evidence, 141–142
  pidgin, 39–40
  Swahili, 40
Lattimore, Owen, 157
Lavalloisian culture, 135
Lavallois-Mousterian culture, 236
Lavigérie (Cardinal), 6
Law(s). *See also* Government;
  Political systems
  in African societies, 95–99
  courts and, 95–96
  dispute settlement and, 97–98
  lineage systems and, 93–94
  self–help tradition and, 98–99
Legal systems. *See* Courts;
  Government; Law(s)
Legba (Dahomean religion), 118
Legislative councils, Africans on, 245
Leopold (Belgium), 221
Lesotho, 242
Less developed countries (LDCs), 256
Lewin, Roger, 135n
Liberia
  Americo-Liberian conquests and,
    221–222
  military revolt in, 265–266
  refugees from, 268
  settlement by ex-slaves, 215

Lineage systems. *See also* Family
  life
  minimal, 80
  stateless society and, 92–94
  states and, 90
Lingua franca, Krio as, 40
Linguistics. *See* Language(s)
Literacy
  of Fulbe, 209
  historical records and, 166
  spread of, 190
Literature, 52–53
  novelists, 53
  playwrights, 53
Livingstone, David, 6
Lobbo, Ahmadu (Sheikh of
  Maasina), 211
Loi-cadre (framework act), 248
Luanda
  Portugal and, 175
  slave trade and, 184
Luba group, 171
Lumumba, Patrice, United States
  intervention and, 266
Lunda empire, changes in, 177

Maasina, Lobbo, Ahmadu, of, 211
Madagascar
  insurrection in, 247
  military regime in, 266
  slave trade and, 185
Madeira, plantatations and slavery
  in, 181
Mahdi, Mhammad 'Ahmad ibn
  'Abdallah as, 200
Mai Ndombe, Lake, 171
Makolo, Barotseland and, 196
Malagasy language, 39
Malagasy Republic, Orientals in,
  36
Malaria, 29–30, 31
Malawi, 196, 268
Mali
  historical records of, 166
  preeminence of, 167
Mali Federation, transportation
  links of, 237
Malik Sy, 210, 224
Mandela, Nelson, 249, 268
Manikongo Mzinga Kuwu, 175

Maps and mapping
  genealogical, 80–81
  market places and, 110
  social, 79–81
  use of, 34–35
  Western vs. African, 78–81
Maritime revolution, 172–174
  Portuguese traders and,
    173–174
Market forces, and labor, 84–85.
  See also Economy
Marketing, trading compared with,
  105–106
Marketing boards, 260
Market places, 107–109
  policing and quality control in,
    108
  religious activities and, 108–109
  in rural Africa, 113
  social aspects of, 109
  systems of, 109–110
Markets
  and market places, 102–105.
    See also Market places
  principle of, 103–104
  spread of, 110–113
Marriage. *See also* Family life;
  Women
  bridewealth and, 69–71
  and Tiv (Nigeria), 74
Marxism, 258
  and Africa, 14
  in Angola and Mozambique,
    265, 266
Mascarene Islands
  Orientals in, 37
  slave trade and, 185
Masks, 57
Matrilineal descent groups, 72.
  See also Women
Mauritius Island, 37
Mecca, 159
Medicine
  diseases and, 28–31
  and European colonialism, 219
Medina, 159
Mediterranean islands, slavery in,
  181
Mediterranean populations, in
  Africa, 136

Men. *See also* Family life;
  Polygyny; Women
  imported as slaves, 187
  trade and, 106
Menelik (Ethiopia), 222
Meroe, 155
Metallurgy, 145–146. *See also*
  Minerals
Metalworking, spread of, 144
Mfecane
  Cape Colony and, 197
  conquest of, 226
  in southern Africa, 194–195
  states founded by, 194
Middle East, development of
  agriculture and urban living
  in, 140–143
Migration. *See also* Diffusion
  early agriculture and, 141
  of Fulbe, 208–209
  and genetic changes, 142–143
  languages as evidence of,
    141–142
Migratory labor, 85
Military, lack of preparedness for
  independence and, 262
Military coups, 7
Military dictatorships, 262–263
Military innovation
  African-based, 193–194
  Boer secondary empire and,
    196–198
  European-based, 192–193
  in 19th-century Africa, 192–194
Millet, spread of, 144
Minerals, 26–28. *See also* Iron
  Age
  copper, 26–27
  diamonds, 27
  economic development and, 236
  gold, 26
  growing importance of, 27–28
  iron ore, 27
  metalworking and, 144
  mining of, 170
  oil, 27
  resources of, 257
Minimal lineage, 80
Mining. *See also* Labor; Minerals
  of copper, 27

economic development and, 236
  of iron ore, 27
Miocene Period, human origins
  and, 133
Mirambo-ya-Banhu, 202
Missionaries
  Portuguese, 174–175
  from Sierra Leone, 215
  Westernization and, 215
Mitochondrial DNA, 134
Mkrumah, Kwame, 255
Mobutu, Joseph. *See* Mobutu Sese
  Seko
Mobutu Sese Seko, 248, 263, 255
Modernization, 254–256
Mogadishu, trade and, 163. *See
  also* Somalia
Mombasa, 201
  Portuguese fortress in, 177
  sack of, 177
  Turkish raids on, 177
Monetary systems, 112–113
Money, economic change and,
  111–112
Monogamy. *See* Polygyny
Monomotapa Empire, 172
Monophysite Christianity, 155
  in Egyptian and Syrian
    provinces, 158–159
Monotheistic religions, 116
Moots, 97–98. *See also* Law(s)
Morocco, growth of power, 176
Mosquitoes. *See* Malaria
Mousterian culture, 135, 136
Mozambique
  fighting in, 268
  independence of, 240, 249, 265,
    266
  Portugal and, 176, 177
  slave trade and, 184, 185
Msiri, 202
Mtethwa, military innovation of,
  193
Muhammad, 159
Muhammad 'Ali, 198–199
Muhammad 'Ahmad ibn 'Abdallah
  (Egypt), 200
Multi-centric organizations,
  stateless societies as, 94–95
Multi-racialism, 247–248

Muqaddimah (Ibn Khaldun), 157
Museums, African arts in Western,
  60–61
Music, 51–52
Muslims
  struggles with Christians,
    176–177
  in West Africa. *See* Islam
Mwenemutapa, 172
  destruction of, 196
  Portugal and, 177
Myth, and religion, 119
Myths about Africa
  Africa as land of jungles, 7–8
  African races and, 11–13
  national political alliances and,
    13–15
  news reporting and, 7
  savage Africa, 8–11
Myungu-ya-Mawe, 202

Namibia, successes in, 268
Natal
  African culture of, 198
  Nguni peoples of, 193
  trade and, 173
  trekboers and, 107
National Assembly (France),
    African representatives in,
    249
National Council of Niger and the
    Cameroons, 247
Nationalism, 240–243
  goals of, 242
  in West Africa, 227
National Liberation Council
    (Ghana), 262
Native Reserves, in South Africa,
    85–86
Natural disasters, 7
Ndebele, 196
  conquest of, 226
Neanderthal Man, 132
Near East, agriculture and,
    142–143
Negroid peoples, 136
  migration of, 144, 146
Negro peoples, 35
Nembe, slave trade and, 184

Newly industrialized countries (NICs), 256
New World. *See* Americas; Slave trade
Nguema, Macias, 263
Nguni peoples, 193
  warfare and, 194
Nigeria. *See also* Tiv people
  Brazilian influence in, 216
  British trade in, 214
  bronze sculpture from, 55
  civil war in (1967–1970), 164
  ex-slaves in, 215
  Hausa trade and, 106
  Ibo in, 224
  Ife bronzes in, 27. *See also* Ife bronzes
  jihads and, 210
  oil and, 257
  population in, 25
  Portugal and, 175
  protest in, 245
  sculptures of, 54–56
  spread of Bantu-speaking peoples and, 146
  Tiv of, 80
Niger-Kordofanian language group, 39
Niger River, 18, 19
Nile River, 18
Nile Valley, agriculture in prehistoric, 142
Nilo-Saharan language group, 39
Nilotes, language of, 39
Nilotic sudan
  Caucasians in, 36
  European conquest of, 219
  Islam in, 164
  secondary empire in, 198
Nkatha Freedom Party, 243
Nkrumah, Kwame, 247
  political parties and, 262
Noble Savage, myth of, 8
Nok culture, sculpture and, 54–55
Nomads, 24
  agriculture and, 141
  camels and, 149
  Fulbe as, 208–209
  Islam and, 159, 162
  raids by, 156–157

and sedentaries, 156–158
Noncentralized society, 89
North Africa
  camels in, 148
  Ottoman Turk control in, 175–176
  Tijanyya of, 211
  traders from, 169
North America, mixture of African cultural and racial heritage in, 13. *See also* Americas; United States
Novelists, 53
Nubian kingdoms, Christian, 163
Nubian states, 155
Nupe, jihad movement in, 211
Nyamwezi
  trade by, 201
  warlords of, 202
Nyasa, Lake, 18
Nyerere, Julius, 255, 263
  "African socialism" of, 258–259

Oases
  agriculture in, 148
  importance of, 157
Obote, Milton, 263
Oil, 27. *See also* Minerals
  and economic development, 257
Old Stone Age. *See* Paleolithic Period
Old World Culture Area, 143
Oman
  as naval power, 201
  Portugal and, 177
Onchocerciasis (river blindness), 28–29
Orange Free State, 194. *See also* South Africa
  British annexation of, 220
Ordeals, for dispute settlement, 98
Organizations, labor and, 83–86
Oriental peoples, 35, 36–37
Oromo, invasions by, 177
Orthodox Church, 159
Oryza
  glaberrima, 143
  sativa, 143
Ottoman Turks, 198–199
  North African control by, 175–176

Portugal and, 176
Ovimbundu people, slave trade and, 184
Oyo
empire of, 188
jihad movement in, 211

Painting, 53. *See also* Art(s)
Pakistan, independence for, 246
Paleolithic Period (Old Stone Age), 135–137
Paleomagnetic evidence, of human origins, 133
Parenthood, 74–75
Pastoralism
of Fulbe, 208–209
nomads and, 156
Paternalism, 231
Patrilineal descent groups, 72
Patriotism, 255–256
Peacekeeping, by European governments, 233–235. *See* Government, under colonialism
Peking Man, 134
Pemba, trade of, 201
Peoples of Africa, 35–37. *See also* Race(s)
Caucasian peoples, 35, 36
Ethiopian/Somali (Hamite, Erythriote), 35, 36
Indian peoples, 35, 36
Khoisan peoples, 35, 36
Negro peoples, 35
Oriental peoples, 35, 36–37
Pygmy peoples, 35
People's Republic of Benin, 215
Persia. *See* Sassanian Empire
Persian Gulf
Portuguese trade and, 177
slave trade and, 185
Philippines, independence for, 246
Pidgin languages, 39–40
Piltdown man, 132
Pitt-Rivers, African arts and, 60
Plantations, slavery and, 181, 185
Plants, diffusion of, 141–142
Plateau Tonga (Zambia), 79
Playwrights, 53
Political alliances, in Africa, 13–15

Political centers. *See* Kingdoms; State(s); centers by name
Political dissent, slavery and, 188
Political institutions, 88–99
and economy, 78–86
indigenous, 89–95
stateless societies and, 89, 92–95
Political order and disorder, 261–263
Political systems, European colonialism and, 94
Political violence, 265–267
Polygyny, 65–69. *See also* Family life; Men; Women
divorce and, 67
social status of women and, 67–69
Polytheistic religions, 116
Population
growth of, 257
railroads and, 237
as refugees, 268
in sub-Saharan Africa, 25
Population decline, and slavery, 181
Portugal
art of, 58
destruction of sphere of influence of, 196
impact on Africa, 174–178
impact on coastal region, 177
independence movements and, 249
independence of colonies, 240
Kilway attack by, 177
maritime trade of, 173–174
and Ottoman Turks, 176
slave trade and, 185, 188
trade control by, 177
Portuguese language, 40
Potassium-40 dating, of human origins, 132–133
Pottery, of Nok culture, 54–55. *See also* Art(s); Sculpture
Poverty, AIDS and, 31
Prayers, 122
Precolonial century, 192
Prehistory. *See* Agriculture; Migration; Stone Age cultures

Priesthood, 116
Property, social relationships and,
    81–83
Pulo, Umar Tal, of, 211
Pygmy peoples, 35, 36
    Bantu languages and, 146

Qadirīyya (brotherhood), 207, 210

Rabih Zubayr, 199–200
Race(s). *See also* Peoples of Africa
    "Cape colored" as, 197
    and culture, 11–13
    human origins and, 137
    migrations and, 142–143
    peoples as, 35–37
Racism
    culture and, 152
    in South Africa, 240
Railroads
    economic development and
        236–237
    national unity and, 237
    population growth and, 237
Rainfall, 22–23. *See also* Climate
    civilizations and, 167–168
Rain shrines, 79
Rassemblement Démocratique
    Africaine (RDA), 247
Rebellion. *See* Independence
    movements
Reciprocity, economies and, 112
Redistribution, economic
    institutionalization and,
    112–113
Red Sea, 18, 159
    Portuguese trade and, 177
    Portuguese-Turkish conflict over
        trade in, 176
Refugees, 267–268
Religion, 116–125. *See also*
    Christianity; Islam
    art and, 57
    brotherhoods in West Africa,
        206–207
    Christianity, Islam, and,
        123–125
    and colonization of Bunganda,
        225
    conversions to Christianity,
        174–175

conversions to Islam, 159–160
correlation with social group,
    116
decline of conversionism and,
    231
descent groups and, 73
divination in, 120–121
dogma in, 119–121
Egyptian, 142
enslavement by, 180
independence toward churches,
    244
Islamic jihads and, 210–213
Islam in Africa, 161–164
market places and, 108–109
Monophysite Christianity as,
    155, 158
monotheistic, 116
moral content of, 118–119
polytheistic, 116
prayer and, 122
rise of Islam, 158–160
ritual in, 116–117, 121–122
sacrifices in, 116, 121–122
as solution to religious
    problems, 120
themes of, 117–119
witchcraft and, 122–123
RENAMO, 266
Republic of Congo-Kinshasa, 264,
    266. *See also* Zaire
Resources. *See also* Agriculture;
    Minerals; Soils
    availability of, 25
    and economic development in
        colonial Africa, 235
    iron, steel, and, 27, 145
    minerals, 26–28
Reunion Island, 37
Rhodesia. *See also* Zimbabwe
    British South African Company
        in, 226
    food production in, 25
    independence and, 248, 249
    labor in, 85–86
    Soviet intervention and, 266
Rice, African and Asian, 143
Rift Valley, 18
    cultures of, 136
Riots. *See* Independence movements

Ritual, religious, 116–117,
121–122
River blindness. *See*
Onchocerciasis
Rivers, 18–19
Roads and highways, economic
development and, 236–237
Roman Empire
Eastern, 158
fall of Western, 158
Romans
civilization of, 54
road system of, 148
Roots (Haley), and myths about
Africa, 10
Rubber, demand for, 236
Rudolf, Lake, 18
Rwanda, 242
peasant risings in, 261

Sacrifices
human, 122
religious, 116, 121–122
Sahara, 20
migration and genetic changes,
142–143
nomads, sedentaries, and,
156–157
prehistoric, 142
Stone Age cultures and, 137
trade along coast, 173–174
Sahel, drought in, 7
Sailing. *See* Ships and shipping
Salt, trade in, 170
Sanhaja Berbers, 162
San peoples, 10–11, 36
Khoisan and, 136
language of, 37
São Tomé
plantations, slavery, and, 181
Portugal and 175
Sassanian Empire, 159
Savage Africa, myth of, 8–11
Savanna, 20
civilizations in, 168–169
cultures of, 136
history of southern, 170–172
records from northern, 170
Savimbi, Jonas, 266
Angola civil war and, 267

Schistosomiasis, 29, 30–31
Scholars, Fulbe, 209
Sculpture, 53–54. *See also*
Bronzes
aesthetics of, 58–59
bronzes as, 54
of Kingdom of Benin, 54–55
in Nigeria, 54–56
types of, 54
Seasons, 22
Secessions, 243
frontiers and, 264–265
Secondary empires
Boer, 196–198
of Buganda, 202
of Bunyoro, 202
Congo Independent State as,
221
in East Africa, 201–204
between 1884–1908, 221–222
Ethiopia as, 222
Liberia as, 221–222
limitations of, 199
Mfecane and, 194
military technology and, 193
from north, 198–201
in Transvaal, 219–220
Union of South Africa as, 222
weaknesses of, 200
Zanzibari trade network as, 202
Second World War. *See* World
War II
Sedentary peoples
Fulbe as, 208–209
nomads and, 156–158
Seers and diviners, for dispute
settlement, 98
Segu, 213
Selassie, Haile, 266
Sembene, Ousemane, 39
Semitic languages, 39
Senegal
French in, 214
Portugal and, 175
rulers of, 225
Senghor in, 263
Senegalese people, trade of, 106
Senegal Valley
Fulbe in, 208–209
Takrur in, 169

Senegambia, gifts in, 112
Senghor, Léopold, 255, 263
Sesame crops, 143
Seyyid Said, 201
Shaba, 171
    state in, 202
Shaba province, slave trade and,
    184
Shaka (Zulu ruler)
    military and, 193–194
    wars of, 194
Shifting cultivation, 23–24
Ships and shipping
    Portuguese trade and, 173–174
    revolution in, 172–174
    trade and, 183
Shire River, 18, 19
Shona, conquest of, 226–227
Shrines, in market places, 109.
    See Rain shrines
Sierra Leone
    culture change and, 215
    as settlement colony, 214
Slaves and slavery, 180–190. See
    also Slave trade
    adaptation of Africans to climate
        and, 182
    Afrikaners and, 197
    from America, 215–216
    Boer secondary empire and, 196
    convicts and, 181
    European, 180–181
    European change in African,
        183
    as labor source, 181
    Liberian settlement and, 215
    myths about Africa and, 9–10
    origins of African, 180–182
    Portugal and, 175
    self-perpetuating slave
        population, 187–188
    warfare as cause of, 188
Slave trade
    abolition of, 187–188
    in Africa, 182–185
    African participation in,
        182–183
    to Brazil, 185
    to Caribbean islands, 185
    demand for, 185

demographics of, 187
destinations of, 184–185
duration of, 188
in East Africa, 201
European conquests and, 192
growth and incidence of,
    185–188
impact on Africa, 188–190
price of slaves and, 187
to United States, 185–186
in West Africa, 206, 213–214
Sleeping sickness. See
    Trypanosomiasis
Smallpox, 28
Socialism, Nyerere and, 258–259
Social problems, religion as
    solution to, 120
Social relationships, mapping of,
    78–83
Society. See also Culture(s);
    Institutions; Political
    institutions; Social
    relationships
    under colonialism, 82
    family life in, 64–75
    labor and, 83–86
    law in African, 95–99
    non-familial kinship groups in,
        72–75
    role of arts in, 56–57
Sofala, trade and, 177
Soils, and agriculture, 23–26
Sokoto, 211
Somalia. See also Mogadishu
    refugee problems in, 268
    revolution in, 266
    Soviet Union and 266–267
Songhai, 167
    Hausa cities and, 210
    time of troubles in, 176
Soninke people
    dry period and, 169
    trade diasporas of, 106
Soninke state, Ghana as, 155
Sotho, Lesotho state and, 196–197
Sotho chiefdoms, Nguni groups
    and, 194
South Africa, 7
    abolition of apartheid in, 249

African National Congress (ANC)
in, 243, 246
African political party in, 246
apartheid in, 232
Caucasians in, 36
economic development of, 238
gold in, 26
Industrial and Commercial
Workers Union of Africa,
246
labor in, 85–86
non-racial elections in, 268
racism in, 240
society in, 196
Soviet intervention in, 266
Union of, 222
Southeast Asia, independence
movement in, 246–247
Southern Africa
Afro-European relations in, 198
Boer secondary empire in,
196–198
Mfecane in, 194–195
Southern savanna, history of,
170–172
Soviet Union
and Africa, 13–14
influence of, 266–267
intervention by, 266
Soyinka, Wole, 39, 53
Spain, abolition of slavery by, 188
Specialization, regional, 170
Special purpose money, 111–112
Stabilized labor, 85
State(s)
Ghana as, 166–167
as indigenous political system,
89, 90–91
in southern savanna, 170
Stateless societies, 92–95
law in, 96–97
as political organization, 89
Steel, 145
Stereotypes, and race, 12
Stimulus diffusion, 143–144
Stone Age cultures, 135–137
Straits of Melaka, 172
Strikes, in South Africa, 246
Subordination, as European
attitude, 231–232

Sub-Saharan Africa. *See also*
Peoples of Africa
agricultural revolution in, 143
culture of, 152–164
iron technology in, 145
Islam in, 161–164
peoples of, 35–37
population and food production
in, 25
states in, 155
Subsistence areas, 41–45
Subsistence economy
defined, 103–104
in Sahara, 142
tensions in, 45
Sudan
caliphate in, 201
civil war in, 265
history of western, 166–169
time of troubles in, 175–176
Swahili coast, slave trade and, 185
Swahili language, 164
education in, 40
Swahili peoples, trade by, 201
Swazi, military innovation and,
196
Swaziland, 196, 242

Tabora, trade and, 201
Takrur, 155, 169
historical records of, 166
Islam and, 162
Takruri, 208
Tanganyika, Lake, trade and, 201
Tanzania, 196
"African socialism" in, 258
Nyerere in, 255, 263
Portuguese impact on region,
177
states in, 202
Swahili language education in,
40
trade and, 201
Tarīqa (brotherhoods), 206–207
Taxation, in African kingdoms, 91
Technology
colonization and, 218–219
comparative progress of,
153–156
development of, 190

and economic development in
colonial Africa, 236
gunpowder and, 174
impact of, 14–15
impact of Western, 202–204
Industrial Revolution and, 192
maritime revolution and,
172–174
military innovation and,
192–193
Territoriality, 78–83
Theater
literature and, 52–53
masked drama and, 57
Things Fall Apart (Achebe), 224
Third World, 6
Tigrinya, 267
Tijani Empire, 211–213
Tippu, Tib, 202
Tiv people, 25, 224
courts and moots of, 97–98
family life of, 73–74
lineage system of, 80–81
minimal lineage and, 80
Togo, ex-slaves in, 115
Tonal languages, 37
Torday, African arts and, 60
Touré, Samori, 225–226
Touré, Sékou, 227, 263
Town meetings, 97
Trade, 102–113. *See also* Market
places; Markets; Minerals;
Portugal; Slavery; Slave trade
of Abbasid Caliphate, 161
African protest over, 245
disease and, 32
distance from desert ports and,
170
Dutch East India Company and,
196
in East Africa, 201
European forts for, 183
geographical barriers to
maritime, 173
growth of, 155–156
Indian Ocean ports and, 170
Islam spread by, 206
in ivory, 184
Kilwa control of, 177
literacy, Islam, and, 169

maritime revolution and,
172–174
in market places, 109–110
outside influence and, 163–164
Portuguese-Turkish conflict
over, 176
process in 16th century, 183
and regional specializaiton, 170
ship trade as, 183
by Sierra Leone Creoles, 215
transportation and, 237
West African commercial
revolution and, 213–214
of Western Sudan, 169
Zanzibari network in East
Africa, 202
Trade diasporas, 105–106
Traders, impact on languages,
39–40
Trade winds, 173–174
Trading, marketing compared
with, 105–106
Transportation. *See also*
Communication; Ships and
shipping; Technology
camels as, 148–149
caravans and, 148–149
economic development and,
236–237
markets and, 107
Transvaal, 194. *See also* South
Africa
British in, 219, 220
Trekboers, 197. *See also* Boer
secondary empire
Tribalism, 240. *See* Nationalism
"Tribe"
as concept, 34
and "tribalism," use of terms,
10
Tripoli, 175
Tropical regions
medical improvements and
European colonization in,
219
slavery and African vs.
European survival in, 182
soils of, 23
True levirate, 71
Trusteeship, 231

apartheid and, 232
Trypanosomiasis (sleeping
    sickness), 30
Tsetse fly, 30
Tuareg nomads, 156, 210
Turks. *See* Ottoman Turks
Turuq (brotherhood), 206
Tutsi peoples
    Bantu languages and, 146
    revolt against elite, 261
Tutuola, Amos, 39

Uganda
    Amin in, 263
    dictatorship in, 263
    Great Britain and, 225
    Obote in, 263
    progress in, 268
    trade and, 201, 202
Ujamaa (community), Nyerere
    and, 258–259
Ujiji, trade and, 201
Ulama, 206–207
Umar Tal (Sheikh), 211, 213, 224
Underwood, Leon, Nigerian
    sculptures and, 55
Unilineal descent groups, 72–73
Union of South Africa, 222
United States. *See also*
    Afro-Americans
    abolition of slave trade, 187
    African settlements by ex-slaves
        from, 215
    African studies in, 6–7
    influence of, 266–267
    intervention by, 266
    Liberia and, 222
    Philippines and, 246
    slave trade to, 185–186
Urban civilization, 153–154
Urban development,
    transportation and, 237
Usuman dan Fodio, jihads and,
    210–211

Value judgments, culture and,
    152–153
Vegetation, climates and, 19–23
Victoria, Lake, 18
    empires near, 201
Vietnam, independence and, 247

Violence
    in market places, 110
    nationalism and, 243
    in 1994, 267–268
    political, 265–267
Volta River, 18
Voortrekkers, 198

Wagadu, 169
Wangarawa, 106
Wars and warfare
    military innovation and,
        192–193
    by Shaka, 194
    slave trade and, 188
Weapons. *See also* Wars and
        warfare
    and European colonialism,
        218–219
    innovations in, 193
West
    African ambivalence toward,
        234–235
    African arts in, 60–61
    impact on Africa, 14–15
West Africa
    annexations in, 220
    coastal commercial revolution
        in, 213–214
    coastal trade of, 173
    French, 247
    fringe Westernization in,
        214–216
    Fulbe in, 208–210
    Islamic reform in, 206–207
    jihads in (19th century),
        210–213
    kingdoms in, 90–91
    marketing system of, 109
    Portugal in, 175
    Touré as jihad leader, 226
West African National Congress,
    247
Westminster model, 88
    democracy and, 262
Whites, as South African labor,
    85–86
Widows
    in American and Western society,
        71–72

inheritance in Africa, 71–72
Wife. *See* Bridewealth; Polygyny;
Women
Witchcraft, 122–123. *See also*
Religion
disputes and law, 97–98
Witwatersrand, gold in, 219
Wolof language, 106
Women. *See also* Family life;
Polygyny; Widows
and farming, 44
as marketers and traders, 106
as slaves, 182, 187
social status and polygyny,
67–69
widow inheritance and, 71–72
Woodworking. *See* Sculpture
Work. *See* Labor
World Bank, 260
World Health Organization, 28
World War I, annexations before
and after, 221
World War II, 240
independence movements after,
247
Writing, of languages, 39
Written language, historical
records and, 166

Xhosa people, 197
Cape Colony and, 197, 198
resistance by, 244–245

Yao, slave trade and, 184
Yaws, 28, 29
Yellow fever, 29, 31
Yoruba people
ebi of, 82
land, property, and, 81–82
trade by, 215

Zaire, 264. *See also* Belgian
Congo; Congo; Republic of
Congo-Kinshaa
Congo as, 255
mining in, 170
Mobutu in, 263
slave trade and, 184
state in, 202
trade and, 201
Zambezi River, 18, 19
Zambia
Kaunda in, 262
Makolo in, 196
mining in, 170
Plateau Tonga of, 79
successes in, 268
Zamfara, 210
Zanzibar
as British protectorate, 204
revolt against Afro-Arab elite in,
261
Seyyid Said in, 201
slave trade and, 185
trade of, 201–202
Zimba, raids by, 177
Zimbabwe. *See also* Rhodesia
Caucasians in, 36
combined action in, 227
food production in, 25–26
independence of, 249
mining in, 170
successes in, 268
Zongos (trade enclaves), 106
Zulu
age-grade regiment of, 193
military strength of, 194
Nkatha Freedom Party of, 243
Shaka's wars and, 194
Zwaya peoples, 209

Also available from Waveland Press . . .